PRAISE FOR
ISHI IN TWO WORLDS

"Remarkably lively and interesting."
Atlantic Monthly

"Absolutely fascinating."
Chicago Tribune

"This magnificent biography of the lone survivor of the Yahi Indians shows man at his best."
San Francisco Examiner

"A moving, poetic document."
Christian Science Monitor

"A most remarkable biography. . . . It is also a real source book of central California ethnology and a detailed record of this example of acculturation which is in most respects without equal in today's anthropological literature."
American Anthropologist

"Let me put it to you in these terms: if you read no other book this year, you must read this one. . . . Mrs. Kroeber's portrait of Ishi . . . is so beautifully done. It is a biography of the first order: no hint of false sentimentality, no romanticizing."
Los Angeles Times

"A classic of North American anthropology."
Saturday Review Syndicate

"The story of Ishi is indescribably sad. Theodora Kroeber has told it concisely, factually, sympathetically, and beautifully. She has avoided the excesses of pathos or condemnation to which such a story lends itself. The book is one of the most fascinating ones about Indians I have ever read."
Ethnohistory

It is nearly a half century since Ishi startled the Modern World by accidentally wandering into it from the Stone Age. There follows an account of all that is surely and truly known of him. What he believed and felt and did in the modern world and, earlier, in his own world are the bone beads of his story. The stringing of such of these beads as could be recovered onto a single strand has been my task. Surprisingly, the circle of his life's necklace appears whole despite its many incompletions.

The history of Ishi and his people is, inexorably, part of our own history. We have absorbed their lands into our holdings. Just so must we be the responsible custodians of their tragedy, absorbing it into our tradition and morality.

ISHI
in Two Worlds

A BIOGRAPHY OF THE LAST
WILD INDIAN IN NORTH AMERICA

by Theodora Kroeber

With a New Foreword by Karl Kroeber

UNIVERSITY OF CALIFORNIA PRESS
Berkeley   Los Angeles   London

University of California Press
Berkeley and Los Angeles, California

© 1961 by The Regents of the University of California

Copyright © 1961, 1989 by the Estate of Theodora Kroeber-Quinn;
from *Ishi in Two Worlds*, published by the University of
California Press; reprinted by permission of the author's Estate
and the Estate's agent, Virginia Kidd.

Foreword by Karl Kroeber © 2002 by
the Regents of the University of California

ISBN 0-520-22940-1 (ppb.: alk. paper)

Library of Congress Catalog Card Number: 61-7530

Printed in the United States of America

12   11   10   09   08   07   06   05   04   03
     10   9   8   7   6   5   4   3   2

The paper used in this publication meets the minimum requirements of
ANSI/NISO Z39.48-1992 (R 1997) (*Permanence of Paper*). ⊗

To My Husband

ALFRED LOUIS KROEBER

1876–1960

NEW FOREWORD BY KARL KROEBER

Ishi in Two Worlds: Forty Years Later

Ishi in Two Worlds, the first historical and biographical work of then-60-year-old Theodora Kroeber,[1] although a harbinger of "sixties culture," was very much a product of the late 1950s. At that time, American Indians were just beginning to recover—economically, educationally, politically, and culturally—from the devastations wrought by the savagery of the white conquest of their continent. The violent extermination of Native Americans was seventy years in the past; they had been granted full citizenship in 1924; their populations and self-respect, if not their economic conditions, were on the rise; and they had begun to gain legal redress for past injustices. At the same historical moment, the orientation of American anthropology was shifting from concentrating on preserving evidence of Native traditions, institutions, and languages from mindless destruction by whites to attending to conditions of current Indian life and its recent history. Forty years later we can perceive that the extraordinary impact of the 1961 publication of *Ishi in Two Worlds* derives from Theodora Kroeber's subtle embodiment of such pivotal transformations in the painful history of white-Native American relations.

The book helped to popularize Boasian anthropology, which had emerged in the final years of the nineteenth century under the leadership of Franz Boas as a reaction against the systematic extermination of Native peoples by Europeans expanding their power across the New World. By 1890, the United States' advance westward had annihilated a majority of the several hundred distinct cultures that flourished in North America before the arrival of Columbus and had pushed to the edge of extinction most of the remaining tribal groups. The Boasians' intellectual opposition to these exterminations was rooted in the eighteenth-century anti-Enlightenment ideas of the Protestant German Johann Herder. Boasians subscribed to Herder's view that every human culture is equally unique and equally precious; they treated each Indian culture, however materially puny and tiny its population, as profoundly valuable because a singular, original human achievement. This view put them in opposition to modernist celebrations of abstract "primitivism" and Freudian claims for meta-cultural psychological universals—and it even challenged self-justifications of United States' expansionism, such as the ideal of an "American melting-pot." By the late 1950s, greater appreciation for the value of diverse lifestyles had made people increasingly sympathetic to this "oppositional" orientation of American anthropology. Anthropologists were also becoming more concerned with the deplorable condition of Native peoples resulting from persistent injustices practiced against them by whites. Of particular relevance to *Ishi in Two Worlds* were the California Indian Land Claims Commission hearings in the mid-1950s. The Indians won this legal fight (although they were inadequately recompensed financially), proving that their right to California lands had been unjustly violated; and in following decades they successfully prosecuted other land claims through American courts. Theodora Kroeber's husband, Alfred Kroeber, as the leading authority on traditional California Indian cultural history, was asked to appear as an expert witness for the the federal government *against* the native claimants. He chose instead to testify at length *for* the Indians. His effectiveness as a witness for the Indians, however, depended upon his extraordinary knowledge of their past history, which had been the principal focus of his work. Theodora began writing *Ishi in Two Worlds* in the wake of the Land Claims Commission hearings at the urging of Robert Heizer, who had worked closely with Kroeber in preparing his testimony.[2]

Theodora became absorbed in trying to recover something of the uniqueness of Ishi's personality, but her long acquaintance with anthropology reinforced her sensitivity to how individuality is always realized through interaction with historically shaped social conditions. And when she examined the circumstances into which Ishi had been born and how his people had been treated when he was a growing child, she was horrified. When she wrote this book, there were few popular accounts of the extermination of Native peoples, and her story of the killing of the Yahi remains one of the most damning histories of these slaughters—in part because she avoids abstract words such as "genocide." She keeps the story agonizingly particular. She never lets us conceal from ourselves by generalized terms the primary horror of such events, which is the robbing and murdering and torturing of individual human beings. The immediate success of her book is closely linked to the emergence at the beginning of the 1960s of popular revulsion against such brutalities of ethnic prejudice, feelings that helped to shape, for example, the emerging Civil Rights movement.

But the book is free from ideological didacticism. It concentrates on the man's personality, displaying, for example, informed sympathy for Ishi's intimate connection to the land his people inhabited. Theodora knew the country first hand, having come from a family of miners, ranchers, farmers, and shopkeepers who in one fashion or another had lived in intimate contact with the land of the Western United States. Her account of Ishi's life of concealment, a necessarily imaginative reconstruction, carries conviction because her experience included long acquaintance with a natural world that is no mere refuge from urbanization, not a place to be visited briefly as the spectator of an Indian ceremony, but a complicated environment within which one continuously works and lives, and which over time even shapes how one dreams and imagines.

Moreover, she knew the white exterminators first hand. Her family background made her familiar with the cattlemen, farmhands, lawmen, bounty hunters, miners, drifters, and the rest who conducted the massacres and private killings. Never retreating to generalizations to mask the emotional horror of such events, she focuses her story on particular people whom, without excusing, she makes believable and understandable. The true ghastliness of these events is that they were carried out not by alien monsters but by people shockingly like you and me. As long as we can think and talk about exterminations in impersonal terms—referring to them as crimes of Nazis, or Turks, or Stalinists, or Mongol hordes—we shield ourselves from truly confronting the hideous fact that particular men do these murders, men who may well be hard-working and keep their promises, love their wives, and are conscientious in rearing their children.My mother had never before written any biography or history. She was at sixty a complete amateur, and she had not, of course, known either Ishi or my father during their years together. She was reluctant to undertake the project, and would not have done so without the urging of Heizer, who years before had come to Berkeley to pursue studies Alfred Kroeber then judged of small value: the archaeology of California Indians. Heizer stuck to his guns and changed Kroeber's mind, and convinced others in diverse disciplines, such as the innovative historian Herbert Bolton and the physiologist Sherburne Cook (who pioneered study of Native American demography), of the interdisciplinary value of California archaeology. In 1947, after my father's retirement, Heizer was one of the scholars appointed to replace him, and he immediately set about establishing the California Archeology Survey, which continues to grow and flourish. Heizer's historical, demographic, and archaeological activities made him acutely aware of the brutal destruction of California Indians, first by the Spanish and then, even more ferociously, by the Americans. No state in the Union surpassed the Golden State in systematically and shamelessly harassing, murdering, and stealing from its native inhabitants. Helping my father prepare testimony for the Indians Claims Commission intensified Heizer's anger at such practices (which had not, alas, entirely disappeared), and more energetically than ever he set about publicizing the injustices suffered by Native Californians, especially since the Gold Rush.[3] His interest in getting my mother to write the history of Ishi was infected by these moral/emotional commitments.

Yet, as she tells in the afterword, Heizer helped her most by refusing to judge what she wrote, and by not advising how she should organize her material. If there were references to be sought out, suggestions for how to discover something, the possibility of supplying data she needed, he was unfailingly helpful. He sustained and supported but never interfered, not least because as the project developed he increasingly admired her intellectual sensibility, so radically different from yet complementary to his own. Through the writing of *Ishi in Two Worlds* Heizer and my mother developed a profound friendship, which led to later collaborative work on the beautiful *Almost Ancestors* (1968) and the indispensable *Ishi the Last Yahi: A Documentary History* (1979)— the latter of particular importance to my mother because it enabled her to articulate some issues she had kept out of *Ishi in Two Worlds* as distracting from its primary focus, the personality of Ishi.[4]

Although gifted with intuitive psychological acuity and a sensitive imagination, fiction in the usual sense was not my mother's forte. It is not irrelevant, I think, that it was difficult for her consciously to lie. The fibs so necessary to most social intercourse she never carried off with skill. It was not that she was outspoken, one of those people who say what they think and damn the consequences. To the contrary, her unusual perceptiveness about other's feelings made her alert to what would distress or embarrass them; I don't believe she ever deliberately said a spiteful or hurtful thing. History and biography were in some ways appropriate fields for her. Like my father, she found individual persons more interesting than anything else in a world full of interesting phenomena. Her wide experience with people of diverse ages and classes and cultures stimulated and refined her remarkable gifts of psychological insight, but also trained her to recognize the limits of such perceptions. She was keenly aware of the danger of believing one understands the inner life of another. Her account of Ishi, though never superficial, never denies an ultimate core of which we know nothing, the enigma of his peculiarly terrible personal experience (including what she describes as his sexual starvation). She makes us feel, moreover, that what we cannot know of the man derives not merely from his special experience and his upbringing in a different culture, but simply from the fact that he was a complex human being. She never violates this "normal" mysteriousness of individuality. Again and again she suggests possibilities without asserting the kind of definitive conclusions common in many later commentaries by both Indians and whites.

In judging how this elderly novice achieved the effects she did, one needs to consider her historical method, which she illustrated in characteristically sensuous fashion. She tells how, on a blazing hot winter afternoon in the Nazca Desert of Peru in 1926, her husband, Alfred,

> much excited, brought from a near-by opened grave several dozen pottery shards. Pouring them carefully into my lap, he said, "Look! Beautiful! Pure Nazca 3. See if you can make sense out of them."
>
> During the hours until darkness took over, and again the next day under that heady sun, I worked, using now a hollow in the sand, now a mound of sand as mold, sorting, fitting, discarding the pieces which belonged to other pots. At last, before me, sand-shored and fragile, stood a double-spout, cat-God Nazca 3 jar, pregnant with beauty and significance. . . . A reconstruction, whether of pottery-shards or other historical event, is a creative process of sorts. If it is an honest putting together, with patient and unforced absorption . . . it becomes . . . historic truth.[5]

This is an approach probably few historians today will applaud, although her conception of the historian's task parallels that of the celebrated historian-philosopher R. G. Collingwood. Like Collingwood, my mother thought that the writing of history is finally an imaginative act, and that the holism of narrative is the only mode of discourse able to account for both the coherence and contingencies that constitute specific human experiences. As the singular artistry of each Nazca pot can be reconstructed only by an imaginative response to the truth of its unique total form, so the full historicity of any person can be recovered only through some imaginative understanding of that person's individualized wholeness. It is an irony of Ishi's astonishing life that it compelled my mother to tell his story as only a tiny fragment (although the dramatically painful conclusion) of his people's larger history. Yet it was fortunate that the task of telling his story fell to one so perceptive about the difficulties and rewards of imagining a wholeness implicit in shattered bits of evidence.

Her book was simultaneously biography and history, because one was incomplete without the other. Beyond the darkening narrative of the Yahi and Ishi, my mother includes the bright if distant glow of the long, long pre-history of all California Indians, "copper-colored people on a golden land." The result is an impression of a vast continuity which highlights how little we know of Ishi's life. This deepens the sorrow of his story, because we feel in the death of the man the disappearance of thousands of years of Yahi family life, the loss of the Yahi impoverishing by that much the diverse antiquity of all California Indians.

Simultaneously, the evocation of ancient culture enables us to understand how Ishi could with such swiftness adapt so positively to the modern world. Considering what had been done to his society, one marvels at how successfully Ishi resisted becoming a displaced or marginalized person; he yielded to neither self-pity nor resentment. He was an irrefragably civilized man. At his first formal dinner in San Francisco, just days away from the Oroville jail, he made no mistakes in etiquette. His culture put a high premium on mannerly behavior. He watched the white man's particular protocols (as he would if visiting another Indian culture); his training in disciplined formality made the adaptation unstrained. Saxton Pope's daughter told me that what she remembers best from having meals with Ishi when she was a child was how good his manners were, even as he behaved at table with energetic spontaneity, making no secret, for example, of his fondness for the jelly her mother served. Because Ishi was so civilized a person, he could quickly overcome what would seem almost insuperable differences between his native heritage and twentieth-century urban life.

Luck, my mother observes, landed him in the Hearst Museum. There he was among people who enjoyed their daily work and therefore were congenial to Ishi, whose culture was founded on the pleasure of familiar social tasks neatly and efficiently carried out, qualities reflected in the fashion in which he ordered and protected his personal possessions. Because he was civilized, he would have liked neither the routinized life of a factory or office nor the enforced mindlessness of reservation existence, but he could feel at home in a place where hand-made artifacts were so highly valued and cared for.

My mother emphasizes, though, how troubled he was at learning that the Museum contained human bones, and she vividly depicts his distress when he wandered into the hospital morgue. Contrarily, he was fascinated by what he saw when Pope invited him *into* the operating room to observe his surgery close-up. Unlike most present-day readers, Ishi was experienced at butchery and dissection (for example, to obtain sinew), and he could appreciate both Pope's purposes and his skill, as when Pope saved a patient by removing his kidney. Here as throughout the book, we perceive Ishi actively participating, whether his immediate experience involved revulsion, excitement, bafflement, curiosity, or quiet pleasure.

The persistent attention to the liveliness of Ishi's responsiveness, to the irrepressible vitality within this reserved and self-controlled man, has escaped many commentators, even Thomas Merton, who judged *Ishi in Two Worlds* "a moving and significant book, one of those unusually suggestive works that *must* be read."[6] He found "challenging and awe-inspiring" my mother's speculation on the "long concealment" of Ishi's people, and he felt that her suggestion that the Yahi found strength to survive in "the circumstance that their sufferings and curtailments arose from wrongs done to them by others" compelled any thoughtful reader to think about the then-ongoing war in Viet Nam. Ishi-inspired meditation on that war, he asserted, forced one to understand the real meaning of Kennedy's "new frontier," and to recognize ominous puritan overtones in the vigilante language of contemporary American patriotism.

Merton's response was surely a valid one, yet it carries us away from Ishi, making polemical use of him, whereas the enduring power of *Ishi in Two Worlds* arises from a less ideological aim: to absorb us into contemplating the unique experience of an individual civilized in a highly particular way. Like other commentators on the book, Merton ignores its descriptions of Ishi's skill at manual crafts. My mother found these difficult to write, yet her book's unusual appeal derives in good measure from her success at helping us to understand *how* Ishi made bows and arrows, shaped projectile points, and operated the fire drill. In our society, to be sure, there is a diminishing number of people who give a damn about how anything is done or made. But Ishi's "stone age" culture might better be called a culture of hand-craftsmanship. My mother's descriptions of the way Ishi worked with his hands offer modern readers insight into a key quality of Yahi character/behavior that sustained Ishi through the decades of concealment and his final years in San Francisco, where he found continuous satisfaction and pleasure in practicing his skills at creating out of stone and bone, wood, grass, sinew, and skin the artifacts upon which his culture had depended for thousands of years.[7]

An integral relation of Ishi's temperament to the "manual tact of a kind that only experience can teach" was required, for instance, in creating fire with a wooden drill, for the "fire must be coaxed out of the unwilling wood—coaxed and nursed." In working the drill "haste, violence of motion . . . will accomplish nothing, nor will indifference . . . or a moment's let up." What is demanded is "strength, continuity, and rhythm" for which "Ishi's patience, perseverance, and delicate control were precisely the requisite qualities" (187). I know of no more lucid articulation than this of the conjunction of individual behavior with learned, traditional skills in a society where one makes for oneself the tools by which to produce artifacts that simultaneously distinguish oneself and one's culture.

This attention to the fusing of biography and cultural history probably helped my mother to ignore possibilities for discovering opinions about Ishi that might have been gleaned in the 1950s from Northern California native peoples, not only from Yana descendants (by the time she wrote there were no longer any speakers of Yana) but also from neighboring tribes with whom they had interacted. In 2002 such information would be especially valuable, because *Ishi in Two Worlds* has played a major role in the shifting Native American judgments on Ishi over the past forty years. Amongst whites, research stimulated by the book has produced a wealth of new knowledge about the Yana and neighboring tribal groups, as well as new facts of Ishi's life in San Francisco. The publication of *Ishi in Two Worlds* in 1961, for example, evoked personal responses to my mother from people who as children had known Ishi in San Francisco. Their accounts, especially that of Fred H. Zumwalt, Jr., have revealed new aspects of Ishi's life in the city outside the museum, above all with what success he related to a diversity of children.[8] Ishi's friendships with young people, however, will come as no surprise to readers of this book, for the impression it evokes is of a man possessed of that genuine maturity which allows an adult to give and receive pleasure from being with children. This is one reason *Ishi in Two Worlds* is likely to endure as what Lewis Gannett in his original introduction called it, a literary classic.

Part of what Gannett meant is also suggested by my mother's insight into the contingencies that underlie Ishi's history, how easily it might never have come to pass:

> [H]e was as a stone skipped randomly across the surface of a quiet pond. He might have died from starvation or violence and disappeared without a trace, the world none the wiser.

But he did not die. Rather, quiet riffles of contact and influence formed round him in widening circles, carrying him to
foreign and unimagined shores. (148)

The ever-widening circles of influence initiated by Ishi include,
my mother understood, the various ways in which people have
responded and will respond to his unusual story. A strength of *Ishi
in Two Worlds* is that she recognized her telling to be but one version, one perspective, because historical circumstance and personal
interest inevitably determine how any past event is perceived and
assessed. For her, the subsequent *Ishi the Last Yahi: A Documentary
History* was valuable because it emphasized a diversity of perspec-
tives she had judged inappropriate for her first book. Thus the
concluding item in this documentary history is the notice of Ishi's
death published in the *Chico Record*, March 28, 1916:

> "Ishi," the man primeval, is dead. He could not stand the
> rigors of civilization, and tuberculosis, that arch-enemy of
> those who live in the simplicity of nature and then abandon
> that life, claimed him. Ishi was supposed to be the last of a
> tribe that flourished in California long before the whites
> reached these shores. He could make a fire with sticks, fash-
> ion arrowheads out of flint, and was familiar with other arts
> long lost to civilization. He furnished amusement and study
> to the savants at the University of California for a number
> of years, and doubtless much of ancient Indian lore was
> learned from him, but we do not believe he was the marvel
> that the professors would have the public believe. He was
> just a starved-out Indian from the wilds of Deer creek who,
> by hiding in its fastnesses, was able to long escape the white
> man's pursuit. And the white man with his food and cloth-
> ing and shelter finally killed the Indian just as effectually as
> he would have killed him with a rifle. (242)

The rhetorically dramatic placing of this death notice (containing
so much with which my mother disagreed) is revealing of her

awareness of the intrinsic conditions of all historical biography. Yet the item and its placement should not startle anyone who has taken as seriously the brief paragraph of acknowledgments that opens the volume and that concludes:

> Howsoever one touches on Ishi, the touch rewards.
> It illuminates the way.

In *Ishi in Two Worlds* she wished her readers never to lose sight of the wanton destructions that permanently obscure much more we *might* have known of Ishi and his people. The period of three or four thousand years ago (today's linguists, who have found some weaknesses in glottochronology, might double that age), when there may have been a single Hokan language spoken by Ishi's's ancestors, she recognized could be evoked only conditionally. So of the Yana then she says:

> [I]t is to be presumed that they lived freely in the open valley, going up into the hills, which to Ishi were a year-round home, only seasonally in the course of following the deer from valley to hills to mountains. There must have been a wide dispersal of Hokan-speakers as part of the drama of change which resulted in the appearance of many new languages within the old Hokan mold. This may well have been the time of the greatest creative florescence of the Yana. . . . (17)

We can *know* Yahi culture "only at that last moment before its extinction, when it was become meager and flickering."

By her unfaltering vision of the senseless loss and suffering upon which Ishi's impressive behavior was built, she convinces us that he was not merely a conventionalized "starved-out Indian" on the run, but a man who with "little room for choosing, . . . made choices as courageous and enlightened as the scope of his opportunities permitted" (230). Although writing from a firmly defined perspective of time, place, and personality, she argues for no cause other than an effort to understand a man attractive but

reserved, attractive because reserved. Her only agenda is to articulate, as clearly as the blurred and eroded evidence allows, a
chiaroscuro portrait of a strong man of goodwill, generosity, and
patience, yet a person volatile, and characterized by what she
aptly calls élan, a man who underwent an experience for most of
us nearly unimaginable, but which her account makes almost too
poignantly imaginable.

Almost. What surprises me rereading the book forty years after
its first publication is that its final effect is not depressing. My
feeling is not of tragic closure, but, almost incomprehensibly,
of amazement at the productive resiliency of Ishi's spirit. My
mother enables us to catch what was positive in Ishi's reluctance
to speak words of farewell, his profound empathy with the ongo-
ingness of life. The book, at least to a reader of advanced age,
carries some of Ishi's wisdom over to oneself, offering recognition that the destiny of every individual life, and every way of life,
participates in a continuity of the natural world's ceaseless vitality: "You stay, I go."

KARL KROEBER
New York
January 12, 2002

NOTES

1. From this book many people have learned that no one knows "Ishi's" real name. I confront a slightly analogous difficulty, because my family and I, and all our intimate friends, *never* referred to my mother as "Theodora" but always as "Krak" (rhymes with "lake") or more frequently "Krakie," a nickname derived from her maiden name.

2. It was Heizer who persuaded my mother to write about Ishi. Alfred Kroeber had no wish to recall the loss of a friend, the pain of which remained acute because my father was gifted with an astounding memory even at the age of 80. Moreover, he only rarely reminisced; he was too entranced by immediate activities to spend time yarning about his personal past. More than anyone else I've known, he lived enthusiastically in and for the current moment—one reason he was such an interesting and entertaining father at every stage of my life. In the late 1950s he was as occupied with as many ongoing enterprises as ever, ranging from studies into relations between modern German and English poetry (including translating Housman into German) to persuading the National Science Foundation to fund a project to make movies of contemporary California Indians.

3. Heizer's work ultimately resulted in several publications, notably *The Destruction of California Indians* (1974; reprint, edited by Alberto L. Hurtado, Lincoln: University of Nebraska Press, 1993), which concentrates on the period 1847–1865; and the invaluable *Federal Concern about Conditions of California Indians, 1853 to 1913: Eight Documents* (Socorro N.Mex.: Ballena Press, 1979). Heizer contributed much to the development of California Indian history (with special emphasis on white-Indian relationships) by compiling bibliographies and encouraging graduate students to enter this field.

4. She and Heizer also collaborated with Albert B. Elsasser on *Drawn From Life: California Indians in Pen and Brush* (Socorro, N.Mex.: Ballena Press, 1977), a remarkable work that includes more than 300 reproductions of paintings and drawings of Native Californians from 1599 to 1880.

5. "About History," *Pacific Historical Review* 32:1 (February 1963), 2–3.

6. "Ishi: A Meditation" first appeared in *The Catholic Worker* in February 1967; it is reprinted in Merton's *Ishi Means Man* (Greensboro, N.C.: Unicorn Press, 1976), 25–32, from which my citations are taken.

7. Ishi also happily made use of new materials, for example coming to prefer glass to obsidian for arrow points, just as he found a hand vice better than his big toe for holding some things. Most American Indian cultures are distinguished by their adaptability, and any competent workman welcomes an effective tool or superior materials.

8. *Ishi in Three Centuries*, ed. Karl and Clifton Kroeber (Lincoln: University of Nebraska Press, 2002), includes the Zumwalt memoir as well as recently discovered facts about Ishi's life in San Francisco.

FOREWORD
TO THE ORIGINAL EDITION

Think, if you will, of all the Indians who have emerged from fact, fancy, and fear to take their places in the pantheon of the American imagination: in history Squanto, who fed the Pilgrims; Pocahontas, who loved an Englishman; Chief Logan the eloquent; Sacajawea, the girl-mother who guided white men across the Continental Divide; Sequoia, who invented an Indian alphabet; Crazy Horse, who outfought Custer; and in fiction Hiawatha and the Last of the Mohicans. They are not many; and there is not one of them whose story haunts the imagination more than Ishi's.

Ishi was, literally, a Stone Age man, the last of a "lost" tribe, when, only half a century ago, he stumbled into twentieth-century California. Undoubtedly Ishi anticipated death as a result of his arrival in an enemy world, but almost miraculously he came to the hands of T. T. Waterman and Alfred L. Kroeber, anthropologists who were among the few men in the country equipped to understand his dilemma and his personality. It is almost as miraculous that Ishi should today find a biographer able to tell his story with the scrupulous integrity, the poetic insight, and the sense of historic drama which give Theodora Kroeber's book its unique radiance.

For Ishi to adjust to what Mrs. Kroeber calls "the wilds of civilization" was as remarkable as for Mark Twain's Connecticut Yankee to settle down in King Arthur's England, or for a modern astronaut to survive in the worlds of outer space. It is far easier to romanticize such a story than to understand it.

The "discovery" of Ishi, "the last wild Indian," was well advertised in the newspapers of 1911, and in the next five years thousands of visitors watched him chip arrowheads, shape bows, and make fire by his age-old techniques in the halls of the modern museum where he so oddly made his home. And when Ishi died he had his "obits," some loosely journalistic, some semiscientific. But in 1916 the idea of a race dying out had for most Americans romantic rather than imminently realistic overtones, and Ishi was soon forgotten. Two world wars have since given new poignancy to the phrase "death of a race," as well as to the conception that patterns of life other than our own may have validity and significance.

This book, as the author herself says, is like an archaeologist's reconstruction of a bead necklace from which some pieces are missing, others scattered. She puts together two necklaces: first, the story of a tribe that survived almost unchanged, along the streams of the Mount Lassen foothills, from what we call the Age of Pericles to the period of our gold rush; of its decay and its murder. The second necklace is the story of Ishi's adjustment to the trolley-world of San Francisco—proof, as the author says, that Stone Age man and modern man are essentially alike.

Alfred Kroeber, who had been Ishi's trusted friend, was at his wife's side when she was assembling the materials and writing this book; without the light his mind threw on Ishi's it could hardly have been written. Modern historical research also aided the author; so did her own family memories of old California traditions. But the warmth and understanding with which Ishi's story is told give this book its special quality. It can, I think, without exaggeration, be called one of the great American stories, a contribution not only to our history but to our literature.

LEWIS GANNETT

PREFACE

Theodora Kroeber Speaks for Herself

It was late in August, 1960, when I wrote *Finis* to my biography of Ishi. Only then did Alfred Kroeber, my husband and principal live informant about Ishi, read the manuscript through. He declared himself satisfied.

He died in October, 1960, without having seen the book, published a year later. I shall always be grateful that Kroeber read the final manuscript; he knew that a permanent account of his friend Ishi was at last on record.

For me, the writing of Ishi's biography was responsibility, not pleasure. I was relieved when it was completed—as well done as I could do it—and was content to forget the long, now finished task. I could not know that ahead of me lay the real experience of Ishi: the greatest human experience of my life.

It came by way of letters, telephone calls, announced and unannounced visitors. Men. Women. Young. Old. Children. Not "important" people in the wordly or the academic meaning. Few bookish or intellectual ones among these people from all stations of life and levels of education, background, interests, and cultures.

All sorts of people came, wanting sometimes to question, more often to talk, to express complex reactions, to philosophize, to wonder, even to cry—shamelessly, men and women—to put into words their feeling for Ishi's humanity. His humor. His understanding. His patience. His beauty. His tragedy.

Before this great need to share feeling with me—and it continues to this day—I feel humble; grateful to them, to Ishi. And by way of them and Ishi I declare myself confident of the goodness and humanity of the men and women and children of my time and place.

Theodora Kroeber

ACKNOWLEDGMENTS

It is usual for an author to single out from multiple indebtednesses for completion of a task of research and composition the person "without whose constant advice and help" the particular work "could not have been done." The author of *Ishi* must in honor mention first Robert F. Heizer, without whose total refusal to have anything to do with the ordering and writing of this book, it would never have been done.

Heizer, Professor of Anthropology and Director of the Archaeological Survey of the University of California, had inherited as it were the sense of responsibility of the elders of the department for seeing to it that, sometime, somehow, Ishi's biography be written before all memory and all record of it were lost. To this end, he had begun long since the collecting of various and varied source material, which, when I said I was ready to make a try at the biography, he gave to me. Heizer might properly have felt that his ordering of the invaluable miscellany gave him proprietary rights over its use. I began my work honoring such feeling. He sensed this within a week, and put a stop to it. "It is *your* book you must write. Work in your own way, not in mine. Satisfy yourself, not me," was what he said, freeing me to browse and wander and absorb according to my own slow, amoeba-like way of containment and understanding of data, with order and meaning very gradually taking shape and contour—a process which I find to be in part tense and at the forefront of consciousness, in part vegetative and subconscious. When, at long last, I wrote *Finis,* Heizer gave the manuscript a complete and critical reading.

To the staff of the Archaeological Survey, and particularly to Albert Elsasser, I am indebted for the finding of books and maps, and for the intangible gifts of time and interest.

Sacramento Daily Transcript, April and May, 1850

Siskiyou Chronicle, May, 1859

Red Bluff Independent, April, July, August, 1862

Oroville Register, August 29, 30, 31 and September 1, 2, 4, 6,
    and 7, 1911

Chico Daily Exchange, August 29, 30, 31, 1911

Sacramento Bee, August 29, 1911

San Francisco Call
San Francisco Chronicle } August 29–September 6, 1911
San Francisco Examiner

Stockton Record, June 20, 1925

Sacramento Union, October 2, 1927

Chico Enterprise Record, November 7, 1956

CONTENTS

Part One: ISHI THE YAHI

Prologue: OUTSIDE THE SLAUGHTER HOUSE

The story of Ishi begins for us early in the morning of the twenty-ninth day of August in the year 1911 and in the corral of a slaughter house. It begins with the sharp barking of dogs which roused the sleeping butchers. In the dawn light they saw a man at bay, crouching against the corral fence—Ishi.

They called off the dogs. Then, in some considerable excitement, they telephoned the sheriff in Oroville two or three miles away to say that they were holding a wild man and would he please come and take him off their hands. Sheriff and deputies arrived shortly, approaching the corral with guns at the ready. The wild man made no move to resist capture, quietly allowing himself to be handcuffed.

The sheriff, J. B. Webber, saw that the man was an Indian, and that he was at the limit of exhaustion and fear. He could learn nothing further, since his prisoner understood no English. Not knowing what to do with him, he motioned the Indian into the wagon with himself and his deputies, drove him to the county jail in Oroville, and locked him up in the cell for the insane. There, Sheriff Webber reasoned, while he tried to discover something more about his captive he could at least protect him from the excited curiosity of the townspeople and the outsiders who were already pouring in from miles around to see the wild man.

The wild man was emaciated to starvation, his hair was burned off close to his head, he was naked except for a ragged scrap of ancient covered-wagon canvas which he wore around his shoulders like a poncho. He was a man of middle height, the long bones, painfully apparent, were straight, strong, and not heavy, the skin color somewhat paler in tone than the full copper characteristic of most Indians. The black eyes were wary and guarded now, but were set wide in a broad face, the mouth was generous and agreeably molded. For the rest, the Indian's extreme fatigue and fright heightened a sensitiveness which was always there, while it masked the usual mobility and expressiveness of the features.

It should be said that the sheriff's action in locking Ishi up was neither stupid nor brutal given the circumstances. Until sheriff Webber took the unwonted measure of keeping them out by force people filled the jail to gaze through the bars of his cell at the captive. Later, Ishi spoke with some diffidence of this, his first contact with white men. He said that he was put up in a fine house where he was kindly treated and well fed by a big chief. That he would eat nothing and drink nothing during his first days of captivity Ishi did not say. Such was the case; nor did he allow himself to sleep at first. Quite possibly it was a time of such strain and terror that he suppressed all memory of it. Or he may have felt that it was unkind to recall his suspicions which proved in the event groundless, for Ishi expected in those first days to be put to death. He knew of white men only that they were the murderers of his own people. It was natural that he should expect, once in their power, to be shot or hanged or killed by poisoning.

Meanwhile, local Indians and half-breeds as well as Mexicans and Spaniards tried to talk to the prisoner in Maidu, Wintu, and Spanish. Ishi listened patiently but uncomprehendingly, and when he spoke it was in a tongue which meant no more to the Indians there than to the whites.

The story of the capture of a wild Indian became headline news in the local valley papers, and reached the San Francisco dailies in forms more or less lurid and elaborated. The story in the *San Francisco Call* was accompanied by a picture, the first of many to come later. In another newspaper story, a Maidu Indian, Conway by name, "issued a statement" that he had conversed with the wild man. Conway's moment of publicity was brief since the wild man understood nothing of what he said.

These accounts were read by Professors Kroeber and Waterman, anthropologists at the University of California, who were at once alerted to the human drama behind the event and to its possible importance, the more particularly because it recalled to them an earlier episode on San Nicolas Island, one of the Channel Islands of the Pacific Ocean some seventy miles offshore from Santa Barbara.

In 1835, the padres of Mission Santa Barbara transferred the San Nicolas Indians to the mainland. A few minutes after the boat, which was carrying the Indians, had put off from the island, it was found that one baby had been left behind. It is not easy to land a boat on San Nicolas; the captain decided against returning for the baby; the baby's mother jumped overboard, and was last seen swimming toward the island. Half-hearted efforts made to find her in subsequent weeks were unsuccessful: it was believed that she had drowned in the rough surf. In 1853, eighteen years later, seal hunters in the Channel waters reported seeing a woman on San Nicolas, and a boatload of men from Santa Barbara went in search of her. They found her, a last survivor of her tribe. Her baby, as well as all her people who had been removed to the Mission, had died. She lived only a few months after her "rescue" and died without anyone having been able to communicate with her, leaving to posterity this skeletal outline of her grim story, and four words which someone remembered from her lost language and recorded as she said them. It so happens that these four words identify her language as having been Shoshonean, related to Indian languages of the Los Angeles area, not to those of Santa Barbara.

Another reason for the anthropologists' particular interest in the wild man was that three years earlier, in 1908, some surveyors working a few miles north of Oroville had surprised and routed a little band of Indians. After hearing of this incident, Waterman with two guides had spent several weeks in an unsuccessful search for the Indians: the wild man of Oroville might well be one of them.

On August 31, 1911, Kroeber sent the following telegram: "Sheriff Butte County. Newspapers report capture wild Indian speaking language other tribes totally unable understand. Please confirm or deny by collect telegram and if story correct hold Indian till arrival Professor State University who will take charge and be responsible for him. Matter important account aboriginal history."

The sheriff's office must have confirmed the report promptly: Waterman took the train to Oroville the same day. That he and Kroeber correctly "guessed" Ishi's tribe and language was no *tour de force* of intuition. The guess was based on field work with Indians all up and down California; they knew that Oroville was adjacent to country which formerly belonged to the Yana Indians; presumably the strange Indian would be a Yana. He might even be from the southernmost tribe of Yana, believed to be extinct. If this were true, neither they nor anyone so far as they knew could speak his language. But if he were a Northern or Central Yana, there were files of expertly recorded vocabularies for those dialects from two old Yanas, Batwi, called Sam, and Chidaimiya, called Betty Brown.

With a copy of Batwi's and Chidaimiya's vocabularies in his pocket, Waterman arrived in Oroville where he identified himself to Sheriff Webber and was taken to visit the wild man. Waterman found a weary, badgered Indian sitting in his cell, wearing the butcher's apron he had been given at the slaughter house, courteously making what answer he could in his own language to a barrage of questions thrown at him in English, Spanish, and assorted Indian from a miscellaneous set of visitors.

Waterman sat down beside Ishi, and with his phonetically transcribed list of Northern and Central Yana words before him, began to read from it, repeating each word, pronouncing it as well as he knew how. Ishi was attentive but unresponding until, discouragingly far down the list, Waterman said *siwini* which means yellow pine, at the same time tapping the pine framework of the cot on which they sat. Recognition lighted up the Indian's face. Waterman said the magic word again; Ishi repeated it after him, correcting his pronunciation, and for the next moments the two of them banged at the wood of the cot, telling each other over and over, *siwini, siwini!*

With the difficult first sound recognition achieved, others followed. Ishi was indeed one of the lost tribe, a Yahi; in other words, he was from the southernmost Yana. Waterman was learning that the unknown Yahi dialect differed considerably but not to the point of unintelligibility from the two northern ones of his list. Together he and Ishi tried out more and more words and phrases: they were beginning to communicate. After a while Ishi ventured to ask Waterman, *I ne ma Yahi?* "Are you an Indian?" Waterman answered that he was. The hunted look left Ishi's eyes—here was a friend. He knew as well as did his friend that Waterman was not an Indian. The question was a tentative and subtle way of reassuring and being reassured, not an easy thing to do when the meaningful shared sounds are few. Between meetings with Ishi, Waterman wrote to Kroeber from Oroville:

This man [Ishi] is undoubtedly wild. He has pieces of deer thong in place of ornaments in the lobes of his ears and a wooden plug in the septum of his nose. He recognizes most of my Yana words and a fair proportion of his own seem to be identical [with mine]. Some of his, however, are either quite different or else my pronunciation of them is very bad, because he doesn't respond to them except by pointing to his ears and asking to have them repeated. "No!" *k'u'i*—it is not—is one. "Yes!" *ähä,* pleases him immensely. I think I get a few endings that don't occur in Northern Yana on nouns, for example. Phonetically, he has some of the prettiest cracked consonants I ever heard in my life. He will be a splendid informant, especially for phonetics, for he speaks very clearly. I have not communicated with him successfully enough to get his story, but what can I expect? He has a yarn to tell about his woman, who had a baby on her back and seems to have been drowned, except that he is so *cheerful* about it.

Waterman misunderstood. In the excitement and relief of having someone to talk to, Ishi poured out confidences and recollections which Waterman could by no means comprehend even with the aid of an elaborate pantomime. Ishi's seeming pleasure was not in the recollected event, but was rather a near hysteria induced by human interchange of speech and feelings too long denied.

Waterman's letters continue:

We had a lot of conversation this morning about deer hunting and making acorn soup, but I got as far as my list of words would take me. If I am not mistaken, he's full of religion—bathing at sunrise, putting out pinches of tobacco where the lightning strikes, etc. I'll try rattlesnake on him when I go back after lunch. It was a picnic to see him open his eyes when he heard Yana from me. And he looked over my shoulder at the paper in a most mystified way. He knew at once where I got my inspiration. . . . We showed him some arrows last night, and we could hardly get them away from him. He showed us how he flaked the points, singed the edges of the feathering, and put on the sinew wrappings.

Even before Waterman had established a thin line of communication with Ishi, the sheriff had become convinced that his prisoner was neither insane nor dangerous. There were no charges against him; he did not properly belong in jail. The question was, what in place of the shelter of the jail was there for him? Waterman offered to take him to San Francisco. Phones and telegraph wires were kept busy for the next forty-eight hours between Oroville and San Francisco, where the University's Museum of Anthropology then was, and between the museum and Washington, D.C.

While these negotiations were going forward, the sheriff, at

Waterman's suggestion, sent a deputy to Redding to find and bring back with him the old man, Batwi, to act as interpreter-companion to Ishi. Batwi came, and although he patronized Ishi outrageously, he was for the present a help. He and Ishi could communicate in Yana, not without some difficulty, but quite fully. Meanwhile, the Indian Bureau in Washington telegraphed permission for Ishi to go to the University's museum whose staff was to be responsible for him at least until there was opportunity for fuller investigation. The sheriff of Butte County was greatly relieved; he at once made out a receipt of release from the jail to the University. This remarkable document seems not to have survived the years of moving and storing in odd corners which has been the fate of the museum files and specimens.

In any case, Waterman, Batwi, and Ishi, with the release and government permission, left Oroville on Labor Day, September 4, arriving in San Francisco somewhat before midnight. There remained to Ishi four years and seven months of life, years which were to pass within the shelter of the museum walls at the Affiliated Colleges, or in the hospital next door when he was sick.

Ishi was the last wild Indian in North America, a man of Stone Age culture subjected for the first time when he was past middle age to twentieth-century culture. He was content that it should be so, participating as fully as he could in the new life. Before examining more closely those astounding few years and what one Stone Age man contributed in so short a time to our understanding of man as such, let us go back to the years of childhood, young manhood, and middle age—almost a whole lifetime. These were years spent by him without experience or understanding of a way of life other than that of a tiny fugitive band of fewer than a dozen souls at most, opposing their ancient Yahi skills and beliefs to an unknown but hostile outside world.

There came the time—months, perhaps two or three years before August, 1911—when Ishi was the only one remaining of the little band, violence from without, old age and illness from within, having brought death to the others.

Ishi's arrival at the slaughter house was the culmination of unprecedented behavior on his part. A few days earlier, without hope, indifferent whether he lived or died, he had started on an aimless trek in a more or less southerly direction which took him into country he did not know. Exhaustion was added to grief and loneliness. He lay down in the corral because he could go no farther. He was then about forty miles from home, a man without living kin or friends, a man who had probably never been beyond the borders of his own tribal territory.

Our task is to piece together all that is known of Ishi's life before that day: from his own account of it; from what was learned of it on a camping trip with him in his own home country; and from the miscellany of rumor and fact and speculation as reported by surveyors, ranchers, rangers, and other white residents of Butte and Tehama counties. It is an episodic story, incomplete, and loosely strung across lacunae of time, ignorance, and events too painful for Ishi to relive in memory.

That Ishi should have crossed the boundaries of his homeland, and continued on into the unknown, means to be sure that he had also reached and crossed certain physical and psychic limits. But to begin to understand how profoundly disturbed he must have been, we must know how aberrant such behavior was, not for Ishi the man merely, but for Ishi the Yahi. His life becomes more of a piece if we step back from it, as from the detail of a face or feature in a painting, to focus briefly on the whole of the canvas, bringing its background and pattern into perspective. To understand Ishi's values and behavior and belief, and his way of life, we must know in a broad and general way something of his heritage: the land and people of Indian California.

Chapter 1

COPPER-COLORED PEOPLE
ON A GOLDEN LAND

The stubborn and enduring land of California has changed less than its people. From an aeroplane the "coloured counties" are seen spread out like a giant relief map. Mount Shasta looms to the north, Mount Whitney to the south; the Sierra Nevada forms a wall to the east; and beyond Whitney, where the Sierra appears to go underground, the desert takes over. There are the long interior valleys; and there are the tumbled, rough, and wooded Coast Ranges through which rivers and creeks break to the sea. Below, incredible, lies the vast and varied land, its mountains and deserts empty and mute today, while over the accessible valleys and coastal plains a congested and diverse population clusters close to a few centers like wasps around heavy-hanging nests. A constant stream of automobiles, looking from the air like lines of black ants on the march, fills the passes over the Sierra barrier, moving westward to the favored spots. The hills are empty except for lumbering operations wherever there is a good stand of trees; the mining towns of the Mother Lode and the old rancherias are shabby and deserted, or have been taken over by "summer people." The banks of rivers and creeks are empty save for sporadic invasions of fishermen; and the desert is without human occupants except for a citified overflow which follows in the wake of air-cooling installations, swimming pools, and motels.

What would an air view have revealed in the days of the gold rush? The same lines of black ants moving in the same westerly direction over the same passes, on horseback, and in covered wagons drawn by oxen, traveling more slowly than today's immigrants but with the same doggedness as these later ones, heading in part for the same centers, in part stopping in the hill country where ranches, mining camps, and saw and grist mills were scattered along streams and in the forests.

Hovering over the same land, but continuing our flight back in time, we view another trek, this one on foot or on mule and horseback, coming up from the south, northward along the rim of the sea. The time is the 'seventies of the eighteenth century, and the travelers, Spaniards pushing out of Mexico, keeping a sharp eye for a sheltered and sunny and likely spot for mission, rancheria, or presidio as they move slowly on.

If we take a last backward flight in time, the Spaniard is no longer seen. This is the time before his coming; the golden land belongs wholly and undisputedly to its native sons and daughters. No lines of black ants move over the high passes or come up from the south in this view. Indeed, we must fly low to see the narrow trails meandering beside a stream, or across country to an oak flat, or up into the hills. At first there seem to be neither houses nor people, but presently a frame with surf fish strung on it to dry on a sunny beach, a clearing in the trees, a thin blue wisp of smoke from a wood fire, serve to guide the eyes to the weathered roof of a low redwood house, to an earth-covered circular house, to a thatched house, to a brush shelter. We see an old woman tending the fire outside a house, a man spearing fish beside a stream, a half-grown boy paddling downstream in a dugout canoe. A young woman, her baby in a basket carrier on her back, gathers wild iris on a hillside; a hunter brings down a deer with bow and arrow. These people step noiselessly over the ground, barefoot or in soft deerskin moccasins, and their naked or near-naked copper-colored bodies blend in semicamouflage against the colors of the earth. Such clothes as they wear, a skirt of shredded bark, a buckskin breechclout, an occasional fur or feather cape, also blend into the natural background. Their voices, whether in ordinary conversation, or in song or prayer or mourning cry, are light-toned, neither harsh nor loud.

The high mountains are empty. But people are living in the hills as far up as oak trees grow and wherever manzanita and other berries are abundant, and wherever there are deer; along fish-filled streams; and where a river flows into the sea; and on the desert. Even so unlikely a place as Death Valley has men who call it home.

Back on the ground and again in the twentieth century, we turn to maps and estimates and reports to learn something more of these ancestral peoples whom we have glimpsed distantly through time.

We have seen that they lived on parts of the land which modern men do not find habitable or attractive, although at no place were their numbers large. The population of Indian California was small: over the whole of the state there were probably no more than a hundred and fifty thousand people, perhaps as many as two hundred and fifty thousand. (In 1860, ten years after the beginning of the gold rush, the white population of the state was already three hundred and ninety thousand.) There are, to be sure, estimates of the pre-conquest population of California which run higher, but the archaeological remains from village and burial sites point to numbers close to those given here. There is no evidence, as there is in the Southwest, in Mexico, in Yucatan of the Mayas, that a once much more numerous people suffered disaster and decimation. Nor do the histories, legends, myths, or stories of any California Indians speak of ancient wholesale famine as do the old as well as the modern chronicles of China and India.

These one or two hundred and fifty thousand native people constituted twenty-one known nationalities, or small nations, which were in turn further separated into subnationalities, and these again into tribes or tribelets to a total number of more than two hundred and fifty—exactly how many more can never be known because of the obliteration in modern times of whole

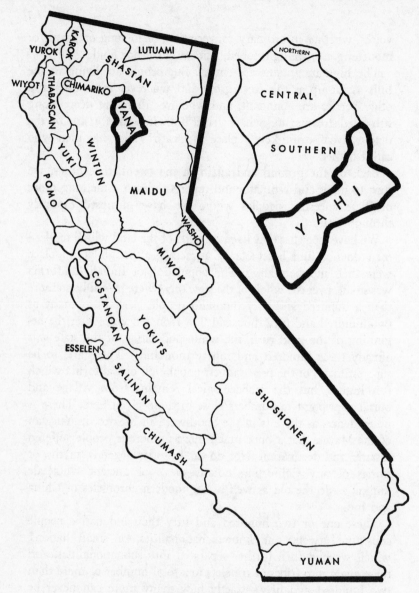

INDIAN CALIFORNIA

Inset shows the Yana territory with the Yahi lands in the far south.

peoples and cultures by Spaniard and Anglo-Saxon alike without record of tribal name or affiliation. Many of these subgroups were of course few in number and inhabited only a small area. Their numbers were almost unbelievably small beside the territorial and population figures for modern nations, but they were nonetheless true nations in their stubbornly individual and boundaried separateness and distinctiveness one from another.

One of these nationalities was the Yana. There were probably no more than three thousand of Ishi's people, perhaps only two thousand,—not many to constitute a nation to be sure, but more people than live today along the favorite streams and on the village sites of the ancient Yana. And few in number as they were, even by California standards, the Yana followed the current pattern of culture fragmentation in being further sub-subdivided into four groups: Northern, Central, Southern, and Yahi (Ishi's group), each with its own geographic boundaries, its own dialect, and its own set of specializations and peculiarities of custom.

There were and are, for the whole of Indian North America, six great linguistic superfamilies, each made up of numbers of separate stocks or families of speech. Each family usually consists of several languages which differ so much one from another that their common origin can be determined only by comparative linguistics study; the superfamilies are even more varied than the large Indo-European stock or family with its Romance and Germanic and Slavic and Hindi divisions. Of the six superfamilies, five were represented in California, and contained among them twenty-one basic languages which were, for the most part, as mutually unintelligible as are German and French; and many of them were even more unlike than these two. But this is not yet the whole of the story, since the twenty-one languages further separated and elaborated themselves into a hundred and thirteen known dialects. These dialects varied, some of them, only so much as New Orleans English from the English of Boston; others so greatly that to know one would not make the other accessible, as with Swedish and German. Only parts of the Sudan and the island of New Guinea offer so much language variety within comparable areas. Or, to demonstrate the congestion of tongues another way, there are twice as many Indian languages on record as there are counties in California today.

We know that such extreme linguistic differentiation takes time. Spoken language is in a sense always changing, since each speaker of his tongue imprints on it his imperceptibly individual voice and accent and choice or rejection of particular words and usages, but the changing is as drops of water on the stone of fixed grammatical form. Ishi's California must indeed have been an old and long-settled land.

Remains of Dawn Man or of some Dawn-like man, his bones or his stones, are proclaimed from time to time as having been found on the Pacific slope, but if Dawn Man or any of his near relations once lived in California, they have yet to be rediscovered. California's first people so far as is presently known were American Indians, ancestors of today's Indians and in no significant way different from them. And they have been in California a long time; by our standards of mobility and compared with our brief history, immemorially long.

The Yana have probably been in northern California for three or four thousand years. There are those who would double this figure, but in the present state of knowledge three thousand years as a minimum is a tentative, conservative figure arrived at, surprisingly, by way of a recently accepted branch of language study known as glottochronology. Put simply, glottochronology is a study of the rate at which the meaning of words changes, and the inferences to be drawn from such changes. It began with analyses of old and documented languages such as Sanskrit, Anglo-Saxon, or Chinese, comparing the old language in each case with its living descendants, to find the rate of change from cognate to new terms of the same basic meaning. Rates of change studied thus far vary little one from another, and their average, used as the norm of change, is applied to comparisons of pairs of other related languages to find the time which has elapsed since their separation or first differentiation. A technique for learning the history of a language thus becomes a technique also for learning something of a people's political or culture history.

Yana belongs to the Hokan superfamily, one of the six superfamilies of North America. The glottochronology of Hokan confirms and sharpens other evidence that Hokan-speaking people were old in California. Apparently Ishi's ancestors were occupying wide stretches of the upper Sacramento Valley and its tributaries at a time when there was a single Hokan language. At some time, three or four thousand years ago, this single language fragmented into ten or a dozen separate languages within the same geographical territory and amongst the original speakers of Hokan.

There is no evidence of other people having disputed the territory and its occupation with the ancestral Hokans; it is to be presumed that they lived freely in the open valley, going up into the hills, which to Ishi were a year-round home, only seasonally in the course of following the deer from valley to hills to mountains. There must have been a wide dispersal of Hokan-speakers as part of the drama of change which resulted in the appearance of many new languages within the old Hokan mold. This may well have been the time of the greatest creative florescence of the Yana and other Hokan peoples.

After two or three thousand years, "barbarians" from outside, Wintun or others, who were by then stronger and more numerous than the older population, engaged in one of their own thrusts of history making, invaded Yana country, occupied the richer parts of it, and pushed the smaller, older population back into the hills.

We turn now to archaeology to decipher a curiously half-lit corroboration of this early Yana history. Paynes Cave on Antelope Creek and Kingsley Cave on Mill Creek, both in Ishi's own country, and some smaller village and cemetery sites closeby have been excavated and their bones and tools studied. Charred wood, bone, and other substances from these presumably old and undisturbed sites have been tested and assigned absolute as well as relative dates, within one or two hundred years of exactness, by measuring their carbon fourteen content against that of recent, similar material. This is a satisfactory dating technique, over long periods, because carbon fourteen is an unstable compound which decomposes at the rate of 50 per cent in fifty-five hundred years. This dating is supplemented by a comparison of styles and any changes in styles over time. Together, the two lines of evidence, which in this case converge reasonably, suggest that the Yana territory of Ishi's lifetime and of the gold rush era had been occupied only occasionally a thousand years ago, but continuously since then. In other words, it would seem to have been not much more than a millennium ago that the Yana surrendered their valley holdings to become truly and wholly a hill people.

But we must leave scientific measurement and historical reconstruction to its specialists, and move on, closer to Ishi's time, realizing meanwhile that it is the scientist and the historian who remind us that the pace of the ancient world was no doubt pedestrian as compared with the modern world with its lightning changes, but that wherever there is life there is change. History was being made by Ishi's ancestors and their enemies as surely as it is today: languages came into being and spread and shrank and died; peoples migrated and made a way of life which was dominant and which then receded. The telescopic view into the old world cannot be made sharp, except perhaps when we hear a momentary echo of old Hokan in Ishi's recorded voice and Yahi speech, or when we hold in our hands an "old-fashioned" stone knife whose style was abandoned for something "new" a thousand years ago. The focus may be fuzzy; it is at least a look at a world in flux and motion, never wholly static; contoured and stereoscopic, never flat; even as our own moving, changing world.

What, then, of the Digger Indians who are supposed to have been the aborigines of California, to have spoken a guttural language, and to have managed barely to maintain a miserable existence by eating the roots which they dug from the unfriendly land with that most generic of tools, the wooden digging stick? Alas, the Diggers are a frontier legend, like the Siwash Indians of the

Northwest, Siwash being a blanket term growing out of a mis-hearing of the word *sauvage,* the French trappers' designation for Indian. Nor was there a Digger language amongst all the babel of tongues.

There is another frontier legend which dies hard: that the hills and streams and valleys of California yielded a grudging and sorry living to their native sons and daughters. The Spaniards and Mexicans did not so misunderstand the golden land, in part because they were never wholly detached from the soil in think-ing or occupation, and in part because California is not unlike much of Mexico and Spain. The Forty-niners, veteran contenders against mountains, high plains, and deserts, were without interest in the land as such, which appeared to them inhospitable, dry, barren. In the course of their continental trek, they had come to look upon food not as something to be grown or harvested, but as meat to be shot on the hoof, and as flour, sugar, coffee, and beans to be carried as part of one's pack and replaced in "Frisco" or Sacramento or at some other urban center.

The legend may have been prolonged in defiance of known fact through inertia, legends easily becoming habits which are hard to break, and through its usefulness in salving a not quite good conscience over the taking of land and lives. If the land was lean and the lives miserable then the wrong done was so much the less, or no wrong at all.

The term Digger continued to be used to refer to Indians other than those one knew. I have heard my grandmother, who came to Amador County to teach school in the early 1850's, and became a rancher's wife there, speak affectionately and correctly of her Miwok Indian neighbors, and disapprovingly of the strange Dig-ger Indians who from time to time used to wander in from a distance asking for work or perhaps only for food. Digger remains to this day a term of derogation, like "nigger."

Digger also defines however crudely and inadequately, one occupation of California Indians which the Forty-niners must have seen over and over again. The Indians did no planting, being hunters, fishermen, gatherers, and harvesters of grains and seeds and fruits and roots which grew wild in their natural habitat and uncultivated state—diggers if you will. The digging stick was used, customarily in the hands of women who were forever going off into the hills or meadows for maidenhair and sword ferns, for squaw grass and pine root, for redbud and hazel, and for all the stems and plants and grasses which they wanted for making baskets. And the digging stick, as will be seen, helped them in season to get some of the fresh vegetables of which they were fond. Only the aberrant Mohaves and Yumas, who live on the Colorado River, have always been agriculturists of sorts. That is, they planted many of their food stuffs—not like the hard-working and true farmers of the Southwest: the Hopi, Zuni, and Rio Grande pueblo Indians—but like the people of ancient Egypt, by dropping the seeds of corn and beans and squash into the red ooze exposed by the seasonal flooding and retreat of the river, and allowing the crops to grow under the blazing sun with a minimum of attention from the planters. But the Colorado River Indians were different also—and fortunate—in having no Forty-niners.

We have seen that the varied land once supported separate little nations, rather like Greek city states at least in size, in enclaves of inland valley or rough hill-country or woods or desert or along streams or beside the sea. And we have seen that these village states set themselves off further one from another by a growth of language barrier. The peoples differed in physical type, some being broad and stocky with round faces, some slim and tall with high-bridged noses, but none resembled the Plains or woodland Indians. Some lived better than others, and with more leisure; some buried their dead while others practiced cremation. Customs and beliefs varied from tribelet to tribelet, but nonetheless underlying their differences was a certain characteristic "set," a profile of a life which, broadly speaking, fits all of them and fits no Indians east of the Sierra Nevada. It was anciently a different world, from the crest of the Sierra westward to the

Pacific Ocean, as indeed it continues in oddly telling ways to be different today.

In some part, larger or smaller depending upon how one weighs it, the differences ancient and modern are born of the climate which is Mediterranean and subtropical. For the Indians this meant that during many months of each year outdoor living with only the lightest of shelters was comfortable, and that in most seasons they wore no clothes at all, a little front apron of bark and the ubiquitous brimless round basketry hat satisfying the requirements of modesty for a woman, while a man wore nothing at all except perhaps a deerskin breechclout. The buckskin shirt and leggings to be found to the east were not needed here and did not exist; an ample apron or skirt of buckskin for the women and grass or buckskin sandals with a wildcat or rabbit or feather cloak thrown over the shoulders when it was cold did very well for both men and women and completed their wardrobes except for beads and other ornaments, and ritual and dance regalia.

This was the area where, for whatever reason, basketry design was most elaborated, and the possibilities of baskets as utensils were most exploited to the almost total neglect of wood and pottery. Baskets were used for carrying and for storing all sorts of food and materials; they were the only cooking utensils; and they were the trays, plates, bowls, and mugs of dining. The creative impulse found expression most usually in basketry; also in the intricate fashioning of feather capes and headdresses; and in occasional beautifully wrought obsidian knives made from a single obsidian flake. These knives, two, three, or four feet long and correspondingly heavy, were held to be sacred and reserved for ceremonial use.

The great staple food of the California Indian was acorn flour made into mush or bread. The acorn, of which some half dozen or more edible varieties were recognized, meant to Indians what rice means to Cantonese Chinese, or maize to Mexicans. After acorns came salmon, fresh or dried and in large variety; and after salmon, deer meat, again fresh or dried. Other fish were of course eaten, and game larger and smaller than deer, and for the coastal people there was added all the rich variety of seafood. Ducks and geese were much liked. Pine nuts, hazel nuts, buckeye, manzanita berries, wild raspberry, huckleberry, plum, grape, elderberry, barberry, and thimbleberry were enjoyed in season, and some of them were dried and stored. There were sage and tarweed and clarkia seeds, and a host of other seeds small and large and, in season, the earth-oven roasted roots of the camas, annis, tiger lily, and brodiaea were a welcome addition. Certain grubs and worms were roasted as delicacies; also grasshoppers as in modern Mexico. Snakes were not eaten, nor so far as is known, were frogs.

But far deeper than food preferences and response to climate is the psychological set of the California cultures. To judge by their descendants, the ancestral California Indians who made the Far West their permanent home had found their way in the first place, and stayed on, in order to realize an ideal of a separatist and static arrangement of life. The most conspicuous feature of this life, at least to our view, is the preference for a small world intimately and minutely known, whose utmost boundaries were within reach by boat or on foot, a few days journey at most. Outside worlds were known to exist, of course. A man knew certain of his neighbors, sometimes when the neighbor's tongue had dialectic relation to his own so close that communication came readily, or sometimes when two worlds shared adjoining stretches of the same river, for example, and were similar enough in their ways to feel some identification even though they spoke different languages, as with the Yurok and Karok Indians along the Klamath River. But anything, everything that belonged within a man's own world, including its corpus of legendary event going back to the most ancient times, was better known and was more important than any person, place, or happening across the border.

By and large, no one voluntarily left his own and familiar world for a strange one. It was terrifying and dangerous to enter a community as a stranger. You were properly suspect, the inference being that your own people had put pressure on you to leave because of some crime you were guilty of. At best you would be without family or friends or influence or status, and forced to learn to speak a foreign language, if you were allowed to remain at all. There was always the chance that you would be killed, or ordered to move on.

The California Indian was, in other words, a true provincial. He was also an introvert, reserved, contemplative, and philosophical. He lived at ease with the supernatural and the mystical which were pervasive in all aspects of life. He felt no need to differentiate mystical truth from directly evidential or "material" truth, or the supernatural from the natural: one was as manifest as the other within his system of values and perceptions and beliefs. The promoter, the boaster, the aggressor, the egoist, the innovator, would have been looked at askance. The ideal was the man of restraint, dignity, rectitude, he of the Middle Way. Life proceeded within the limits of known and proper pattern from birth through death and beyond. Its repetitive rhythm was punctuated with ritual, courtship, dance, song, and feast, each established according to custom going back to the beginning of the world, an event which, along with subsequent events having to do with setting the way of life, was well known and fully recounted in the peoples' oral but elaborate and specific histories.

It was not an easy life, but it was a good one. The hunting and fishing and gathering, the endless labor of preparation of foods and hides, the making of baskets, tools, and implements and the always vexing problem of storage, required the industry and skill of both sexes and of young and old; but there was some choice and there was seasonal and ritual variety. There were lean times, but the lean like the fat times were shared with family, friends, and tribe. Life was as it had always been.

Chapter 2
A LIVING PEOPLE

In the foothills of Mount Lassen and along the streams that flow from the mountain west and southwest lies the Yana country. Here, east of the Sacramento River and south of the Pit River, within the angle of the coming together of the two streams, is an area roughly forty miles in width and sixty miles in length. The Yana's southern border stops just short of the Feather River; its western, six to ten miles short of the Sacramento, shunning the level valley.

The Yana were fewer in numbers and poorer in material comforts than were their valley neighbors, whom they regarded as soft, lax, and indifferent fighters. Like hill tribes in other parts of the world the Yana, too, were proud, courageous, resourceful, and swift, and were feared by the Maidu and Wintun peoples who lived in the lowlands.

The Lassen foothills are unlike the open, gently rising foothills of the Sierra Nevada. Mount Lassen belongs to the Cascades, a range whose underlying rock is basaltic, not granitic, formed from volcanic action, some older Cenozoic, some recent, Lassen being itself an occasionally active volcano. There are fir and pine forests in the higher parts, the forest below twenty-five hundred feet giving place to great expanses of boulder and broken rock that cover plateau-like, barren hills. Where the forest cover thins out, the streams have cut precipitous gorges, some of them to a depth of a thousand feet. There are oaks and scrub pines interspersed with the boulders, and there are occasional lush meadows. Beginning at about a thousand feet, there is as dense a chaparral growth as is to be found anywhere on the western slope. It is an

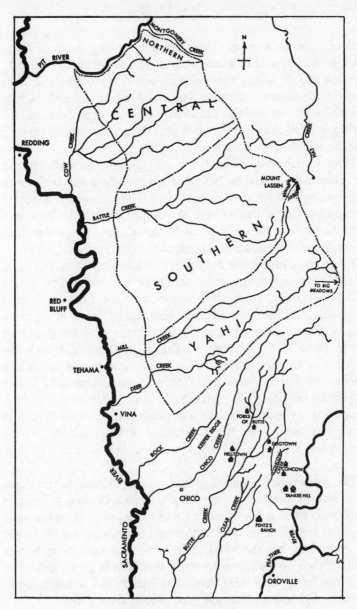

THE FOUR YANA TRIBELETS

area of heavy winter rainfall with snow coming down as far as does the forest; cold in winter; hot in summer; and cut across by streams which, unlike most of California's, flow full and swift even in the summer months. These streams are all rich in fish, especially salmon, and the Yana knew when to expect the heaviest spring and fall runs in each creek and river, and how far up each one the salmon were accustomed to go.

How, it may well be asked, in a land so unaccommodating, did the Yana maintain themselves? It was a precarious life, with never quite enough within their own borders. They foraged and hunted far up Cow Creek, Battle Creek, Antelope Creek, Mill Creek, and Deer Creek, and all the way up Mount Lassen, *Waganupa* they called the mountain, Little Shasta, their particular landmark.

There was considerable neighborly exchanging. Outsiders came to the Yana salt meadows to gather a season's supply of the "black" salt there, a salt which was used by the Yana as a special seasoning. And the Yana gathered acorns, and fished in the territory of their near neighbors. Their relations with the Atsugewi living along Hat Creek were friendly, as they were with the Achomawi on their eastern flank: these were people much like themselves. But the wealthy Wintun in the Sacramento Valley feared the periodic raids of the Yana into their own fat hunting country; and the Maidu to the south considered them a fierce and dangerous people: the age-old attitude of the lowlander to the hungry hill dweller who has a sure retreat behind him, and little to lose.

The pattern of marginality, then, was an old one to the Yana, who were accustomed to a hard and uncertain life and to fighting stubbornly for that life when they had to. But until the white man began to hem them in, the Maidu might fear them, and life might be precarious, but the whole of the two thousand or so square miles of their own undisputed world was open to them; and when they needed to, they went beyond as friends and welcome, or as enemies, fighting and raiding, but among their peers.

The crazy courage of the Yana was common talk even among their neighbors who hated and feared them most; and it was through these neighbors that their reputation as stubborn and fierce fighters reached the first white settlers, before they themselves had occasion to meet any Yana. White men had arrived in California with secondhand, often firsthand experience of the courage and pride of the Plains Indian warrior. This warrior was tall and handsome, with strongly marked, craggy features. His arrogant seeming, cold mien was dramatized in the flamboyant feather war bonnet which he wore. Thanks to the Spaniards, he was mounted and carried firearms not conspicuously inferior to those of the emigrants. He led war parties, took scalps, counted *coup,* and told of his exploits around the campfire afterward, in formal, boastful, expressionistic, declamatory prose.

The first white settlers, remembering the Plains Indians, thought that they knew what the Maidu and Wintun meant when they warned them that the Yana were fighters. They could not have been more mistaken. The people who fought to keep the white man from the Lassen hills were rarely above middle height, their features were rounded, and their expression typically bland. They were unmounted and unarmed, had never heard or dreamed of the art of scalping, and did not themselves curse or boast, secretly despising the white man for his propensity to do both.

The Yana had no weapons of war as such. When they defended themselves or when they took the aggressive against an enemy, their arsenal was no more than the tools by which they lived, used for the duration of the conflict as weapons: bow and arrow; spear; knife; harpoon; rock and sling. In all of California, it was only the Indians along the Colorado River who possessed a weapon as such, a war club.

Yana courage and pride were rather of the communal sort, the nearest modern equivalent of which would be the guerilla or resistance fighter. The Yana had maintained themselves against odds, using the tactics of surprise, speed, and secrecy. These same tactics, used by Ishi and his little group, prolonged the history of the Yahi a half century against fantastic odds.

The four linguistic divisions of Yana appear within the boundary lines of Yana territory on the map, page 25. Yahi, Ishi's dialect, is shown as the southernmost area; Batwi's country, Central Yana on the map, was less than thirty miles from Ishi's, but he and Ishi encountered dialectical differences great enough to make conversation somewhat difficult and aggravating to both of them. Each regarded the other's dialect as an outlandish and inferior misuse of his own language, but recognized it as his own, however barbarized, quite as a Heidelberger regards and recognizes Plattdeutsch.

Nor were these difficulties of Ishi's and Batwi's owing to either man being incompetent in his own tongue. Both men were satisfactory linguistic informants, a role requiring some intellectual grasp of the elements of a language which is in process of being written for the first time in phonetic transcription and by a person who does not himself control the language. The speaker must have accuracy and clarity of pronunciation, and great patience in the endless repetition of the words and sounds required of him, and some sense at least for the grammar, the internal structure of his language. (Needless to say, he need not be conscious of the structuring of the words and phrases as he uses them in natural speech.)

It may be with Yana as with French, that it can be understood only with exact articulation, for Yana has the peculiar nicety of separate dialects for women and for men. Such duality of speech is so rare as to have been authenticated by linguists no more than two or three times anywhere in the world. A near equivalent is known for certain Carib Indians in the West Indies, the difference from the Yana being that Carib-speaking men invaded islands of Arawak-speaking peoples, either killing the men and staying on to marry the women, or carrying the women off to yet other islands. Accounts differ; quite possibly it happened both ways. Anyway, the women were Arawak speaking and persisted in their native speech, even to teaching it to their daughters while their sons spoke the Carib of their fathers, thus forcing bilingualism on the men, a neat revenge. With the Yana, the sex distinction is made within a single language, developed at some unknown time and within the tribe, in response to what societal or psychological exaggeration of a bent or preference, we can only speculate. It may not be without some meaning in this context to note that the Yana and other Indians of interior northern California marked the coming-of-age of both girls and boys with elaborate ritual and social observances. Maturation was looked upon as perhaps the most important and most dangerous of life's traumas; it was hedged about with ceremony and taboo, and boys and girls were not allowed to play together or even to sleep under the same roof once they began to mature. It is also a specialization of Yana that a brother and sister addressed each other in the plural form—the Yana *vous,* never its *tu,* the impropriety of the use of the singular having to do with its too great familiarity.

Infants of both sexes were cared for by the mother with an older sister or a grandmother helping. Their first speech was that of the women's dialect, always spoken by women, and by men and boys when in the presence of girls or women. As a boy grew older and was independent of nursing care, he was taken by his father or older brother or uncle wherever they were going, for longer and longer times each day. By the age of nine or ten, well before puberty, he was spending most of his waking hours in male company and was already sleeping in the men's house. Thus he learned his second language, the men's dialect.

It is as difficult to explain a linguistic trait without becoming technical as it is to explain how music is written or the rules for playing a game. Briefly—and my source is the linguist, Edward Sapir—the male form is longer than the female, and a characteristic of the male dialect is the addition of a final syllable of its own to the fundamental, root form of a word. This trait has led Leonard Bloomfield, another linguist, to suggest that the women's dialect is the more infantine, since the female form is most commonly a reduction in the final syllable of the theoretically fundamental form of the word. Sapir, however, warns against any rationalization, either by the Yana themselves or by linguists, of psychological causality, because of the structural fact that the dialectic differences occur in complete words, not in suffixed elements as such, and that the female as much as the male is a conventional dialect within a dialect—each is a completely formalized system. There was a further, nonstructural distinction in pronunciation: men talking to men spoke fully and deliberately; when speaking with women a "clipped" style of utterance was preferred. All in all, Sapir concludes that there are or have been in the world few if any languages in which this splitting of a dialect has been so pervasive and so thorough.

For example, the male form of the word for "person" is *yana,* pronounced with stress on the first syllable, the second syllable crisply finished without dropping the voice; in the women's dialect, it becomes *yah,* a single syllable, but the final sound, the *h,* a protracted, rough-breathing, sounded *h.* Or, take the word for "grizzly bear," again a two-syllable word in the male form, *t'en'na,* the syllables separated by a glottal stop; it becomes *t'et,* single syllable, in the female form. Or, there is a phrase such as "See me!" which is *diwai-dja,* male; *diwai-tch,* female. In single word examples such as those given here, the common root seems to dominate over the divergent endings, but in full sentences, endings determine much of the nature of the flow of speech from word to word, thus greatly heightening the dialectic difference in the sounds of the male and female forms, and probably accounting for the different voice quality which the men brought to their pronunciation of the women's language.

In addition to distinctions made in word endings, there are also some verb stems which are different in the two dialects. "A man goes" is *ni;* "a woman goes" is *'a;* "a man dances" is *buribu;* "a woman dances," *djari-dja.* There are many of these.

Of course, every Yana woman knew the men's dialect as well as her own. The sex-differentiated dialects would be obstructive to understanding only to a non-Yana speaker, not to men and women whose tongue it was and who constantly heard the two variants, even though the female speakers used but one of them. The convention of speaking proper Yana, man to man or man to woman, and of knowing but never using words which you overheard, is not a matter of mastery in a single lesson, nor need the present account go more deeply into its niceties and subtleties. As for Ishi, even in his hunted life he maintained the old linguistic deference and adaptation of speech to the sex of the person spoken to so long as there was any Yahi man or woman for him to address.

There remains a psychological aspect of this language peculiarity which is not subject to proof, but which should not be dismissed. The surviving Yahi seem never to have lost their morale in their long and hopeless struggle to survive. Could the language have played a role in this continuing tension of moral strength? It had equipped its speakers with the habit of politeness, formality, and exact usage freighted with strong feeling for the importance of speaking and behaving in such and such a way and no other, a way which did not permit slovenliness either of speech or of behavior.

The sex-duality in language and the institution of the men's house, both point to the large role played by the father in his son's upbringing, and to the mother's responsibility for the daughter's training. Taboo limiting and directing the father's behavior upon the birth of a child was only somewhat less than that imposed upon the mother. Customarily not present at the birth, the father's activity was nonetheless oriented to it. He gathered wood according to ceremonial rule for the fires built to care for mother and child. At dawn he ran a course which took him into the higher hills where he prayed on the days preceding and following the birth. Both husband and wife observed prolonged periods of sexual restraint and of dietary and other restrictions to insure the infant's protection from sickness and danger. None of this behavior is peculiar to the Yana except in detail, but the impression remains of an unusual mutual involvement of both parents in family matters, accentuated perhaps because the tribal numbers were always small, with intimate, close-knit family and village units.

The use of the formal address between brother and sister suggests the Freudian fear of incest and a bolstering against it, but it must be seen in its perspective of being merely one of a series of proscriptions of formal behavior. A man did not look directly at, or continue for any time a *tête-à-tête* with either his mother-in-law or his daughter-in-law, and a woman was equally circumspect toward her father-in-law or her son-in-law. It would be naïve and inaccurate to interpret this restraint in the light of our mother-in-law jokes. To speak directly to a mother-in-law or father-in-law was to fail in respect toward them. The Indian attitude to their elders was much closer to that of pre-commune Chinese veneration of age than to the modern American fear and disparagement of both the look and the fact of old age.

The single family house was conical in shape, its framework of poles overlaid with slabs of bark, either cedar or pine, and banked with dirt to a distance of three or four feet for added warmth. At the center posts, which were the highest point, the house might be ten feet high, inside measurement, no more, and with a total diameter at ground level of eighteen or twenty feet. Inside, there was a circular pit, dug to a depth of three or four feet, and ten or twelve feet in diameter. Within the pit were the fireplace and the baskets, ladles, stirrers, and other cooking utensils. Here the family cooked and ate and slept when the weather was too cold for outdoor living. Tule mats lined the floor and walls; blankets, clothing, tools, hunting gear, and baskets containing various materials hung from the walls or were stored on the ledge which encircled the pit. There was a small, ground-level covered entryway for children, and for the grownups, a notched ladder-post which went from the pit up to the top of the house, and through the smoke hole. In such a house a man, his wife, children, and perhaps a grandfather and a grandmother lived, cooked, ate, and slept.

The Yana were polygynous in theory, and sometimes in practice. When there were two wives, they occupied the same house. Neither myth nor other record indicates tension between plural wives beyond the expectable strains of housemates. So far as it is possible to analyze this occasional polygamy, it seems to have gone with a man's being an unusually good hunter and provider, hence both wives drew credit from the marriage. When, as was usually the case, the wives were sisters there was no complication of a double set of in-laws. Presumably, when there were marriageable bachelors available, the second sister married outside. If husbands were in short supply, to be a second wife, whether or not a sister of the first wife, was an acceptable arrangement.

There were sometimes larger houses in which two or more families or a numerous and extended single family lived. In any case, quarters were crowded, and some formalization of relations between in-laws, and siblings, and between men and women, would seem an aid to amicable living. The institution of the men's house takes on an enlarged role in this view of the family. It was something between the modern men's club, a school, and a church. It got the men out from under foot, giving the women an opportunity for sociability among themselves, and for doing their own work. The separate small house to which a woman was required to retire alone for the duration of her moon periods may well have served to give her a welcome rest from the impingements within the "big" house. She cooked only for herself during her six days of retirement, and many chores were done for her, since she was proscribed from doing them herself.

The exaggeration of the importance of whatever was physiologically and functionally characteristic of women not only colored the relations between men and women but also it varied and elaborated them, made them formal and patterned. Without it, given the cramped quarters and a great deal of repetitive monotony in life, the interpersonal and sex relations might have suffered from laxness, or boredom, or amorphousness. There are more ways and sometimes more effective ways than those of sheer animal extroversion to introduce variety and interest and a certain pleasant tension to living; formalization is surely one of them. The Hawaiians memorized their family trees for as many generations back as they knew or could imagine them. Homesick Englishmen dressed for dinner on the dusty plains of India and in the remote jungles of Africa. The California Indians of the interior valleys and foothills elaborated behavior patterns centering on sex, maturation, birth, and periodicity; the Yana added to these some complicating linguistic wrinkles of their own.

There was a pan-California phenomenon which also affected interpersonal relations: the Indians did not have large families; the population, until the Caucasian invasion, remained fairly constant. This meant that children were desired and welcomed, and that parents and grandparents had time and love to lavish on them. This may have been true for North America as a whole, but the same gentleness and permissiveness and ease of the parental attitude toward children did not operate equally the country over. A part of this pattern is also the attitude to the mother before, during, and after childbirth, and this is true for all North America. Nowhere was it expected, or indeed allowed, that the mother should at once be up and back to work. She was kept to her bed and to a special diet, cared for by her mother or another older woman and by her husband until the infant's cord had healed and dropped off, by which time the mother would normally have the milk flow and nursing established. Whoever was caring for her helped her also in this, gently sucking off the colostrum if the baby did not do so, and giving the baby a little acorn gruel to suck at until he learned to nurse properly. The "strong woman" tradition of north European peasantry, in which the mother "has" her baby out in the field and returns forthwith to scything or other field work in which she was engaged up to the actual moment of birth, not only was unknown to our Indians;

the idea of such a procedure would have disgusted and outraged their sense of propriety and their understanding of medicine and healing.

Nor is there to be found in California anywhere a source for the traditional picture of the *squaw,* loaded like a pack animal and following behind her leisured and swaggering buck of a husband. Everybody worked hard, but more or less according to strength and capacity, and the division of labor seems to have been fair and reasonable.

The Yana apparently enjoyed recounting their dreams to one another sometimes, as we do when we are not too sophisticate. They might read a predictive significance in dreams after the fact, but the act of dreaming and of recalling dreams was not systematic with them, nor did it attach to mystic belief except for those dreams in which they got power: the vision dreams. Those were something apart, and private.

All the Yana buried their dead in a cemetery close to the home village, except the Yahi who practiced cremation, afterwards gathering the bones and ashes into a basket which was buried under a rock cairn to mark the grave and to keep animals away. The Yana, although not approving of the occasional habit of dead souls to return to the land of the living, accepted with considerable equanimity the fact that they sometimes did so. They were said to visit places dear to them in life; and flowers and whistling might attract them. They might take a drink from water left out at night, hence fresh water was always fetched for household use in the morning. The feeling was that the business of life was with the living. Once dead, the beloved one was started on his journey to the Land of the Dead with ceremony and mourning. That far land must henceforth be his proper home.

The ancient rhythm of Yana days and nights following the moons and seasons in their orderly progression and repetition was the pattern Ishi was born to. He lived it in nostalgic, painful-loving memory even though he could have experienced it fully and undistorted only as a very young child.

The last of the snow moons brought the seasons full circle, and was sure to find the Yana, young and old, at their leanest and hungriest. The indoor tasks of the days of storms were completed, and the storage baskets of acorns and of dried deer and salmon meat, empty or almost empty. An occasional rabbit or squirrel caught at the edge of the snow was insufficient to relieve the gnawing, growing hunger of the last hard days of winter.

The big winds of spring were a welcome announcement of renewal. They were cold and gusty, but they blew around the warm earth-covered houses harmlessly, blowing themselves out, and were followed by warm rain. Then came the miracle. The bare rocks of the plateaus, the hills, and the meadows were painted overnight in the fresh green of new clover. The sun shone warm, and the streams filled with leaping salmon swimming strongly upstream from the sea. While the men speared and netted the salmon, the women filled baskets with the precious clover. There was feasting and thanksgiving. No salmon bones were thrown away: it would have been a disrespect to do so; dried and pounded and ground in mortars, they were eaten thankfully. The ribs of the Yana became overlaid with fat, and babies no longer cried hungrily.

As the clover grew large and tough, the women passed it by. In its place were bulbs, tender enough to be eaten raw or after light steaming. Best of all, there was fresh deer meat, which meant a good strong broth with pieces of meat and young greens floating in it. Spring was a likely time for a family to celebrate a daughter's coming of age. Friends would gather from near-by villages and streams to feast and dance and sing for six days and nights. The Yana, as was true of other hill people, did not have as many or as elaborate sings and dances and tribal feast days as did the valley and coast Indians. A special effort was made for the daughter. Births, deaths, marriages, and most of life's other crises with their ritually prescribed behavior were enacted within the family unit in which several generations might be represented, and were extended to include only the intimate home village group.

There followed the moons of summer, day after day sunny and cloudless, the night sky hung heavy with stars. Before the dry heat was upon them, the Yana women would have built new or repaired old thatched summer houses. The heat becomes intense in the foothills, the temperature ranges from the high eighties to the one hundred and twenties. There is no rain during the summer, and not much breeze, and the sun reflects off cliffs and bare rocks as from overheated ovens. Unhampered by clothes, immune to the ever present poison oak, and living at peace with the rattlesnake and lesser pests, the Yana took their ease in their summer houses as long as the sun stood high, going for a swim several times a day in the always close-by streams, leaving fishing, cooking, and gathering for the early morning hours, and for the long twilight time. For the hot days, the women made a cooling and nourishing drink of pounded manzanita or other berries mixed with water. Men, women, and children slept with only the open thatched roof over them, learning the stars: their place in the cloudless sky; their names; and the stories of how they came to be there. When the heat grew fiercer until even the nights stayed hot, they went for a moon or two's duration far up the slopes of Mount Lassen (Waganupa) where there was coolness under the tall trees, and where the hunting was as it is even today, excellent. There the men hunted in earnest, going off for a day and a night or longer, coming back to camp, laden. And there the women filled the great baskets as fast as the meat was dried; baskets which would be carried, full, down the mountain against the hungry days of winter. Ishi, as long as he was in his own home country, until perhaps his last, sad summer there, made this trip up Waganupa, a trip of four "sleeps" or days it was. He, like the other Yana, knew the mountain as he knew his own hills.

They would be home once more in the villages along Battle Creek and Antelope Creek and the other streams during the time of the unchanging moons, our harvest and hunter moons. The harvest time was the most social season of the year for the Yana. Acorns were ripe, ready for picking, shelling, drying, and storing as were buckeye, and pine and hazel nuts. Everyone took part in the harvesting, villages coming together in temporary camping places, as many as two or three hundred or more people in a single camp. It was during these large encampments of autumn, in the 1860's, that some of the massacres of the Yana by white settlers occurred. At no other time could so many be found together or so exposed, with children and dogs running about more freely and more noisily than was their wont. There was also the fall run of salmon to engage the time and interest of the men, who, having knocked the acorns and pine cones to the ground, went off to fish while the women packed the nuts in storage baskets. Sometimes they stayed up most of the night, working and talking. There would be days for sleeping, later.

This harvest-time sociability was happier and more relaxed and outgoing than that of the springtime. The spring festivities were confined to family and intimates, and there clung about them the pervasive magico-mystical intensity which the Yana and their neighbors felt toward the power for good and evil residing in the female principle with its recurrent moon cycle and association with blood. Also there was the almost frenetic excitement of release from cold and hunger: the religious aspect of thanksgiving. In contrast to these overheightened sensibilities, harvest time was friendly and gossipy and neighborly. What the men and women and children learned and experienced during the days of the big encampments would be the raw material for conversation, speculation, and philosophizing after everyone was home again, and the days drew in: the odd names by which people and tools were called; a different way of shooting a bow; a song of another people.

The first cold rain brought the harvest sociability to a close. Everybody went home to his own stream and to his own warm house. Winter was good, too, if it did not go on too long. The rain moons and the fog moons were a time for repairing and making ropes and nooses, bows and quivers, and arrow and spear points; and for basket weaving. In the long winter nights the men, taking with them the boys who were old enough to understand men's talk, went to the men's house. Here the boys learned the skills and duties which were a man's. They learned as well the proper language for men, and the Yana point of view toward work and war and women, particularly one's wife; and the Yana world-view was made explicit to them. Meanwhile, it was not dull in the house where the women stayed with the babies and small children. The mother and grandmother had work to do, and the daughter must learn not only a woman's skills, but a woman's duty to her husband, and her terrible power for harm should she fail in knowledge and practice of the etiquette and taboo attaching to her sex.

Winter was also the time for retelling the old history of the beginning of the world and of how animals and men were made, the time to hear over again the adventures of Coyote and Fox and Pine Marten, and the tale of Bear and Deer. So, sitting or lying close to the fire in the earth-covered house, and wrapped in warm rabbitskin blankets, with the rain falling outside and the snow moon bringing a light fall down Waganupa as far even as Deer Creek, the Yana cycle of changing seasons completed another full turn. As the food baskets emptied, one by one, and game remained hidden and scarce, the Yana dreams turned to a time, not far off, when the earth would be covered with new clover. They felt an urge to be up and about in an awakening world, while far away in the great ocean which they had never seen, the shining salmon were racing toward the mouth of the Sacramento River, their goal the Yana's own home streams.

Chapter 3
A DYING PEOPLE

The Spanish and Mexican regimes had run their course in California before Indians as remote as the Yana were reached. The most northerly mission to be established was at Sonoma, far to the south and west of the Mount Lassen country, with several coast ranges and many weary, untracked miles intervening between. Moreover, the missions had been secularized before the ready-to-hand valley Indians, easily rounded up and missionized, were in short supply.

The beginning of the end of the Yana might be said to have been in the year 1844, when a spate of land grants was made by the Mexican government in the Sacramento Valley bordering on Yana country. After 1844, Mexico's time of trouble at home and abroad brought to an end any further expansion of Alta California, the thrust which carried Mexican hegemony up valley to the Yana hills being her last as it was her northernmost reach. In due course the United States government confirmed these grants which were for land belonging to two border neighbors of Ishi's people, the *Memponna,* Wintun, on the Sacramento River and the *Nemshua-Mai,* on the lower Feather River—"Wahle Indjins"—as Ishi would have learned to call them by the time he drew the map which indicates the common borders which they and the Yana shared.

Each grant was a strip of land of a few leagues of which a stretch of riverbank formed one side and defined its longitudinal limits. Of the better known grants which impinged on Yana borders, the farthest upstream was *San Buena Ventura,* made to Pierson B. Reading. This grant comprised six leagues of land bordering the west banks of the Sacramento River, within which were the present-day sites of Anderson, Redding, and Ball's Ferry. This land lay abreast the northern Yana.

The grant to Job F. Dye, *Rio de los Berrendos,* also comprised six leagues bordering the east side of the river, a little below and across river from the present site of Red Bluff and continuing south to include the mouth of Antelope Creek, directly west of the Central Yana.

La Barranca Caljada, or *La Barranca Colorado,* extended four leagues along the west bank of the Sacramento and took in the present site of Red Bluff.

Las Flores, given to William Chard, only three leagues in extent, lay along the west bank of the river between Red Bluff and Tehama, paralleling the lands of the Southern Yana.

Rio de los Molinos, or *Saucos,* five leagues granted to Albert G. Toomes, lay along the east bank and included the mouth of Mill Creek and the townships of Tehama and Vina.

Bosquejo, Peter Lassen's grant, comprised five leagues along the east bank beginning just south of Vina and including the mouth of Deer Creek.

Directly east of *Bosquejo* and *Rio de los Molinos,* where valley gives over to foothills, was the ancient border between the valley Indians and Ishi's people, the Yahi.

There were some other grants made in 1844, but farther downriver and south of the Yana hills. It is apparent from the fewness, smallness, and lateness of these grants that American settlers among the sparse valley population of Mexicans and Spaniards were a tiny trickle north as far as the latitude of Mount Lassen, until the gold rush. The always scant Spanish-Mexican population had available to it more rich and accessible pasture land than it could use; neither the vaquero nor the farmer bothered with the lesser resources of the rugged Yana country.

Ishi's grandparents had picked up from their Indian neighbors in the valley a few Spanish words which, incorporated and Yanaized, were not regarded by Ishi as words of foreign origin. For example, his "bad" was *malo,* Spanish, and his word for "woman," *muhéli,* probably from Spanish *mujer.* For the rest, the coming and departure of the Spaniards and Mexicans between the years 1769 and 1848, years of destruction of identity, of decimation and tragedy to the mission Indians, left the little nation of the Yana untouched.

With the signing of the Treaty of Guadalupe Hidalgo by Mexico and the United States in 1848, the Spanish-Mexican phase of the invasion of California ended, to be followed immediately by the Anglo-Saxon, represented as yet in the upper Sacramento Valley by only a few white grantees, their families and households, none of them in Yana country proper. Jim Payne, to be sure, moved from the valley into the hills, settling on Antelope Creek close to a cave which came to be known as Paynes Cave. But this was not before 1875, nor were there many other permanent settlers on Ishi's ancestral land before the late 'seventies and 'eighties.

But with the discovery that the gravel of creek and riverbeds in the red foothill country of California carried gold, what had been a trickle of new immigration became a stream pouring down the western face of the Sierra, a never ending stream as it would seem now, a hundred and more years after its beginnings. The so-called historical or documented period of Yana history began when old and discontinuous trails to oak flats, along creeks, or over low divides, became united into prospectors' trails, and were later widened to allow covered wagons to travel them. One such trail skirts Lassen Peak to the south, passes through Deer Creek Meadows, follows the watershed between Deer Creek and Mill Creek, and continues down Mill Creek to the Sacramento River at Los Molinos, cutting through the rugged but beautiful southern heartland of the Yahi country. (See the map, p. 44.) It came to be known as the Old Lassen Trail, named, as was the peak it skirted, for Peter Lassen, whose rancho near the mouth of Deer Creek was the end of the long, long trek for those emigrants who came west by this route.

In 1850, ten or more years before Ishi's birth, the Yana occupied some 2,000 to 2,400 square miles of land recognized as their own; they and their Indian neighbors distinguished four linguistic, territorial, and cultural groups in the little nation of two or three thousand people—life was as it always had been. By 1872, twenty-two years later, and when Ishi was perhaps ten years old, there were *no* Southern Yana left; and only some twenty or thirty scattered *individuals* of the Northern and Central Yana remained alive. As for the fourth group, the Yahi, they were believed to have been entirely exterminated also, and so they were except for a handful, Ishi among them.

This death of a whole people came after the fiercest and most uncompromising resistance that the intruders were to meet anywhere on the west coast. And, at the bloody heart of this last stand of the Yana, were Ishi's people, the Yahi, a tribelet of probably no more than three or four hundred souls, counting the women, the very young, and the old. How so small, and to the newcomers so unimportant, a fragment of humanity succeeded in involving the United States Army as well as citizen vigilante groups is a tale soon told, a tale which satisfies the Greek ideal of starkness of tragedy and unity of time.

Disastrous to the Indians as had been the Ibero-American invasion of California, it was, all in all, less destructive of human life and values than was the Anglo-American. The earlier invasion remained small in numbers, being in the hundreds to the Indians' thousands. However cruel or culture-bound were many of those who peopled the land, they were nonetheless responsible officers of church or state or military; or they were vaqueros or farmers—answerable to authority, every one. Also, they were Mediterranean in their racial outlook. This meant that intermarriage with indigenes and the emergence of the *mestizo* were regarded as natural results of conquest.

The Anglo-Saxons, by contrast, reversed the ratio of whites to Indians, coming in inundating numbers—there were as many as a hundred thousand of them in a single year. They lacked any formal church control and, during all the fateful years for Indian

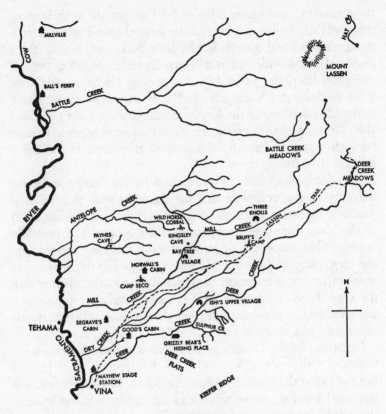

YAHI TERRITORY

The following sites do not appear on any other map: Segrave's cabin; Good's cabin; Bruff's camp (probably Bluff camp on Waterman's map); Bay Tree Village (probably the village at Center ford on Waterman's map); the Three Knolls (close to Black Rock on Waterman's map).

survival, were without adequate state or military restraints, so that both the excesses and cruelties and crimes, and the efforts to bring them under some sort of surveillance and control, were pretty much up to the frontiersmen themselves. Anglo-Saxons tended to racism then as now. A person with a skin color different from their own was thought to be intellectually and morally inferior; marriage with him was an antisocial act, sometimes legally forbidden; whatever the source for a sense of wonder and sacredness, if non-Christian, it was considered to be superstition and to be reprehensible. The early Anglo-Saxon emigrants were of two sorts: one, moral, ethical, and law-abiding, even if the laws were of local manufacture; the other, made up of the floaters, the irregulars, the failures at home, in revolt against the old customary home behavior patterns, and contemptuous of restrictions attempted on the spot by their soberer companions. Among the second group were also the outrightly criminal. Both sorts were in agreement, however, that the Indian was an inferior, and both used him as indentured laborer, slave, or concubine, and deprived him of life as well as freedom if he threatened to be in any way troublesome. White men who married Indian women were regarded with contempt. Half-breeds, especially the unhappy spawn of concubinage and rape, were classed as "natives," with all the disadvantages implicit in that special and by white definition second-class category.

It is with reluctance that the statistics which follow are offered at all, for the nature of the available source material can but rarely yield exact figures. Since all information is from white sources, and since an account of an Indian murder of a white was more acceptable copy than the reverse event, any inaccuracy in ratio will minimize the extent of the disproportion. The author finds a total of not more than twenty authenticated murders of whites by Indians who were or who were thought to have been Yana; six or eight of these killings, however, occurred out of presumable Yana range. This figure agrees closely with Professor Waterman's, who reports a total of twelve. This is not to say that there were no more than twelve or twenty murders of whites by Yana Indians. We have only hearsay and fragmentary record of much that went on in those remote hills and cañons on either side of Lassen Trail. During the years of the destruction of the Yana only some six hundred Yana deaths by violence from white settlers are of record—otherwise, the accounts say "several," "many," "a few"—not exact numbers which yield exact totals, not to mention those deaths of which no formal record survives. The ratios suggested by the meager Yana data, of one white person murdered for every thirty to fifty Indians, understates but indicates the drift of the vital statistics for the bloody years of Yana history: 1850–1872.

It was in the early 'sixties that the whole white population of the Sacramento Valley was in an uproar of rage and fear over the murder of five white children by hill Indians—probably Yahi. But the soberly estimated numbers of kidnappings of Indian children by whites in California to be sold as slaves or kept as cheap help was, between the years 1852 and 1867, from three to four *thousand;* every Indian woman, girl, and girl-child was potentially and in thousands of cases actually subject to repeated rape, to kidnapping, and to prostitution. Prostitution was unknown to aboriginal California, as were the venereal diseases which accounted for from forty to as high as eighty per cent of Indian deaths during the first twenty years following the gold rush. Professor S. F. Cook's series of monographs on Indian-Caucasian relations in California are the principal source for the estimated totals given in this paragraph, his ordering of all known pertinent data being an exhaustive and informed study of population statistics on both the Ibero- and the Anglo-American invasions.

The Caucasians brought with them also the "common" diseases, which included measles, chicken pox, smallpox, tuberculosis, malaria, typhoid, dysentery, influenza, pneumonia, and others, seeding them all willy-nilly through a population wholly without immunity. The mission Indians who had received these same diseases from the Spaniards were already, in 1848, extinct or much reduced; in any case, they had never been in the hill and mining country of Lassen nor mingled with its people. One or another of the introduced infections continued through several generations to kill numbers of Indians. The worst of the decimation—according to Cook an average of sixty per cent for the population of the state as a whole—was, naturally, in the first ten years. In no case did disease alone exterminate a whole people, and exposure to infection fell most heavily upon those valley Indians who bowed before the new order, and whose land was "settled."

Forced migrations account for some hundreds of Yana deaths; but death by shooting and particularly by mass-murder shooting interspersed with hangings were the usual and popular techniques of extermination. The Yahi opposed to this mass murder a courageous and spirited opposition, raiding when they could, killing when they could, and killing where it hurt as they were being hurt. But the taking of a horse, a mule, a cow, or a sheep; a bag of barley; even the firing of a barn now and then and the occasional murder of an innocent child or woman appear in the totals a puny revenge. The story is not a pretty one. It seems proper, at this distance, to confront the facts and the judgments which flow from the facts.

Many of us in California number among our ancestors a grandparent or a great-grandparent who came from somewhere in the "east," either with the Forty-niners or in the later waves of immigration following close upon them, family units these later ones, burdened with wagons and horses and cattle and oxen: men and women moving out from their country's earlier centers, homeless, but looking for a home. We have been taught to regard with pride the courage and ingenuity of these ancestors, their stubbornness in carving out a good life for their children. It is neither meet nor needful to withdraw such affectionate respect and admiration; it is perhaps well to remind ourselves that the best and gentlest of them did not question their right to appropriate land belonging to someone else, if Indian—the legal phrase was "justifiable conquest." However broad and real governmental and popular approval was, this invasion was like the classic barbarian invasions— a forced intrusion upon a settled population, and its replacement by the intruders. Such invasions have occurred many times, and continue to occur in the history of mankind, but also as well in the history of all forms of life; they are a part of the biological urge of each plant and animal to make or to take a place for itself and its descendants. Invasion, then, is a necessitous act in the Darwinian sense of struggle and survival; it is instinctive, primitive, and in itself inhumane.

That the invasion we are examining aroused a maximum of mutual fear and hate, was probably due in the first instance to the opening of a trail through a country before inviolate, and to the habit and psychology of some small part of the Forty-niners who did the opening. The first prospectors, miners, hunters, and trappers to travel Lassen and the other trails were a hard and hardy company. They came unencumbered with women or children; or with baggage beyond what a mule could carry. And they had their guns, by which they lived. They had been further hardened by a rough trip over a wide country not easy or friendly to cross, and their trek had been slowed and bloodied, and ended for some of their companions by Indians who contested their crossing and harried them; these were mounted and armed Indians, seemingly fearless.

In the company of these first comers were the inevitable trigger-happy few whose habit had become to shoot an Indian, any Indian, on sight; who counted *coup* under the slogan, "The only good Indian is a dead Indian," and who were possessed of the special skill of scalping, something previously unknown to California's aborigines. There was one such of whom Waterman writes: "On good authority I can report the case of an old prospector-pioneer-miner-trapper of this region [Butte County], who had on his bed even in recent years a blanket lined with Indian scalps. These had been taken years before. He had never been a government scout, soldier, or officer of the law. The Indians he had killed purely on his own account. No reckoning was at any time demanded of him."

By the time there was a resident and sober and responsible citizenry living in townships in the valley, that is, by the early 'sixties, the Yana—those who were still alive—had learned to distrust every white person as a possible killer out for gratuitous murder. So far as they could, they paid back in kind. Very few of the newcomers settled in actual Yana country before the 'eighties. The rub was that their oxen and cattle and sheep and pigs ranged the hills in such numbers that the native food sources such as the seeds of various grasses and the smaller varieties of oaks bearing acorns within reach of a woman's gathering (and equally of a pig's rooting) were depleted or destroyed. At the same time, the once free and open streams for fishing were appropriated or polluted or both, thus increasingly restricting Ishi's people, who were ordered off at the point of a gun if need be, and pushed back more and more into the inaccessible cañons of their streams. Hydraulic mining poured thousands of cubic yards of silt into the Sacramento River. This ruined many hundreds of acres of farming land in the valley, and diminished the size of the salmon runs up the tributaries where the Yana lived. The rich, open meadows on which these foothill Indians depended for varietal seasonal foods were tramped out, and the sometimes widely placed stands of large acorn oaks were increasingly denied them.

Always close to hunger, they became hungrier. They had raided beyond their borders and fought when they had to during all their history, if reciprocal land use between neighbors broke down. They raided and fought back now with every skill and device they could muster, having learned some new techniques from those who were responsible for the wholesale killings, scalpings, kidnappings, and rapings which were visited upon them and their near neighbors during the first years of emigrant travel over "Old Lassen Trail"—not so old then. The Yana image of the white man became fixed during those days when it was a careless boast that "You can't tell one Indian from another." The

Yana found themselves, too, indifferent to making distinctions between one white person and another.

In actual fact, both the Yana and the new settlers did make distinctions. Indians were blamed, with or without evidence, for every out-of-the-way killing, for every cabin burning, for every stealing of stock or tools or clothes. But never the close-by Indians, "our" Indians: it was Indians at a distance, "wild" Indians who had done the deed. The Mill Creeks, as Ishi's people, the Yahi, were by then called, came in for maximum blame. They were actually responsible for more depredation than were other Indians; the valley Indians had feared them in the old days, and passed along their fear to their white neighbors; in any case, the Yahi were "wild," refusing to be "our" Indians to anyone. There seems to have been a discernible pattern among the stealings and murders committed by the Yahi: time after time they returned to the same ranch or cabin or stock pen or range; some they never troubled. Beyond this, they stole when they were hungry and cold; they murdered after murder had been done among them, so nearly as one can read the evidence. Of this, Richard Gernon, a surveyor in Red Bluff, who spent many years working in and about the Mill Creek country, says in a letter to Professor Waterman, November 3, 1914: "You have been misinformed about them [the Mill Creeks] robbing my camp. . . . It is a remarkable thing, that the white men who hunted the Mill Creek Indians, between the years 1854 and 1865, have always had their camps robbed in after years. And those who never hunted those Indians never had anything stolen from them by the Indians." It is to be noted that the same names appear and reappear in the stories of reprisals and counterreprisals. Some people showed a predilection for Indian scouting and vigilante service, others did not, and were involved only when fear following upon women and children being made the victims of Yahi revenge roused a whole countryside.

Of the twenty-two years, 1850–1872, the first ten after the gold rush might be said to have been the years of preparation. In

those years, between disease and murderings and loss of free movement, the Yana became a desperate people. And the new settlers,
their stereotype of the Yana as fixed and inaccurate as the Yana's
of them, were exasperated by raids on their stock and destruction
of their property, and fearful for their lives. Along Deer Creek
and Mill Creek it was as elsewhere in California: the years of
the Civil War were also the years when the clash between the
Indians and whites reached its climax, breaking out more and
more often into open hostility and violence after ten years of increasing tension. The outcome at this distance is seen never to
have been in doubt. The Indians were doomed. But to those
embroiled or close at hand, Indian and white, the inequality
of the struggle was not apparent.

It is to the journals of J. Goldsborough Bruff that we turn today
for a living description of Yahi country in 1849, and for a picture
of the kinds and conditions of men, women, and children who
traveled over the Old Lassen Trail that year. Bruff was a drafts-
man in the Bureau of Topographical Engineers in Washington.
Taking leave from his job and his wife and children for what he
believed would be a lucrative venture of eight or nine months
duration, he organized and led a party of sixty-six men to the
"gold fields," choosing the Oregon-California Trail for the Sierra
Nevada crossing.

He continued to lead his party as far as the ridge which divides
Mill Creek and Deer Creek. There, owing to loss of mules, sickness, and the disaffections of hardship and the incompatibilities
of men on expeditions, the party as a unit broke up, the men
going their ways individually to the "settlements" in the valley.
Bruff, who by this time was unwell and crippled with rheumatism,
elected to remain with their otherwise abandoned provisions and
possessions, most especially from his point of view—and ours,
today—his own journals, drawings, and maps. Only one of the
company chose to stay with him. The stay in "Bruff's Camp"
was to have been a matter of days. Some of the party were to
return from Peter Lassen's rancho, only thirty-two miles away at

the mouth of Deer Creek, with Bruff's own valuable riding horse, which he reluctantly loaned one of them, and with wagons and mules to move the two men and all the property to the valley.

In the event, Bruff's horse was never returned to him nor did a rescue party put in an appearance on Mill Creek. He was abandoned to starve in the hills, which he very nearly did. From October 22, 1849, to April 4, 1850, Bruff lived in the heart of Ishi's country. His first companion, and after him a second one from a passing emigrant party, left him to go for help. One died in the hills, and the other was not able to get horses and supplies and to return to him. Sick and discouraged himself, Bruff sat alongside the Lassen Trail during the weeks of late autumn while emigrants streamed past him, telling him their stories, occasionally giving him a little tea or rice or tobacco, leaving their weakened mules and oxen and steers in his care, their wracked and broken wagons, and even a sick child, whom he cared for until it died, and then saw to its decent burial. They warmed themselves at his fire, slept in his beds improvised from abandoned wagons; and hungrily devoured his fresh venison.

Then winter with its raw wind, cold rain, and snow was upon him and the stream of travelers over the trail dried up. Alone except for his little dog, "Nevada," and sick, he determined, once spring brought a warmer sun and the new clover, to make a try for the settlements. Carrying only a gun, a small amount of ammunition, a knife, and his precious load of journals, he left camp. It took him five days to "come in." He was starving and badly crippled. A less determined man would have given over the effort.

To the reader curious to know what the emigrants were like toward the end of a trek begun with such extravagant hopes, Bruff is recommended reading. His picture is specific, circumstantial, and compassionate, and it puts into our hands some sort of answer to the question of how and why people of principle, many of them, and of good upbringing and antecedents, some of them, could act toward their Indian predecessors on the land with such ferocious inhumanity and brutality. The answer, in part at least, is that between frustrated cupidity, cholera, scurvy, dysentery, starvation, filth, exhaustion, and disillusionment, they arrived in California already dehumanized and brutalized in their behavior to one another and to strangers alike.

Gold seems to work on the human psyche to its undoing. The Reverend Walter Colton, Alcalde of Monterey, is quoted as saying in 1848, "The people are running over the country and picking it (gold) out of the earth, just as a thousand hogs let loose in a forest would root up the ground-nuts." Of those who stopped at his camp, Bruff writes, "Many I recognized as old acquaintances as far back as Pittsburg: large companies [they were then], with fine animals, a great amount of provisions and stores, and smiling faces; now scattered, broken, selfish stragglers, thin with hunger (and) anxiety." He told of one grandfather who, sick with scurvy, was dumped from the family wagon and left to die beside the trail. He watched a man hammer into useless scrap the tools he could carry no farther—if he could not use them, neither should Bruff nor anyone else. There were those who burned the precious pasture grass when their own animals died. Mules, cattle, sheep, and horses were stolen in great numbers, branded and added to the herds of a sub rosa group or groups recruited from the criminally inclined and disaffected members of emigrant parties.

Bruff fed, warmed, doctored, cheered, and buried the dead of these people. Not one offered to take him the thirty-two miles to the rancho. On his trek out of the hills in April, he met one party of prospectors coming into the hills—strong men and well-provisioned. They gave him a piece of bread spread with salt-pork grease when he stumbled, starving, across their trail, and shared the next morning's breakfast with him, but refused him even such modest provisions as he would need to see him into the valley.

Now it is a curious circumstance that Bruff, the earliest white man to live in Yahi country as far as is known, should never have been molested by, nor himself molested, any Indian or Indian cache or encampment. Daily he saw the thin blue smoke from their fires as they no doubt saw his. He came on the prints of their bare feet, as they must surely have kept a mental record of his booted tracks; he knew where grew their grass and acorns—he himself made acorn bread—and he knew the fallen log over which they crossed and recrossed Mill Creek. He knew intimately the gorge of the creek, its open spaces and its precipitous walls, but there is, in the whole of his journal record, only one encounter with an Indian in Yahi country, and this was when he was on his way out. The Indian was probably, but not certainly, a Yahi. His description includes as well a cannibal fantasy, inspired by seeing bare footprints on the trail, apparently fresh ones. It is an example of the phenomenon of unconscious response to the trauma of prolonged starvation, which, by the way, has nothing at all to do with brutalization as such—no man was ever less brutalized by his experiences than Bruff—nor has it to do with the religious, fetish-istic, and highly selective cannibalism practiced by certain peoples in particular rituals. Writes Bruff on April 8:

> On striking the road, I was astonished to see the fresh tracks of an indian [*sic*]. He was pigeon-toed, and I judge small. Oh! if I can only over take him! then I will have one hearty meal! a good broil! I examined my caps, they were good. I felt relieved, it gave me additional strength; to think I might soon get a broil off an indian's leg! I could not but laugh, when I thought of it,—the expressions I have heard, how people would starve to death rather than eat human flesh! Fools! how little could they form an idea of the cravings of hunger! Let them be placed in my circum-stances, and see how soon they would discard such silly ideas! My mouth fairly watered, for a piece of an indian to broil! And I continued to look out sharper for one, than for any other game. As I came along, was compelled to halt, and rest, at every thing on which I could also support my knapsack. Feet quite sore, shoulders very sore, and would fail alto-gether, but for the hope of shooting an indian, to eat. Stag-gering, and resting every few paces,—on the indian trail still, at last reached Dry Creek, at the base of the hills, eight miles, about, from where I parted with the company yesterday.

[The prospecting party.] On descending to the wagon ford, I loosened my packs and threw myself down exhausted. On recovering, I eat my last small piece of candle: giving the wick to the poor pup.—She eats grass, just now eat a cartridge paper, and is busy gnawing a black leather strap. She runs to me, looks in my face, wagging her tail, and whining, as if upbraiding me for permitting her to starve. I am very drowsy, but cannot lay down yet. A fine day. [The reference is, plainly, to the fineness of the weather.]

Bruff relates how the next day, April 9, he managed to ford the stream, and being almost out of the hills, buried his knapsack which he could carry no farther. Writes Bruff:

In a quarter mile more, I met a low square-built indian, very dark, and had slight mustache; he had just emerged from a deep gulch on the left. He was nude, except a kind of fig-leaf, had a knife, a quiver full of arrows on his back, and a bow in his hand. He was accompanied by a small black indian dog. I spoke to him in Spanish, but he did not understand me. I then made signs that I was hungry— starving, and wanted something to eat, which he comprehended but gave me to understand he had nothing, and was on his way to Dry Creek to shoot birds. My pup was following his dog, and I worried myself much to get her along; so glad was she to meet one of her own specie, I had to make signs to the indian to drive her back—beat her with his bow: —which he did. While he was going off, I turned round, thought of eating him; he was then about thirty or forty paces; but I could not shoot the poor wretch in the back: besides, he had done me a favor. So I proceeded. Could this have been a mountain indian?—the one I trailed, and wanted to eat? I dare say.

Chapter 4
EPISODES IN EXTERMINATION

Peter Lassen's trail was soon abandoned as a route to the "gold fields," the advantage of its low pass through the mountains cruelly offset by the rough trek down the backbone of Ishi's country. There, where the long overland trip might be considered to be all but over, horses and mules slipped and broke their legs, and oxen went crashing off the narrow ledges down vertical cañon sides carrying the heavily loaded carts and wagons with them. For each ridge crossed, another loomed ahead with a turbulent and dangerous stream between, whose ford was meant neither for mules nor cattle nor carts. Nor was it possible to get off the trail. One cart, stuck or with a broken wheel, would back up traffic for miles behind, quite in the modern mode. Camp had to be made practically on the trail; the occasional meadows and flats and hollows were inadequate to the accommodation of stock and people, day after day, week after week. And the travelers were very hungry—perhaps redskins could penetrate the surrounding chaparral—it would not yield to a white man whose revolver and bowie knife were of little use. He needed a machete, and patience and time, none of which were then part of his equipment.

Although the trail fell into disuse as part of a transcontinental trackway, it offered a direct and known route from the Sacramento Valley into the Yahi heartland, whose wholeness and privacy were permanently breached. The conflict had been set up; the Indians who lived along Deer and Mill creeks had a "bad name" with the whites in Vina and Tehama and Red Bluff and in the ranch houses and prospectors' cabins. Ishi's people sensed that they were threatened as never before in their long and sometimes turbulent history.

The battle ground at first extended west of Mount Lassen to the Sacramento River, between Montgomery Creek and the north fork of the Feather River, and involved all four subtribes of the Yana. Episodes in extermination are truly the materials from which a surrogate for history must be pieced together. Much, probably most of the details are not to be recovered, and what there are can be structured to make a coherent story of only a regrettably jerry-built sort. Its geographic limits are known, as is its time span: the opening year being, of course, 1849. By 1865 the Northern, Central, and Southern Yana were eliminated from the struggle; only the Yahi, Ishi's tribelet, remained.

Because the episodes which follow float free in certain of their parts, or contradict one another, or are found in embarrassingly elaborated and mutually exclusive versions, a word should perhaps be said of and for them. They compose, so far as the author knows, the responsible source material for the matters of which they treat. They come in travel accounts, newspaper stories, government records, and the oral and written recollections of men and women who played a role, sometimes a key role, in the events described. Waterman's monograph *The Yana Indians* (1918), is the principal single coördinating source for the miscellaneous material, and must remain so. The over-all presentation offered here follows Waterman closely. Where it departs from him, except to supplement with sources not available to him, the reasons for, and the steps of departure, have been explicitly explained so that the reader seriously interested in this aspect of Ishi's story need not break his head over the occasional differences. (See the Notes, pp. 239–240.)

There are inconsistencies and gaps in the record, particularly since much of it comes from "remembered" events. The would-be biographer or historian soon learns to accept with reserve positive identifications of persons, of kinship relations, and of exact dates. Bizarre and violent happenings are likely to be remembered with a burned-in sort of vividness, and the season of the year becomes attached to the memory, clothing it, as it were, whereas the year and the exact order of event, long afterward, may become displaced in memory, as a tribal type or an age parallel may be transformed into a firm identification of a person or a relationship.

The temptation recurred to summarize the spotty and refractory material, and so save the reader the long wade ahead through muddy backwaters of scholarship, but over it all flits the shadow of Ishi, tenuous at first, then ever longer and more immanent, quickening the least as the most horrific of its parts. It seemed that without such light as these events throw on his people in the decade before his birth and all the years of his own life excepting only the last four and a half, it would not be possible to know the man Ishi nor to understand the days of his life after he left the Oroville jail.

As early as 1850, only months after the beginning of the gold rush, and more than ten years before Ishi himself was born, Ishi's people, although not yet mentioned by name, were beginning to appear in the local papers. The *Sacramento Daily Transcript* of April 5, 1850, carried a story plainly pinpointing Yahi Indians in Yahi territory. It reads as follows:

We have been informed by a gentleman from Deer Creek, that one day last week, some twelve men, who had been soldiers in the Mexican War, attacked a party of Indians whom they accused of stealing animals, and killed four or five men and one squaw. The Indians, after running some time before their pursuers, turned around, seeing so few in chase, and the pursuer became the pursued, until they gained a stronghold in a rocky part of the mountain, where the Indians attacked them furiously, wounding, it is believed fatally, two of the whites, one in the shoulder and the other in the arm. The siege lasted two days, during which the Indians lost seventeen men and one squaw, besides those before mentioned. A man called Bill Ebben is the leader of the assailants. A party of two hundred was organizing at Deer Creek, and was expecting to start in pursuit last Thursday morning.

In a journal entry for December 14, 1850, Bruff reports a clash between whites and Indians, the latter surely Yahi. Bruff was in Tehama (or Vina) where he met "in a refrectory [*sic*]," two of his friends just arrived from Lassen's Rancho. They told him that several of Peter Lassen's vaqueros had gone, two or three weeks earlier, from the Rancho to Deer Valley to round up Lassen's stock which was pasturing there. Bruff's two friends had followed some days later with extra saddle horses for the trip out with the stock. They found the vaqueros, but without a single ox or cow, all of which had disappeared after having been rounded up by them. Together, the party tracked the stolen stock into the gorge of Mill Creek, "to the spot where I had so often watched the smoke from Indian fires," says Bruff. They reached an Indian village—indubitably Yahi—which they attacked, killing the Indians who were there and burning the village. Beyond mention of one dead ox, "full of arrows," Bruff does not say whether the other animals were found, nor does he say how many Indians were killed.

Waterman's account begins with events in 1851. Typical of many then and later is the first episode whose Indian victim was probably but not surely a Yana. A Mr. Pentz, who appears prominently among the organizers of expeditions against the Yana in succeeding years, was one day early in 1851 somewhere along Concow Creek. There he met on the trail an Indian whose attitude became "threatening and belligerent," as Waterman got the story, and who was summarily killed by hanging. (Presumably Mr. Pentz did not effect this quick retribution single-handed.)

In 1853 occurred one of the first of the mass murders of Yahi, this one under Pentz's leadership. It was triggered by the stealing of one (or several) cows. Pentz and his men gave chase and before they were through twenty-five or more Indians were dead—some shot, some hanged. It is to be remarked of this foray that the white people in Dogtown through which Pentz's party went, refused to join him, although the more usual response was for any miners or cowboys or idlers about town with time on their hands to join a party if it passed their way while "out for scalps." A second party led by Pentz later in the same year went out in response to alleged raids along the north fork of the Feather River. They netted fifty or sixty scalps on this trip, the question being, whose scalps? The Feather River is south of Yana country; the Yahi the nearest "wild" Indians. But much handier and safer for scalping were the Maidu who lived peaceably and accessibly along Concow Creek and the Feather River.

The 1850's were hard years for the Yana. On their exposed flanks their numbers dwindled, what with the wholesale practice of indenturing and kidnapping, and a heavy toll from venereal diseases. The Yahi, relatively protected from these border hazards, were beginning to feel the first serious deprivation which would before long bring them close to starvation through the loss of their natural fishing, hunting, and gathering grounds. Deer and other game not only were becoming scarce but were shy and hard to stalk, since the crack of a revolver shot—the "breaking" of a gun as Ishi would call it—had sundered the silence of the sling and the bow.

By 1857, the Yahi, known locally as the Kombo, the Maidu name for them, or as Tiger Indians, or as Mill Creeks, were beginning to raid in good earnest, even down into the valley as far away as Tehama. They drove off stock, sometimes they fired a barn or a cabin, and they were credited, probably correctly, with an occasional murder. A growing hysteria of fear spread among the pioneers of the upper valley.

One avenging party of whites, incautious enough to go directly into Yahi territory by way of Lassen Trail to Bruff's old camp was ambushed there. The party retreated without losing any men but also without having inflicted any losses.

Later in 1857 a raid into the valley netted the Indians two or three mules. Some whites gave chase but the Indians took refuge in one of the caves which characterize the overhanging cliff formation along the upper reaches of Mill Creek. This time, too, the Yahi suffered no losses, and they kept the mules. Both the military and the citizen vigilantes, who tried to invade the hill country of the Indians by way of Lassen Trail or by other main routes using the frontal attack technique of open-country fighting, failed much as did the British Redcoats in the Revolutionary War, and for the same reasons. Success came, expectably enough, under the leadership of men who had learned the back country so well that they could travel it almost like the Yana themselves, and who tracked, hid, and attacked in Indian fashion, except that they were armed with guns.

The Indians meanwhile took horses, mules, oxen, cows, and sheep when and where they could, wasting no part of these animals which were food and clothing to them. They made blankets or capes of the pelts, tanned the hides, and made "charqui" or "jerky" of such of the meat as was not eaten fresh. In other words, they treated the introduced animals as they did deer, bear, elk, or rabbit. They seem not to have realized that the animals were domesticated, the dog being the only domesticated animal they knew. They stole and killed to live, not to accumulate herds or wealth, nor did the Indians really understand that what they took was the private property of a single person. Many years later when Ishi was past middle age, he blushed in painful embarrassment whenever he recalled that by white standards he and his brother Yahi had been guilty of stealing.

It was also in 1857 that a company of cavalry, dispatched from Sacramento in response to clamor up valley, is said to have tried a frontal attack against the Yana, and to have been surprised by the unseen redskins, who sent the soldiers scrambling down bluffs and through chaparral in disorderly retreat to the valley floor. The *War Records* do not clearly identify this expedition, but they do mention several occasions when companies of soldiers were sent, during the 'fifties and 'sixties, to "conquer" the Yana. On none of the expeditions, according to the *Records* as well as local popular report, were the soldiers ever able to discover much less to confront the enemy.

Troops were sent only when the civilian white population

panicked and demanded military protection, but, once soldiers were on the spot, it is a curious circumstance that they were given no coöperation. Far from it; the rout and discomfiture of a company of cavalry was thought to be extremely funny. The Indians became for the time "our boys" who were outwitting the uniformed regulars whose frustration and seeming inadequacy was interpreted as a justification for vigilante law. A characteristic of the American frontier was an ambivalence toward governmental and distant authority and toward the military in particular. The settlers between Red Bluff and Vina did not really wish the military to take over the job of destroying the Yana. They preferred to do it themselves. The Pacific Command, reluctantly, and damned for its trouble by local residents, by the Command in Washington, and by the Indian Bureau, took part in the forced removal of numbers of Indians to reservations, but so far as any record shows or any story relates, no member of the United States Army ever shot a single Yana Indian, whose multiple murder remained a home and civilian and strictly extralegal operation.

The years 1857, 1858, and 1859 were those of the greatest belligerency and success of the Yahi and their fellow Yana who were not too exposed. This was before Ishi was born. Like good guerrillas, they struck unexpectedly and swiftly, and for the rest, kept out of sight. Their depredations were credited to the accessible, exposed border Yana, or even more absurdly, to remote groups of valley Indians who had never put up any resistance and had long since been without means or spirit for it.

Yana Indians were indentured in numbers—this was legal in California until 1861—and they were kidnapped and murdered, yet none of these measures stopped their continuing depredations. By 1859, the cry in the settlements was for the physical removal of all Indians. The word went out from Sacramento to Washington that something must be done to appease the white hysteria and to protect the hundreds of peaceable and innocent valley Indians who might become its first victims, for by this time *no* live Indian was a good Indian, or immune from violence. Hastily, but with good intent, a reservation of sorts called Nome Lackee was made ready some twenty miles west of Tehama. Small and not-so-small groups of Indians were rounded up at gun point and herded there, a hundred and eighty-one Southern Yana being the largest number in a single forced migration of which there is record. Nome Lackee was abandoned in 1861, and seemingly with good reason, since all the Indians who had been taken there were either dead or had escaped.

The Southern Yana, much depleted even before the removals of 1859, did not survive after that time as a people. Most of them died from disease, exposure, or the shock of displacement. A few must have lived on, attached to a small band or household of Indians of another tribe. Sam Batwi, for example, was half Maidu, half Southern Yana by ancestry, although he spoke Northern Yana. When the linguist Edward Sapir worked with Batwi, it was to record the Northern dialect to which Batwi was able a few times to add a recollected Southern variant of word or sound. But he had not spoken Southern Yana nor heard it since he was a young child; nor were Sapir or other linguists then or later able to learn of anyone living who knew the dialect.

In 1859 the white settlers were not relying on reservations and the military. From their own number they collected three thousand dollars as a beginning fund to be used to fight the Mill Creeks. The sum was deposited with the storekeeper at the Mayhew stage station on Deer Creek. And it was in the same year— a fateful year for Ishi's people—that the names of two civilian leaders, Robert A. Anderson and his friend and companion Hiram Good occur and recur whenever there was trouble afoot in Yana country. Anderson and Good were natural trackers and scouts who came to know the back country almost as well as did the Indians; and who were, before long, making forays into Yahi strongholds. In 1909 Anderson wrote his memoirs of those years; they were published in Chico under the title *Fighting the Mill Creeks*. Today they are an invaluable source for precisely the subject matter of their title. To read them is to realize that

Anderson saw himself in no such rarefied and noble role as did the men he led. His fighting days began when he was not yet twenty years old. He was sheriff of Butte County at twenty-five. There is more than a touch of Twainian humor in his accounts of his own many unsuccessful expeditions into the hills when the Yahi outwitted and eluded him; of the (to him) hilarious spectacle of a frustrated company, officers and men, returning after weeks of the most arduous chasing up and down lava cliffs, without having so much as glimpsed a fresh spoor of Indian, much less an Indian; of the times when he and his pal Hiram were distracted from their game of trying for Indian scalps by a chance encounter with one or sometimes several grizzly bears. He matched wits and physical prowess with Indians and grizzlies alike: both, in his opinion, "infested" the region and should be cleared out. He and Good, Anderson says, used to argue at length about how the clearing out was to be done. Good was for leaving the women and children alone; Anderson believed that immolation was the only effective way to be rid of Indians, and grizzlies, too, no doubt. Older and presumably wiser men than Anderson subscribed, literally, to his philosophy—they supported him and his "guards" from their own pockets—and it should be said that Anderson writes retrospectively in his memoirs, "It is but just that I should mention the circumstances which raised the hand of the Mill Creeks against the whites. As in almost every similar instance in American History, the first act of injustice, the first spilling of blood, must be laid at the white man's door."

Sim Moak, a faithful and admiring lieutenant, wrote down some of his own recollections of Indian fighting under Anderson, which he titled *The Last of the Mill Creeks and Early Life in Northern California*. Sim it is who tells of the "Hurdy-gurdy girls" who, according to him, were usually German-born, traveled in companies of four girls to one boy accordion player, going from mining camp to mining camp, dancing in the bars to the accompaniment of the accordion, the charge for a single dance with one of them being fifty cents, half to the bar, half to the girl. That the Bertolt Brecht–Kurt Weill opera "Rise and Fall of the City of Mahagonny" was inspired by Moak's account is, of course, highly improbable, but it could have been.

Sim Moak was born in upstate New York and came to California at the age of eighteen in 1863. He was a simple person for whom Indian fighting and the mores of the frontier carried an aura of the romantic and the heroic. Moak reads today like a current television "western"—apparently the myth of hero-pro-tector-sheriff crystallized early. When he retells the story of an expedition or adventure also recounted by Anderson, Moak adds little. But he has some yarns of which Anderson the sheriff does not tell, and we learn from Moak the esteem in which the sheriff was held by his peers. Moak says of Anderson and Hiram Good:

> When I first met Hi. Good and R. A. Anderson, they were in the prime of life. Good was twenty-nine years old and as handsome a man as I ever saw. Anderson was twenty-five years old and as fine a specimen of manhood as one would wish to see. They were large men, shrewd and fearless. They were leaders of men. Anderson was elected sheriff of Butte County, two terms and if Good had lived he could have had any office in Tehama County he wanted. If it had not been for them, more white people living in Butte and Tehama counties would have been murdered by the barbarous Mill Creeks. Their business was never so urgent or time so precious they could not leave all to go forth to avenge the wrongs of the white settlers, committed by the red men. When a party of us settlers would start to clean up the In-dians, we would elect a captain and it would always be Good or Anderson. *The captain always was entitled to the scalps. At one time Good had forty hanging in the poplar tree by his house.* Good was one of the best Indian trailers in North-ern California and a dead shot. [Italics mine.]

Moak describes how Good strung a day's take of scalps:

> After Good had taken all the scalps, he took a buckskin string and sack needle and tied a knot in the end and salted

the scalp and run [*sic*] the needle through it down to the knot, then tied another knot about two inches above the scalp and it was ready for the next one. The string was fastened to his belt and you can imagine a great tall man with a string of scalps from his belt to his ankle.

An early expedition under Anderson's and Good's leadership reached the north side of Mill Creek only a short distance upstream from a Yahi village. There Anderson and his men spent the night unmolested. In the morning, they found the village empty. The Indians had managed, without the intruders having heard anything, to fell a tree across Mill Creek over which the villagers crossed to the south side, thence into the chaparral and out of reach. The expedition pushed north along the creek, very soon picking up the spoor of ten or twelve "warriors" [by which was meant able-bodied men traveling without their families]. This small band of Yahi men, with all the canniness of a mother quail distracting a hunter's attention from her nestlings, lured the whites on, never letting them come up to them, drawing them ever farther away from the Mill Creek heartland. Having crossed much rough country between, and the Battle Creek Meadows, they continued to circle the not inconsiderable base of Lassen Peak to its far side, until in due course they came to Hat Creek. Turning circuitously back, the Yahi made another wide circle which brought them out on Keefer Ridge. A glance at the map on page 25 will show the reader the extent of this trip (each step of which and each of its hundreds of landmarks Ishi later knew as he knew his own hand). Such a trip consumed weeks; some of the raids Anderson led took as long as two months. It is not to be much wondered at that on this particular raid Anderson gave over the pursuit at Keefer Ridge, only traces, never the enemy himself, having once been seen all this while, either going to or coming back from Hat Creek. So soon as the Yahi had shaken their pursuers they went to Anderson's ranch on lower Deer Creek, and thoroughly ransacked it.

As for Anderson and Good, they were not yet so well established in their leadership as they would be later. They felt that they must find *some* Indians to kill, even if they could not catch any Mill Creeks. To this end they continued beyond Keefer Ridge to Chico Creek in Maidu territory. Here they overtook a lone Indian in the hills whom they ran down, killed, and scalped: their first trophy of the journey. A little farther along they came on an Indian village. Surrounding the village, they waited out the night. The first man to come out of one of the houses in the early dawn was, as Anderson saw, not an Indian but a Spaniard. Good nonetheless opened fire, the Spaniard ran, and a second bullet finished him. The gunshots roused the sleeping villagers who ran wildly in all directions. As Anderson put it in his memoirs, "Soon we came in possession of the camp. There was not a bad Indian to be found, but about forty good ones lay scattered about."

The next day, and for some time after, feeling ran high over these killings. The white people living along near-by Butte Creek were much wrought up, for the Indians who had been killed were Maidu, "tame" Indians, friends of the whites. Indeed, one of the wounded Indian women was the wife of the Butte Creek storekeeper. The village was a gathering place for both whites and Indians. Two partly full barrels of whisky were found there: sure evidence that whites as well as Indians frequented the place whether to good or deplorable purpose. In other words, forty gratuitous and irresponsible murders had been committed in cold blood, nor could the Maidu or their white friends call the murderers to account, the latter being handier with a gun, and having the tacit consent of their backers to do whatever they chose or happened by chance to do.

Anderson was, however, learning. These early unsuccessful raids were to bear fruit for him later—and bitter fruit for Ishi's people. In a second expedition, soon after the one which ended in Maidu country, Anderson was back with the Yahi. He surprised a number of them—women, children, and old people with one able-bodied man amongst them. They jumped into Mill Creek as soon as Anderson began shooting, and took shelter under an overhanging bank, in an effort to hide in the only place which offered. The man stayed on land and tried to draw the gunfire to himself, but he was killed before he could give his kinspeople time to escape. Anderson forced them to land at gunpoint and herded them downstream out of the hills and across the valley to Nome Lackee Reservation.

Vigilantes and others continued to kill Indians, many of them Yahi, but the raiding of stock and grain went on during the fall and winter of 1859, and, despite continuing heavy losses, through the early 'sixties. The lone driver of a team of horses or of an oxcart on one or another of the back roads, or a solitary hunter or fisherman or prospector in the hills was from time to time found dead from an arrow wound, the arrow itself, not being expendable, having regularly been retrieved from the corpse.

The probable year of Ishi's birth was 1862. He was born into a difficult world of continuing raids and counterraids; a world of wars and hatred.

In June of 1862, a "citizen's" meeting was held in a ranch house at the Forks of Butte to air grievances against the Mill Creeks and to make further plans toward their extermination. It is to be noted that vigilante meetings are reported as having taken place at private houses somewhere in the hills, although in the valley communities were sheriffs' offices, town halls, and churches in which the public could and for other purposes did meet.

Twenty-four men volunteered at the Forks of Butte meeting to clear the hills of wild Indians. Whether the meeting and its purpose were known to the wild Indians is a matter about which we can only speculate, but there would seem to have been much tension amongst the little bands of Yahi Indians along Mill, Deer, Toomes, and Dry creeks. A teamster was killed by some of them simultaneously with the meeting; and, on the same day or the day after, that is on June 18 or 19, a party of Yahi came across the three children of the Hickok family whose home was on Rock Creek. Two were girls, fourteen and sixteen years of age. They were killed with bow and arrow and left where they fell. The third child, a younger boy, was carried off. Anderson told Waterman that the boy was later stoned to death. Another person in telling the story to Waterman added that the boy's fingers and toes were cut off. Yet other informants alluded in vague terms to his having been cremated. As late as the 1920's, circumstantial, detailed, and mutually different accounts were still being circulated at first or secondhand from old timers in the valley.

Hiram Good and Sandy Young, the latter the boss vaquero for the Bidwell Ranch at Chico, set off at once into the hills to avenge the Hickok murders. They found and killed eight Indians, whether men, women, or children, or whether or not they were Yahi, is not known.

Governor Leland Stanford wrote to the general in command of the Military Department of the Pacific to report particularly the Hickok murders. Troops were promptly sent. From the frightened local whites there was much talk of killing all the Indians, but the troops were under clear orders to protect the "Big Meadows" Indians, as the peaceable mountain-valley natives were then called both from hostile Indians and from *unauthorized white organizations*. Naturally, the commander was in some puzzlement about who precisely had committed the murders. Either he was not empowered to use local scouts or he did not choose to. In September, 1862, United States cavalry in strength covered the length of Battle, Antelope, Mill, and Deer creeks and pushed through and over the rocky ridges and smaller streams between. The white settlers were firm in their demand that the Indians should be "cleaned out." But during the month of September not an Indian was sighted by any member of the company of soldiers. The "signs" of Indian occupation were numerous enough but were two or three weeks old by the time they were found. The Indians were in hiding to be sure, but they were also in motion, and must have kept the mounted soldiers under sharp and accurate observation the whole of the time.

Shortly before the troops arrived, two or three Yahi Indians risked a daylight raid on Anderson's ranch. They took his horses and set the barn on fire. Anderson was at home, and reached the creek so little behind the Indians that the rocks showed their wet footprints where they had forded the stream. Anderson followed on foot up Dry Creek as far as the beginning of the steep ascent of the walls of Mill Creek cañon, but he was never close enough to get a shot. He saw the Indians stop briefly to repack one of the horses with corn and garden truck. The Yahi must indeed have been hungry to risk stopping for a few green vegetables.

In June, 1863, another daylight raid is reported. This time, the Indians took horses belonging to Solomon Gore who, with Anderson, gave chase as far as the defile which leads into Deer Creek cañon. The stolen horses were somehow got up and over the almost perpendicular cliffs and down the other side.

Gore and Anderson, meanwhile, instead of risking a direct pursuit, went around to the east and north, crossing Dry Creek and climbing the ridge which overlooks Mill Creek cañon. Below them they saw Yahi women, unaware of danger, filling baskets with ripe grass seeds. The two men moved cautiously down the steep hillside until they were within a few hundred yards of the women. An Indian lookout somewhere behind and above them gave a warning cry at this point, upon which the women dropped their baskets and ran down the slope, their pursuers following close behind. Where the ground leveled off, the women reached home, one of the villages built close to the water. Gore and Anderson opened fire as Indians, old and young, ran for cover. Seven or eight of them failed to make it and were shot down as they ran.

Soon after this episode, five Indians were hanged at Helltown on the suspicion of robbery. In July of the same year, 1863, came the murder of the Lewis children. A party of Indians "on the warpath," as the account goes, probably meaning a party composed only of men, was reported to have passed through country along Clear Creek midway between Chico and Oroville. The party was thought to have been made up of Mill Creeks; if so, they were well south of their own territory. In any case, these Indians succeeded in kidnapping the three children of the Lewis's who had a ranch nearby. The oldest child, a boy, was killed at once, but a younger boy, and a girl named Thankful, were made to go along with the Indians. It soon became apparent that the little boy could not travel as fast as his uneasy captors wished to go, so he, too, was killed. Thankful, only twelve years old, must have been a sturdy and courageous child, who kept pace with the Indians and who also "kept her head." According to her own account, which she wrote, or perhaps dictated as an old lady in 1915 and which was printed under the title *Captured by the Mill Creeks,* she was the special charge of an old, lame Indian who could himself barely keep up with his companions. Thankful and her guard, already trailing the others, stopped for the old man to shift his load. Thankful watched him closely, continuing to talk to him as he worked, and in the instant when he slipped the pack over his head and could not see her, she ducked behind a boulder, ran downhill, and hid under heavy chaparral where she lay face down. The old man called wildly to her, and to the other Indians who came running back. They beat the bushes with their bows but, afraid to risk a long delay, they left without discovering her. As soon as they were out of earshot, Thankful worked her way on all fours down to the creek at the bottom of the slope. With a sound pioneer woman's instinct, she stayed by the stream, running as fast as she could go until she reached a ranch house, a mile or a mile and a half downstream.

With her arrival, the alarm was given, and while Thankful was being cared for by the women, a posse of men started in the direction she said she had been taken. The men picked up the kidnappers' trail, or a fresh trail at least, which led eventually into Deer Creek cañon. The Indians whom they found in the cañon took to cover; the posse succeeded in taking only a single scalp.

It is impossible to rationalize so dangerous and imprudent an act as this kidnapping except as sheer revenge; and Thankful herself gives a clue. She says that two of the Indians had their heads covered with "tar" and "were terrible to look at." It was Indian custom to cut the hair short and cover the head with pitch when in mourning for a spouse or a near relative. Two Indians, then, were in mourning—and recalling Professor S. F. Cook's statistics —in mourning perhaps for their murdered or kidnapped children.

Following the kidnapping and murder of the Lewis children, another meeting was held, in Pentz's home. A vigilante organization known as the Oroville Guards grew out of this meeting, and "took the field" in considerable numbers. Indians are reported to have been hanged at the Yankee Hill settlement, at Dogtown, and at Bidwell's ranch at Chico. Some three hundred and fifty Indians were also herded together and taken to Yankee Hill, where they were held as prisoners.

Once again the Agent for Indian Affairs for the Northern District appealed frantically to the Military Department of the Pacific. The date of his appeal was July 27, 1863. He asked for troops to "protect and remove" the Indians. He said that armed whites were threatening to exterminate all Indians.

The Army and the Office of Indian Affairs in Washington responded to this appeal with good intent. Nome Lackee Reservation, the only one nearby, was already abandoned and despoiled, hence it was decided to take the Yana Indians to Nome Cult Reservation in Round Valley, Mendocino County, some 115 to 120 miles distant. The plan as outlined must have seemed a good one. It rested on army intelligence to the effect that there were only about a thousand Yana left. With three hundred and fifty of them already accounted for and together at Yankee Hill, there remained the "rounding up" of the six hundred or so still at large, after which, in a single action as it were, they could be removed from Lassen to Round Valley.

The army officers who were involved in the effort to carry out this plan were, many of them, deeply opposed to it, some because they were sure it was not feasible, some because of a suspicion that it was part of a Secessionist plot designed to embarrass the government and that those who urged it were men of bad intent toward both the Indians and the military.

Between ignorance and mutual distrust and haste, the actual

execution of the order of removal was nothing short of a complete debâcle. No proper transportation was provided; the Indians were hastily got together; the military found to its enduring exasperation that those who were loudest in their demand for the removal were unwilling to do anything toward forwarding it; and that no provision whatsoever had been made in Round Valley for the housing and care of the newcomers when they finally arrived there.

A Captain Starr escorted the Indians on their march. He left Chico with four hundred and sixty-one Indians, and arrived at Round Valley with two hundred and seventy-seven. Two were unaccounted for; thirty-two died on the march; and a hundred and fifty were left sick along the trail to be brought in later if they should recover enough to continue the trip. Those Indians who did recover returned home, some reaching Chico ahead of the troops. Of those who were taken all the way to Round Valley little is known. The *War Records* quote one general as saying that it was impossible to keep Indians on a reservation.

The correspondence in the *War Records* pictures the gratuitous disruption, terror, suffering, and death visited on the innocent Indians of that forced migration, but to pursue the details is not to get on with the history of the Yana, against whom it was particularly organized, because there were no Northern or Central Yana actually involved. The whole activity centered around Yankee Hill, itself in Maidu country and well south even of the nearest Yana, who would have been the Yahi; and not a single Yahi was taken. The Yahi remained snugly and, for the moment, safely in their sheltered villages in Deer Creek cañon and on Mill Creek above the gorge while the Oroville Guards and the United States Army made their roundups. Those Indians who were taken to Round Valley, or who started there, were unlucky ones from among the peaceful Maidu and Wintun of the upper Sacramento Valley who got caught in the frenzied and non-selective taking of any and all easily available Indians. There were many white residents who knew this; probably Captain Starr knew it. But between the conflict of motives, and hysteria, this knowledge remained futile.

Captain Starr was back at Camp Bidwell outside Chico. The year was 1864. Word had reached the Pacific Command that the Yahi were expected to attack outlying homesteads in the valley. Captain Starr was directed to apprehend the leaders (of the Yahi attackers) and send them to Alcatraz Island to be confined in the military prison there. Of this directive Waterman says, "This order was a very cool one. The Captain might as well have been ordered to apprehend the northern lights." Troops were duly sent into the Yana hills at intervals during 1864, but failed to find any Indians. The intelligence behind the directive to Captain Starr was that the Yahi were raiding once more and with some success. There were depredations to the south of Deer Creek along Berry Creek and the north fork of Feather River, for which the local Maidu were blamed. Some three hundred Maidu were harried, hanged, shot, or dispersed, not by the army but by the vigilantes. The Maidu were surely innocent. Whatever mischief was done there by Indians must have been the work of Yahi. They stole stock in considerable numbers, and when any of the stolen animals were recovered, as happened when horses could not be made to swim a stream or when carcasses had to be abandoned because the trail was "hot," the animals bore scars from having been shot with bow and arrow, sure evidence that the "hunters" had been Yahi. But it was the murder of two women, Mrs. Dirsch and Mrs. Allen in August, 1864, somewhere in the vicinity of Millville and Balls Ferry, which triggered the unwontedly concentrated and bloody activity of Anderson's and Good's men among the Yana.

In a space of less than five months, between August and December, 1864, three quarters of the remaining task of extermination of the Yana was accomplished. To this end two fully armed companies of guards combed the ridges, streams, and meadowlands from Deer Creek in the south to Montgomery Creek in the north. One of Waterman's informants recalled the year as 1866, but this date was from oral memory fifty years later. The 1864 date has the confirmation of Jeremiah Curtin whose account is detailed and circumstantial as far as it goes, and was gathered and written down only twenty years after the events it describes. It may be reasonably presumed to be correct as to the year, and is a fuller report than Waterman was able to get. Curtin was a traveler and scholar who was by chance in the upper Sacramento Valley during the 1890's, from which experience he wrote a book, *Creation Myths of Primitive America.* Published in 1898, it contains principally a large body of Wintun myths and a small collection of Yana myths, with also a brief summary of how the destruction of the Yana came about, excepting only Ishi's people of whom Curtin had no particular knowledge. Curtin's white informants were also his hosts, as was the custom on ranches and in small country towns in the West where inns and hotels were few, and often poor. Curtin, conscientious in the matter of protecting from possible embarrassment the people in whose houses he had stayed, says: "Nearly all the men who killed the Yana have gone out of the country or are dead. A few are in Northern California yet, and the children of some of the dead ones are living there now. Though one's indignation at the deeds of 1864 be great, there is no use in mentioning names at this hour."

Curtin's careful anonymity is a frustration to the would-be historian or documentarian, particularly since it becomes plain from the tone of the reporting that, for a change, his informants were ranchers who opposed the vigilante program, in principle totally and in practice when they were sufficiently armed and fast on the draw to hold the guards off. Curtin also misread the future: descendants of the anti-vigilantes are today the proud and non-apologetic ones in any discussion of "old times."

Curtin's account has to do with those Central and Northern Yana who were by then on a wide and exposed front *vis à vis* white settlers, and who, whether willingly and freely or not were in fact working for white ranchers and drawing pay for their work. Many of them lived on the ranches where they worked, sometimes in the ranch house itself as domestics, or in near-by bunk houses if they were field workers or were the old people attached affectionally and familially to younger workers.

Curtin estimated from the figures given him that in January, 1864, there were some three thousand of these Yana, counting the women, the old, and the children, and that by the end of the same year their massacre was complete except for remnants of families or bands, or for single individuals. It was from one or more of these survivors that Curtin collected his Yana myths. Again, and unhappily, he does not give the names of his Indian informants.

Curtin's account of the massacres agrees with Waterman's composite story obtained between 1911 and 1914 from old timers, except for the discrepancy in dating as already noted. In both, the murder of the same two women is alleged as the inciting cause; both mention the organization of a second company of guards; Waterman notes that the organization meeting was again held at Pentz's ranch; both say that no effort was made to fix guilt for the murders, and that extermination was the objective. Curtin tells more about the guards below the leader level. They were, he says, a miscellany of the foot-loose, the semicriminal, the hangers-on of saloons and bunk houses. Anyone who wanted to come along was taken, so that among the ragtag of both companies drunkenness, looting, and violence for the sake of violence obtained and were tolerated. His account emphasizes the wantonness of the killings and the opposition of most of the ranchers to it.

The guards stole and sometimes literally tore children and half-grown girls from the arms of their white friends or employers, murdering them in view of anyone who was present except when enough men were at home and heavily enough armed to beat them off. "We must kill them big and little," one of the guards is quoted as saying, "nits will be lice." Curtin recounts some unpleasantly specific details of these encounters. They are of this sort: three Yana men were murdered out of hand while at work in a hay field belonging to a rancher who regularly employed them but who was not at home at the time. His pregnant wife could do nothing to save the Indians, but when the guards came to the house to get their wives the rancher's wife threw herself in front of the three women. The opposition even at its most rash hesitated to get three further victims at the cost of manhandling a white woman. Later, the rancher and his wife managed somehow to secrete the three women in a place of safety; how they did it or where they took them they never told.

It might be supposed that looting could scarcely have been a motive, but such was not the case, for these Indians had their wages in their pockets when they were killed. The guards were known to have collected as much as four hundred dollars in a single "haul." Sadism entered into the violence also. There was one young Yana woman, unusually popular with the white people who knew and employed her, who was dragged by force out of the white man's home where she lived. Her old aunt and uncle who were there with her were also taken, and the three of them pumped full of bullets on the spot. Curtin's informant had counted eleven bullet holes in the breast of the young woman. The man who killed her, and who was well "likkered up," was not satisfied. "I don't think that little squaw is dead yet," he is reported as saying. To make sure, he smashed in her skull with his revolver.

The record piles up—an Indian woman and her baby killed here, three women at another place, twenty Yana of both sexes in the settlement of Cottonwood, and three hundred who were attending an autumn harvest festival at the head of Oak Run. Curtin's informants estimated the number of surviving Yana of pure and mixed blood to be about fifty persons by the time the avenging parties were through with their work in December. Perhaps it is as well that there were not more Curtins reporting during the years when memories were fresh. The pattern becomes as plain with one or two exemplifying episodes as with a hundred, and the imagination sickens before them. Curtin's figure of three thousand Yana in January, 1864, is probably high, since the Southern Yana had been wiped out earlier: there probably were more nearly two thousand Yana in the groups he knew about. His statement that there were at the end of the year about fifty survivors of the massacres (not including the Yahi) may be taken as of a round number exactness. Local ranchers and their wives and children could tick off the survivors by name, for these were the Yana who were married or adopted into a valley tribe, or who lived on white ranches in one capacity or another, many of whom had been hidden from the guards and protected by the ranchers themselves.

From this time, as Waterman says, the only white men to interest themselves in the Northern and Central Yana Indians were travelers like Curtin, linguists, and ethnographers. The cunning and gunpowder of the Indian fighters could now be concentrated on the Mill Creeks—on Ishi and his people in the restricted area between Mill Creek and Deer Creek.

Chapter 5

THE LONG CONCEALMENT

The middle 'sixties and early 'seventies—the era of the Civil War, of Lincoln's assassination, and of the invasion of the South by an army of carpet-baggers—were the years when the clash between Indians and whites in California reached a climax of fear and fury.

These years were also the time when the small boy, Ishi, was being taught Yahi skills, language, manners, law, and religion by his parents and the old men of the tribe. It was to be Ishi's fate to remember Yahi life only within the terror which encompassed and finally engulfed his people. Those Yahi who survived the first decade of the gold rush lived still in their old villages, but they were exposed and vulnerable as never before. Their near neighbors south of Deer Creek were dead or scattered; and to the north, from Mill Creek all the way to the old Yahi border across Montgomery Creek, the ancient Yana world was destroyed: its villages despoiled, its land invaded, its people murdered. In a lonely and lengthy last stand the Yahi contrived to prolong for another half century what may be called the tribal history of the Yana.

The lives of the Yahi and of the white ranchers whose land lay in the valley below and who pastured their stock in the Yana hills were, by this time, geographically interposed one on the other and at hopeless and deadly cross purpose. The white pressure was such that the Yahi were confined to the parts of their country which were inaccessible to stock or to a man on horseback. This meant that to live they were reduced to constant raiding and stealing. When they could not find livestock, they took the food which was stored in sheds or cabins for use at roundup time: they took whatever they could get their hands on. And on a raiding trip one or more of their number, a half-grown boy or one of their able bodied young men or women were as like as not to be picked off with a shot from the gun of a rancher or a herder, or one of the sheriff's men out on a scouting party—an attrition the Yahi could not at all afford. Occasionally the Indians succeeded in a raid of some size. They would take several head of stock or several sacks of grain, or perhaps in their turn they would murder a white woman or a child or a man. This always meant reprisals which were in the event disastrous to the dwindling tribelet.

The Workman ranch was on lower Concow Creek, far below the Yahi. There, Mrs. Workman, her hired man John Banks known as "Scotch John," and a young woman newly arrived from England, Rosanna Smith, were unaccountably murdered, on August 15, 1865. Two days earlier, the peaceful Maidu Indians at Big Meadows had been attacked and some of their young women and girls kidnaped. That a small band as hard pressed as were the Yahi should have undertaken two simultaneous and madcap projects would at this distance seem most improbable. They were believed, however, to have been responsible for both, their guilt attested to by scouts who claimed to have picked up one trail from the Workman ranch and another from Big Meadows, leading straight to Mill Creek. An avenging party of seventeen armed men, among them the wrought-up neighbors of the Workmans, put themselves under Anderson's and Good's leadership.

We might imagine that the Yahi, if only just returned from two bloody expeditions, would have been doubly on their guard. Such was not the case. Anderson and his men made their roundabout way undetected into Mill Creek above the gorge not far from Bruff's old camp—a site much favored by Anderson because its three knolls gave him a natural hiding place from which he overlooked a stretch of the creek and one of the largest of the

Yahi villages. Under cover of a moonless night, Anderson deployed his men in two parties, leading one of them up a steep detour which brought them out onto the three knolls where their gunfire would cover the upstream retreat from the village. Good and the remaining men hid themselves close beside the downstream entrance to the village, which position further commanded the only ford by which the creek could be readily crossed.

Anderson knew to a nicety the terrain, the special features of each village, and the probable behavior of the villagers under surprise attack; these things and more he had learned in the campaigns against the Central and Northern Yana. His execution of the Three Knolls attack was so successful that it almost ended what he called "the scourge of the Mill Creeks," before dawn of August sixteenth. Waiting only until there was light enough for his men to see where they were shooting, Anderson directed a continuous stream of gunfire down from above onto the sleeping village. As he had surmised, the Yahi ran downstream making for the open ford which brought them under Good's fire from below. The terrified Indians leapt into Mill Creek, but the rapid current was a sorry protection. They became targets there for Good's guns, and Mill Creek ran red with the blood of its people. Anderson reported that "many dead bodies floated down the rapid current."

This was, all in all, Anderson's most brilliantly successful attack. Beyond the customary taking of scalps, it may also have had some atrocity embellishments not usual under his command. He does not detail any, but he does suggest them in a single laconic sentence, "The Concow people were intensely wrought up over the horrible atrocities [also never made specific] practiced by the Indians on the white women whom they killed, and I had told them [the Concow people] that they were at liberty to deal with the Indians as they saw fit."

A few Yahi escaped, the small child Ishi and his mother among them. Ishi remembered the morning attack, but he did not talk about it in after years; it may have been then that his father was killed. The attackers ransacked the wrecked village and went triumphantly home, dangling it is not known how many scalps from their belts. Good took with him also a small child whom he found unharmed under a sheepskin blanket when they looted the village. The little boy had six toes on each foot—a peculiarity which seemed to endear him to Good.

Long, long after that August morning, the scarred ground where the village had been remained a shambles of wrecked summer shelters, of overturned food baskets, broken harpoons, and bows amidst the exposed and rotting bodies and at last the whitened bones of the dead. This unnatural neglect of their dead by the Yahi is alone sufficient evidence of how desperate was their condition. They were being attacked again and again at their center, at one or another of their larger villages situated on Mill Creek, from Bay Tree village downstream to the vicinity of Black Rock upstream. This was a concentrated and by Yahi standards a populous area of barely fifteen to twenty miles along the creek and never far from its banks or open fords or overhanging caves and bluffs. Plainly the Yahi were close to the end of their career as trouble makers, their numbers so reduced that any clash, or the loss of a single one of their depleted band made their total annihilation imminent.

It is in Sim Moak's recollections that another punishing attack by Anderson, this one in 1866, is described in much detail. The Yahi must have been desperate, because they were incautious enough to raid a ranch house at midday. The rancher's wife, Mrs. Silva, and a hired man were hiving bees near the house and looked up to see several Yahi, loaded with provisions of one sort and another, climbing out of a window. They got away, but within a few hours Anderson was in pursuit with a number of his regulars, trailing them over Deer Creek Flats and to the far side of the creek despite some delay in making the crossing. The Yahi had taken the precaution of dislodging the logs on which they crossed, which floated away downstream so that the pursuers were forced to rig a precarious and hop-scotch sort of temporary bridge between boulders as a crossing. Perhaps the Indians discounted the white men's competence to do this, and indeed one of the posse barely made it over; perhaps the Yahi did not know they were being followed. In any case, as they neared their home, they kept no rear guard. Without warning, Anderson came over the brow of a ravine above Mill Creek so little behind the Indians that they were dotted along the steep incline below him in a pattern of perfect and helpless targets.

Their slaughter was complete even to the one of their number who was farthest downhill and who took refuge behind a waterfall in the creek. Jake Moak, Sim's brother, could see the outline of a person crouched behind the tumbling spray, and continued to pour shot through the water until he saw the figure collapse into the basin of the falls. This expedition was as sheerly disastrous for the Yahi as it was plain good fun for the Moak brothers. Besides the waterfall episode, with its detail of Jake's going into the stream to retrieve his dead quarry from behind the falls and drag him out onto the bank by his long hair, there is the story of the flower-covered hat and the trip home. Here it is as Sim tells it:

> We all took a load of plunder [which included a flower-bedecked hat stolen from the Workman house and retrieved by Anderson] and packed it out to the valley. Anderson was riding a very small white mule and as we were coming down the stage road one of the party said that Anderson must wear the flowered hat. We untied it from the top of the pack and Anderson being such a large man we had to tie it on his head. We then took a scalp and fastened it on the mule's rump. We met several emigrant wagons going to Oregon. The drivers would stop and the canvas would part, and the women's and children's heads would poke out. It was a sight to see that large man riding such a small mule, the long rifle laid across in front of him and the flowered bonnet and the long haired scalp.

Either in 1867 or 1868, Anderson and his men tracked to a cave a considerable number of Yahi. The different accounts agree neither about the exact date nor about the particular reason alleged for the massacre, but as nearly as can be made out, it was in reparation for a murder. Mrs. Allen's and Mrs. Dirsch's names come up again in this connection but their murder was earlier, and had already motivated the completion of the wiping out of the Central and Northern Yana. All that is known is that the Yahi were tracked to a cave at Campo Seco, north of Mill Creek, and there thirty-three of them were murdered and scalped, making this cave another charnel house of whitening bones to be avoided by whites and Indians.

Neither Robert Anderson, Hiram Good, nor any other of the guards participated in the final mass massacre of Yahi. A party of four vaqueros, J. J. Bogart, Jim Baker, Scott Williams, and Norman Kingsley, were camped at Wild Horse Corral engaged in a roundup of cattle from the Yana hills. One morning toward the end of the roundup they came on a trail of blood. Guessing it was that of a wounded steer, they followed the blood trail which led them in the direction of upper Mill Creek. They found a broken arrow and, a little beyond, the remains of the carcass of a steer. The hunters who had killed the steer had been too pressed to skin it in their usual fashion, and had instead hurriedly hacked off chunks of meat, as much as they could carry, and thrown the rest into the brush to be retrieved no doubt if there was opportunity later.

Having found this much, the vaqueros went back to their own camp, but the next day, with dogs this time, they picked up the trail again and followed it into Mill Creek and upstream to a large cave. In this remote and seemingly safe spot were gathered more than thirty Yahi including young children and babies, well supplied with food, even to fresh and dried meat. They were helpless against the four armed men who forthwith killed them all. Norman Kingsley, as he explained afterwards, changed guns during the slaughter, exchanging his .56-caliber Spencer rifle for a .38-caliber Smith and Wesson revolver, because the rifle "tore them up so bad," particularly the babies. There is today a Kingsley Cave, only about two trail miles from Wild Horse Corral. This is presumably the cave of the last massacre.

With this morning's work done, it was generally believed that the Yahi—the stubborn Mill Creeks whom Anderson and Good had sworn to exterminate—had been killed to the last woman and child. Silence brooded over Mill Creek whose caves had become truly the tombs of its ancient peoples.

Except that the bodies of the victims of this final massacre disappeared complete and clean from the cave.

That the few survivors of the Kingsley Cave disaster might have resorted to burial instead of cremation rites for its victims suggests itself as a possibly necessary compromise, owing to the risk of detection from the smoke of a funeral pyre, or rather from the series of pyres needed for so many corpses. Archaeological evidence within the cave is not conclusive, nor is there other evidence. Ishi implied in any reluctant reference he ever made to deaths or funerary rites that the bodies of the Yahi dead were always cremated according to correct and usual practice. After cremation it was the custom to collect the bones and ashes from the pyre and put them in a shallow hollow among the rocks where a rock cairn was built up to mark the place and also to prevent dogs or wild animals from digging up the bones. The soil of Mill Creek cañon and its caves is thin and not easily dug to any depth with primitive tools. Solomon Gore reported to Waterman that he, in company with a number of other white men, visited the cave soon after the violence there and that there were no bodies, or exposed bones, nor was there evidence of recently dug graves which they could find. Perhaps the customary cremation had, somehow, been managed.

A pioneer rancher, W. S. Segraves, who lived near the head of Butte Creek, also owned a cabin, which he sometimes occupied and used for storage, in Twenty Mile Hollow only a short distance from Hiram Good's place in Acorn Hollow. One morning, Segraves missed several head of cattle. Suspecting that it was Yahi who had stolen them, he got Good, whose last raid this would be, and two other men to go with him to try to recover his stock. The four of them with dogs to help track the Indians, went directly up Mill Creek to a Yahi village about twenty-five miles from the mouth of the creek which they reached in the late afternoon. The village comprised a dozen or so small Yana houses set in a ring in a meadow shaded by overhanging bay trees. It was deserted except for an Indian dog, but showed ample evidence of having been the scene of recent cattle slaughtering operations. Segraves says simply that he and his party made camp there for the night. This village, shown on the map on page 44 as Bay Tree village, was the farthest downstream of the larger Yahi settlements. That it should be deserted and that four white men should occupy it for the night without special precaution indicates how the Yahi situation had deteriorated even in a few months. The next morning, Segraves and his companions continued up Mill Creek. After some hours, they saw a group of fifteen or more Indians coming downstream loaded with baskets of freshly gathered foodstuffs, several women and one man whom Segraves called the Old Doctor ahead of the others. The posse, undiscovered to the Indians, took positions behind trees with their guns cocked. What happened follows as Segraves told it to Waterman:

> As the Indians came abreast of us, we motioned to the squaws to squat down so as not to be in the line of fire. [It was Good who did not subscribe to the killing of women and children.] One old woman, when she saw that the group was covered, did so. A young woman freed herself of her pack in a flash and started to run. The old woman grabbed her and held her. A little girl was also with the old woman, and was held by the hand. The old Doctor tried to get away. Good did the shooting while I called the shots. The first two missed. At the third I called "Distance!" At the fourth the Old Doctor collapsed. The weapons we used were sixteen-shot Henry repeaters, a new weapon at the time.

The old woman, the young woman, and the little girl were taken captive. The others got away. Much behind the first party two stragglers came in, but halted before they were within firing range, and disappeared into the brush. One of them was a middle-aged man, the other a young man or well-grown boy. Segraves liked to think that they were father and son and that the young man was Ishi. Forty years later when he saw Ishi in San Francisco he "positively" identified him as the sixteen- or seventeen-year-old whom he had seen on Mill Creek. He was mistaken. Ishi was a little boy in 1870.

But to go back to Segraves' account, his party, taking their captives with them, returned to Bay Tree village where they again spent the night. In the morning, while they were still in camp, the older of the Indians whom they had seen at a distance the afternoon before, appeared before Segraves with some sort of an offer. The question will occur to the reader as it did to Waterman: why did none of the posse shoot this man as they had shot the Old Doctor? Segraves' answer to Waterman's question was that the man was unarmed. This was scarcely the full explanation, since none of the Indians were "armed." The Old Doctor may possibly have had a bow or a sling with him, but even so, he could not have resisted men with guns, nor did he try to do so. However it was, Segraves listened to what the man said, and although neither he nor Good understood him, they gathered that he was offering to bring all his people to them. To this seeming end, he led the posse back upstream to the scene of the Old Doctor's death and there mounted a boulder from which he called loudly up and down the cañon. Segraves did not of course know what he was saying but the commanding voice would have been heard by anyone there to hear. Then quick and quiet as the flick of a released bowstring, he leaped from the boulder on the side away from the white men and was lost to them in the chaparral. There were no Indians to be seen, and Segraves and Good made no further attempt to pursue them, returning home with their one scalp and their three captives.

The episode remains a somewhat curious one. Segraves had set out to try to recover his cattle. When he found that they were already slaughtered, the old punitive program reasserted itself: there followed a pursuit, a murder, and a taking of captives. The pattern unfolded expectably but there clings about it a sense of wayward half-heartedness. Segraves was not an "Indian killer" at all, and Good was too experienced a one not to know that what would once have been a contest, unequal but somehow worthy of a man of action and courage, had become no contest at all.

The Yahi may themselves have sensed the ambivalence of the white men, otherwise would scarcely have risked the close encounter, whose purpose was almost surely to try if any way opened, to get back the captives. Whatever the Indian was trying to accomplish in taking the whites back upstream, he must have decided that his plan would not work, and so gave up the attempt.

Two weeks later there occurred a probable sequel to this first abortive effort at diplomacy, and a most curious one it was. The same Yahi was again spokesman, coming this time to Segraves' own cabin, after dark, and bringing with him seven women and four other men, the men carrying properly strung Yahi bows in good condition. With much formality, they lined up while the leader made a speech at the end of which each man presented Segraves with his bow. Segraves did not know what was said, but he knew he was being offered some sort of an exchange, perhaps five bows for the three captives. He could not be sure, and in any case the captives were with Good, not with him. Thoroughly puzzled about what to do, Segraves motioned the twelve Yahi along with him to Good's cabin, meaning to leave the decision to Good. Good was not at home, and the party settled down to await his return. There were some of "Good's men" there, that is, some of the guards, and while they all waited together, an incident occurred which put an end of another sort than either Segraves or the Indians could have foreseen to the remarkable vigil. One of the guards, as Segraves told it,

"Took a notion to weigh himself on a set of steelyards. He throws a rope over a limb to suspend the steelyards by, when the Indians take a notion that they are to be hanged. So they all run away and are never seen again."

In reporting the same incident in the May, 1874, issue of the *Overland Monthly*, Stephen Powers, who spent some time in northern California in the 'seventies as a magazine correspondent, wrote, "It was the intention of the hunters, [guards], as one of them candidly avowed to me, to have seized them and secretly put the whole five out of existence [the five Yahi men]. While they were in camp [at Good's cabin] one of the hunters conceived an absurd whim to weigh himself, at which the wily savages took fright, and they all bounded away like frightened deer and escaped." It will be seen from Powers' account that in 1874 the secret intent to do away with the little band of Indians who had put themselves in Good's power was admitted to without embarrassment. It should be said that such was presumably not Segraves' intent, nor do we know that it would have been Good's decision had he been present. By 1915 the motive of murder which lurked as more than a possibility in the incident, had been suppressed or forgotten. But a man's odd whim to weigh himself is the same in Powers' and in Segraves' stories. Deaths by hanging were second only to deaths by shooting all during the violent 'sixties in California. That the twelve frightened Indians should have interpreted the throwing of a rope over a tree limb according to its more usual meaning would not seem surprising. Perhaps a bored guard did want to weigh himself in the middle of the night; perhaps also in the 'seventies it was still good form to rid the country of dangerous savages but was beginning to be frowned upon to do it by trickery.

The ultimate significance of the effort to communicate with Segraves is that it was the first occasion so far as is known when any Yahi made a gesture of compromise and bargaining. Its outcome scarcely encouraged a repetition, nor was there any. The three captives remained with Good; the twelve emissaries from the hills faded into the covering brush, to be seen no more. The time of the concealment had come.

Ishi was a little child three or four years old at the time of the Three Knolls massacre, old enough to remember terror-fraught experiences. He was eight or nine when the Kingsley Cave massacre took place, old enough, possibly, to have taken some part in the cleaning up of the cave and in the ritual disposition of its victims. He entered the concealment in which he would grow up at not more than ten years of age.

The presentation of the five bows was the climactic last act in Yahi history, determinative of the whole of its further course. Five men, the last five able to bend the bow (until Ishi should have grown up), able to fight and to hunt, laid down their arms in an offer of exchange and presumably of peace. Five was the sacred number of most Indian peoples in interior northern California; if five was the sacred number of the Yana, which it probably was, the offering of the bows carried added symbolic and formal meaning. Had the bid been accepted with anything of the courage and imagination of its tendering this story would have another ending, not of necessity a totally tragic one.

As recounted, the one Yahi effort to negotiate with the white man came to nothing. Segraves was left with five bows which he had neither the skill nor the strength to unbend; the captives perforce remained with Hiram Good; the twelve Yahi melted into a night from which so far as the rest of the world was concerned, they never emerged. Survivors of the Kingsley Cave massacre and the encounter with Good and Segraves, they retreated to the inner fastnesses of their own heartland whose gorges and caves and impassable chaparral they shared with occasional elk, with bear, deer, fox, and snake, but with no other human beings. There they constituted what A. L. Kroeber calls "the smallest free nation in the world, which by an unexampled fortitude and stubbornness of character succeeded in holding out against the tide of civilization twenty-five years longer even than Geronimo's famous band of Apaches," and for almost thirty-five years after the Sioux and their allies defeated Custer. These were the years of the Long Concealment. Powers wrote about the Yahi, whom he called the Nozi or the Kombo, during the first years of the concealment. He had talked to Indian fighters in Chico and Tehama and Red Bluff, and had listened to yarns about the fighters' exploits from their friends. Piecing together the stories, Powers arrived at an imaginatively prophetic projection of the tragi-drama the concealment was to become. He says of it:

> They [the Yahi] seem likely to present a spectacle which is without parallel in human history—that of a barbaric race resisting civilization with arms in their hands, to the last man, and the last squaw, and the last papoose. They were once a numerous and thrifty tribe. Now there are only five of them left—two men, two women, and a child. [Powers was mistaken in the numbers left at the time he was writing but again he was accurately prophetic of what would be the numbers and composition of the band a few years later.] No human eye ever beholds them, except now and then some lonely hunter, perhaps, prowling and crouching for days over the volcanic wastes and scraggy forests which they inhabit. Just at nightfall he may catch a glimpse of a faint camp-fire, with figures flitting about it; but before he can creep within rifle-range of it the figures have disappeared, the flame wastes slowly out, and he arrives only to find that the objects of his search have indeed been there before him, but are gone. They cooked there their hasty evening repast, but they will sleep somewhere else, with no camp-fire to guide a lurking enemy within reach. For days and weeks together they never touch the earth, stepping always from one volcanic stone to another. They never leave a broken twig or a disturbed leaf behind them. Probably no day of the year ever passes over their heads but some one of their doomed nation of five sits crouching on a hillock or in a tree-top within easy eye-shot of his fellows; and not a hare can move upon the earth beneath without its motions being heeded and recorded by the watcher's eye. There are men in and around Chico who have sworn a great oath of venge-

ance that these five Indians shall die a bloody death; but weeks, months, and years have passed away, and brought for their oaths no fulfillment.

Withdrawal and retreat had been a Yahi pattern since 1850; the period of concealment meant their commitment to the pattern as a total way of life. The problem is to try to understand what motivated the prolonged concealment, their "almost disembodied life" as Powers called it, in the light of the person Ishi showed himself to be when he finally renounced the known agony for an unknown fate.

Withdrawal is a response congenial to much in the American Indian temperament which leans toward the Yogi not the Commissar, being Eastern and not Western in its orientation: fatalistic, introspective, and introverted. The Hopi Indians, remote on their almost impregnable mesas, responded to both Spaniards and Anglo-Americans by excluding them, a withdrawal psychologically comparable to the Japanese nation's two hundred and fifty years of exclusion; nor has there yet appeared a Perry to breach those mesa ramparts of the Hopi. The Zuni Indians, living in seven accessible villages, were gathered together by the Spaniards into a single large community organized around a mission church. The Zuni continue to live where the Spaniards re-placed them, and they continue to bury their dead in the mission churchyard; otherwise the Spanish-Christian influence has faded except for a single Christian saint who has been allowed living space within the pantheon of Zuni Gods.

Given the intimate separatism of the Californians, it is reasonable to surmise that they would have maintained their identities, some as have the Hopi, some as the Zuni, had there been for them, too, time and place to do so. There was neither; they were visited with annihilation, not interpenetration. Individuals survived sometimes; cultures did not, except along the Colorado River area whose remoteness saved its peoples and their culture for nearly a century longer than elsewhere in the state. It would be sentimentalization to read into the years of desperate concealment a chosen way of life: such choice was never the Yahi's to make. Their choice was between submission with certain loss of identity and probable loss of life, and a finish fight. They chose to fight, withdrawal and concealment being merely the final phase of the unequal fight.

That we know in some detail certain aspects of the concealment and nothing at all of others, is due neither to lack of curiosity and zeal on the part of Ishi's white friends, nor to any uncoöperativeness in Ishi, but rather to inhibiting circumstances, some linguistic, some cultural and very "Yana," very "Indian," some humane. It was incorrect and dangerous to the living and the dead for Ishi to use the name of a dead relative or friend, and circumlocutions were impossibly difficult to Ishi's limited English confronted with his friends' limited Yahi. Any, however informal, census-taking was thus ruled out. Had Ishi's measure of life been longer, he would no doubt have transgressed somewhat the taboo against speaking of the dead, in order to preserve something of their history. This would have come naturally with time as his English and his friends' Yahi became more fluent, all the more since he had a strong sense for participation in whatever was of importance to those about him.

Ishi remembered almost everything that had happened in his lifetime. He was a willing autobiographer, patient and conscientious, yet there is not preserved for the present record the "human interest," the tragical, personal accounts in the detail and circumstantiality which he could have given them, and which some readers will be disappointed not to find. But to be questioned and to talk at length and with any intimacy of his family and people at whose death from starvation or old age or sickness he had stood by, a helpless witness and unhappy survivor, left Ishi depressed and distressed. His friends, seeing how it was with him, forebore to question him, contenting themselves with picking up so much as from time to time Ishi might, unasked, volunteer. And in his own time and way, he told more than a little about certain aspects of the concealment.

We know, for example, only approximately how many people undertook the concealment, and at what ages; we do not know how many of them were men, how many, women; nor do we know the name of a single individual of that small company, not even Ishi's, for Ishi is not a personal name; it means simply, "man."

When Stephen Powers, writing in the *Overland Monthly* of May, 1874, described the escape of the Indians from Hiram Good's cabin as having occurred in the summer of 1870, placing it in time with these words, "There is now wanting only a month of four years since they have been seen together," the two accounts, Powers' and Segraves', agree as to the year. They are within weeks of each other as to the month, and they fit Ishi's description of himself as a child "this high," which again corresponds with the best estimate Doctor Saxton Pope could make from medical evidence of Ishi's age in 1911. The late spring or early summer of 1870 is, then, a time datum firmer than most that we have. It is of help in unraveling the relative chronologies, and it is from this agreement that any estimate of the population numbers of the concealed must take off.

The twelve adults who presented themselves to Segraves are the certainly known Yahi survivors—and the child Ishi—who made up the original group. Waterman, Dr. Pope, and others who were as informed as it was possible to be about the probable numbers, estimated that there may have been as many as fifteen or sixteen in all; that Ishi's cousin or sister, who was not much older (or younger) than Ishi himself, and two or three old people were probably hiding in the brush during the Five Bows parley, unseen by Segraves and the other white men, but close enough at hand to join the twelve upon their retreat from Good's cabin.

There was current in 1915, as in preceding years, a romantic version of the concealment which had it that only five Indians were involved, and the same five, from the beginning. The number had been given the sanction of print by Powers in 1874. Powers' sources for details of the Five Bows incident were secondhand and confused in certain of their parts with other events, or were wrongly reported. According to this version there were two men, two women, and a small boy, who would have been Ishi. Since, as will be seen, there were five and only five survivors for many of the forty years, this stretching to make it for the whole of the time becomes in retrospect not much more unlikely than was the concealment itself.

If any births ever for a time augmented the numbers of those hiding, Ishi mentioned none. The population curve was inevitably and presumably only downward. The survival of the Yahi, with restoration of something more than parity of births over deaths would have been risky and dubious at best, so long as they remained sealed off from other human beings. A species which drops seriously below its customary group numbers and swings far from its usual age and sex distributions only rarely and under unusually favorable life conditions is able to survive long enough to rehabilitate itself and to increase. But the Yahi were not, after all, a "species." They were a macrocosmic nation victimized by the common killers: invasion, war, famine, and intolerance.

Beyond the agreement among those best able to judge what was the probable population of the concealment, there are compelling psychological and physiological reasons for believing that it could not have been undertaken by more than a handful of people. There is the question: In a given situation and circumstance, how many people *can* hide as a single unit? With the disadvantages of the Yahi situation, the answer is: Very few. The Yahi limit would seem to have been only as many as would inhabit one of their smaller villages, a larger number being almost sure to bring down upon itself some drastic debacle, such as another Kingsley Cave massacre.

There is the question: Could the Yana hills, or any land so nearly marginal, support life, with the best hunting and gathering grounds unavailable or despoiled? The answer is: Probably not. This leads to the further question: Was this because there was too little, or because so much time and energy had to be diverted to the elaborate and eternal routines of remaining hidden whatever the activity? And the answer is, surely: Both.

It would seem that the Kingsley Cave massacre and the loss of the precious three captives to Segraves were the events which directly precipitated the concealment. Those who remained were hopelessly crippled not solely because they had suffered the loss of two thirds of their number, but because amongst those two thirds were almost all their young. American Indians in their natural state had no experience of overpopulation: children were important and precious to them at any time, and must have been trebly so to the Yahi who were left in 1870. Nor would babies have greatly complicated their hiding. A baby's cry *may* discover a hideout to an enemy, but Indians are light-voiced; their babies rarely "bawl," their crying being more a whimper, not a far-carrying sound. Even runabout children are quiet, never far from their mother or another adult. When a small child is hungry, he is fed; and he is not left alone. The real hazard to the possible success of the long concealment may have been that those who were left faced a future in which they shared no sure investment.

What became of the captives who were left behind in Good's cabin is relevant to the matter of possible survivors. But the trail of their identity peters out almost before it is found. Good "gave" the three captives to a man living near him in Acorn Hollow. The young woman had a boy born to her who was named or nick-named "Snowflake" or "Snowdrop." This child was pointed out to Powers in Tehama. The variant accounts of the baby's birth, Powers' and Segraves', are given in full in the Notes, page 240f. They are of interest in themselves and as an example of some of the difficulties inherent in hearsay evidence when used as source material. But with the episode of Snowflake's birth, the history of the last three Yahi to be taken captive comes to a close. Whatever their later fortunes may have been, they were blended indistinguishably into that of the white frontier.

Our narrative is come so far that Ishi begins as it were to speak for himself and to recreate for us his life during the concealment. And this is the time perhaps to regard the concealment briefly in its broad, philosophical aspect. The phenomenon of the sealed-off community is a rare but recurrent one in human history. It may be said categorically that it is doomed because of the nature of man, which is social, intermingling, and generalized. A baby raised without hearing human speech or experiencing normal emotional expression and exchange would probably die early, and would in no case develop either speech or other distinctively human and cultural attributes, these being matters which are taught by example and transmitted through imitation and learning. Nor do adults thrive in solitude—we are not hibernating or singly-living animals. And since we are as men the superficially variant members of a single species, an ingrown, inward-looking, and too-specialized community begins to lose health and adherents after a single generation, or goes to pieces through exacerbation of tempers and temperaments which impinge too nearly and too exclusively one upon another.

But these occasional retreats vary enormously in their origins, in their successes, and in the nature of their ultimate failures. The Long Concealment failed in its objective to save a peoples' life, but it would seem to have been brilliantly successful in its psychology and techniques of living. Ishi's group was master of the difficult art of communal and peaceful coëxistence under permanent threat of alarm, and in a tragic and deteriorating prospect. We know from Ishi that men took on "women's work" and vice versa according to need. The sick, the dying, and the bedridden were cared for; the dead were sent on their way with ritual formality, nor did the living neglect to mourn for them.

It is a curious circumstance that some of the questions which arise about the concealment are those for which in a different context psychologists and neurologists are trying to find answers for the submarine and outer space services today. Some of these are: What makes for morale under confining and limiting life conditions? What are the presumable limits of claustrophobic endurance? What temperament and build should be sought for these special and confining situations? It seems that the Yahi might have qualified for outer space had they lasted into this century. They were not too large, nor were they awkward or clumsy or restless; they were skilled and resourceful with whatever materials and means were at hand; they were self-sufficient; and their outlook was duly fatalistic.

In contrast to the Forty-niners whom Bruff describes, whose morality and morale had crumbled, Ishi and his band remained incorrupt, humane, compassionate, and with their faith intact even unto starvation, pain, and death. The questions then are: What makes for stability? For psychic strength? For endurance, courage, faith?

Some of the Yahi sources of strength might be said to be that they were on home ground and that they were already skilled in what they had to do to live. That these were not aspects of first importance Ishi's later ready adaptation to changed locale and culture would suggest. Of very great importance to their psychic health was the circumstance that their sufferings and curtailments arose from wrongs done to them by others. They were not guilt ridden, nor were they "alienated from their culture." Their aims were modest, reasonable, realistic; their egos and ambitions uninflamed; and the American Indian *mystique,* pervasive and unconscious, stood them in good stead.

The twelve years from 1872 to 1884 were without incident or rumor. The concealment for those twelve years was complete. No horses or stock were hunted, no cabins were rifled, no grain stolen; not a footprint, not a telltale bit of ash, or wisp of smoke from a fire was seen; not a single broken arrowshaft or a lost spear point or a remnant of a milkweed rope snare was found on a forest or meadow floor as a sign that Indians were about. Stephen Powers prefigured this hidden life back in 1874, but not even he foresaw that it might go on so long.

The years of Ishi's total disconnection from history were most of the years of his life: a long interlude of stillness. The senses strain to understand what must have been the waking and the sleeping of that time; and if Ishi could not light up for us its traumas and tragedies, he could and did describe and reënact for us, something of its day-to-day living.

The hidden ones fished with the harpoon and the net, and hunted with the bow and arrow, and by setting snares—silent weapons all. They gathered acorns in the autumn, enough if possible to see them through the winter. They ate green clover in April, and brodiaea bulbs in early summer. In midsummer they went to Waganupa, four nights' journey, to its cooler air and deeper shade and more abundant game. For the rest, they lived on upper Mill Creek in small houses camouflaged so that from above, the only direction from which they could have been seen, the bent branches which covered them looked like nature's work. Nearby were storage shelters disguised in the same way, and containing drying frames, baskets of dried meat and fish and acorns, and utensil baskets, tools, and hides. They traveled sometimes for long distances by leaping from boulder to boulder, their bare feet leaving no print; or they walked up or down stream, making of their creeks a highroad. Each footprint on the ground was covered over with dead leaves, obliterated. Their trails went under the heavy chaparral, not through it, and they traveled them on all fours. A cow could not find such trails; even deer sought more open ones. If a branch was in the way it was gradually bent back farther and farther, and if need be severed by charring and wearing through with a crude tool made from splitting a boulder, a slow but silent process. They never chopped, the sound of chopping being the unmistakable announcement of human presence. They kept their fires small so that the smoke dissipated harmlessly through the brush without rising beaconwise above the bay tree canopy, and they covered the site of a camp-fire with broken rock as soon as the fire was out. They went up and down the perpendicular cliffs of Mill Creek cañon on ropes of milkweed fiber—a quick and safe way down, since the cañon was well screened by trees that overhung its rim. They could bring up a catch of fish or a basket of water, or let themselves down for a swim with far less trouble and time than it took to scramble up and down the little branching trails which led to the water's edge. Also, they preferred to use these trails sparingly so that they would not become too plainly marked but continue to appear to be no more than the runways of rabbits or weasels. They ground their acorns to flour on smooth stones and made the staple mush, cooking it in baskets. They wore capes of deerskin and wildcat, occasionally of bearskin. And they slept under blankets of rabbitskins. Ethnologists are agreed that they pursued a way of life the most totally aboriginal and primitive of any on the continent, at least after the coming of the white man to America.

Chapter 6
THE YAHI DISAPPEAR

The years passed. No Yahi were seen and there were no "Indian troubles." New settlers in the valley assured each other that the Mill Creeks had long since been exterminated or had died. They shrugged their shoulders over the mystery of the last massacre as old timers remembered it. Stories never lost anything in the telling, they said. Even the old timers, some of them, agreed. Others were not so sure. A sudden movement in the brush might be a deer or a quail, or it might be a wild Indian.

The back country was changing, it was filling up. By 1884 ranches, saw mills, and small permanent settlements with connecting roads instead of trails mushroomed far upstream into the hills which no longer need be shunned because of fear of Indians, of whom tales continued nonetheless to be told, sometimes making the city papers and growing into circumstantial yarns. The rustling in the chaparral increased; owners of cabins claimed that they were being robbed as in the old days; and once or twice a man or a boy came in with a story of having seen fleetingly a strange Indian.

In 1884 the completeness of the concealment began to crack. After twelve years, the Yahi took to raiding again. By this time they had lost most of their few hunters; hunting and gathering had become ever riskier and scantier in returns. The roads, the ranches, and the new hill population of whites impinged ever closer upon Mill Creek. So, once again, calves were missed, or a sheep would be seen in the flock, unscratched but with arrow points caught in its fleece. And, since the arrows were indubitable evidence that wild Indians were at work, so were the cabins emptied of some of their key contents, but with their canned goods left intact. It was only Yahi, as everyone knew, who took all the flour and barley and none of the canned corn and beans. Perhaps canned goods did not appear to them to be food; or perhaps they had once tried some which was spoiled.

It may seem odd at this distance, but it was the raiding of provisions which irritated the cattlemen far more than did the stealing of stock. When a sheep or a calf was successfully "hunted," its owner suffered a loss; when a cabin was stripped of its stored supplies, inconvenience and frustration were added to loss. Pack loads of stock feed, beans, coffee, sugar, bacon, flour, and canned goods were taken to the hill cabins and sheds where they were stored to await the annual roundup. A vaquero might have to search for the scattered cattle and sheep in difficult and remote parts of the hills, and it was understood that at need he was to dip into the supplies in any cabin whether or not it belonged to his boss. But if the Yahi had been there ahead of the vaquero, there would be neither barley for his horse, nor flour for himself. In the more remote areas, and it was those which the Yahi favored, a cabin or two lacking these staples sometimes made a return to the valley for replacements necessary, and that could mean that the roundup would have to be made all over again.

By the 'nineties, Ishi and the two or three companions still able to raid with him must have known precisely the time of arrival of a pack train at a particular cabin: there were some cabins which they seem to have robbed regularly season after season. They also knew that the risk of discovery and death out-of-hand was greater by far than if they were quietly to snare a sheep or a calf. But it was in spring that the pack trains came, and it was in spring that the ground was still covered with snow and that the remnant band was not merely hungry, but starving.

Mr. Norvall, the informant who in 1915 told Waterman about visiting Kingsley Cave after the massacre there, described for him also one of the late Yahi cabin robbings. As he recalled it, it was one day in April, 1885 that he heard someone in his cabin on lower Dry Creek. He went to investigate, and as he came closer he saw four Indians one after another climb out of the cabin's single window. They obviously were not expecting to be confronted by him, and finding themselves caught, lined up quietly against the cabin wall, leaving the next move to him. They had taken only old clothes from the cabin, perhaps because it contained no food except canned goods. One of the four was a young woman wearing three old jumpers of Norvall's and apparently little else. One was an old man, who had taken a shabby overcoat and an ancient rifle barrel from the cabin. There were two young men, one of whom had a crippled foot. Norvall remarked to Waterman that "Rafe Johnson did that," the reference being to the story that "Rafe" was supposed, some years earlier, to have wounded an Indian child in the ankle. The fourth person was Ishi. The woman pointed toward Mill Creek and said something which Norvall thought was *Dos chiquitos papooses* which would be a pidgin Spanish meaning two small children. Norvall was friendly, indicated by signs that the Indians could keep their pathetic loot, and waved them off. They disappeared, and he saw no more of them. Toward fall of the same year, the cabin was again entered. Nothing was missing from it this time, but Norvall found two Yana baskets left there on the table. These he took to be a gift of gratitude for his earlier friendliness, treasuring them as keepsakes until 1915 when he gave them to the University museum as part of an "Ishi" collection.

D. B. Lyon of Red Bluff related to Waterman also in 1915 an experience he had had in 1889 when he was a young boy, and which certainly involved someone of the Yahi band, perhaps Ishi. Lyon did not say how old he was at the time, probably in his early teens to judge by the anecdote. He was hunting one day on Big Antelope Creek when he heard a rustling in a clump of buckeye. His dog sniffed it and went in but came out uneasily, so Lyon knew that whatever was there was not a deer or rabbit. A noise as of tomcats fighting then came from the buckeye. Lyon threw a rock into the clump, and hit something which responded with a very human "grunt." Encouraged by this, Lyon circled closer, finally edging under the buckeye where he stumbled over a bundle which must have been dropped only seconds ahead of him, the warm sweat of recent handling still clinging to it when he stooped to open it. It consisted of a sheepskin pelt wrapped around half a dozen legs of freshly slaughtered sheep, and a small buckskin bag. As he bent over the bundle, two arrows passed just above his head, one splintering on a boulder, the other falling to the ground in front of him, while a third grazed his cap brim. Whoever was shooting had the distance perfectly and was correcting for height. Hanging onto his treasures, and scooping up the spent arrow from the ground, he ran, nor did he stop until he was well away. When he emptied the contents of the buckskin bag at home, he found it to be a complete Yahi arrow-making outfit. Like Norvall, Lyon still treasured the pelt, the arrow, and the bag with its tools when he told their story to Waterman. Now they, too, form part of the museum's "Ishi" collection. As for the sound as of tomcats fighting which Lyon described, the Yahi experience of domestic house cats was nil, but Ishi and his people could imitate bird songs and wild animal calls and growls, which they used to bring an animal to them or, as in this incident, to scare one off.

It was Lyon who recounted to Waterman one version of the "poisoned wheat" story which turns up in various guises and attributed to different people. According to Lyon, it was Elijah Graham who left a sack of poisoned flour, plainly labeled as poison, in his hill cabin. Many of the white settlers disbelieved that there were Indians in the hills, or were inclined to think that the considerable robbing and pilfering was not done by Indians. The poisoned flour promptly disappeared, which circumstance Graham (or whoever the initiator was in any telling of the tale) took for proof that it was Indians who had made off with it. This is a conundrum without an answer. The story's popularity may have stemmed from the number of people around Red Bluff and vicinity who failed to share Elijah Graham's faith that it was only Indians who were illiterate.

It was in 1894 as Lyon recalled it that he and his brother tracked someone through the brush toward Mill Creek cañon. The tracks were made by unshod human feet, wide across the toes, with an imprint of deep creases and cracks. These were probably made by a Yahi. To escape the white boys, the pursued one had jumped from the top of the bluff into a bay tree below, and by so doing quickly put a good length of sloping cañon wall between him and the boys. They may of course have imagined this feat, but very likely it happened as Lyon said it did. Ishi's friends of later years were to learn that heights, narrow ledges, and sheer drops bothered him not at all.

The decade of raiding which began in 1884 came to an end ten years later as inexplicably and as suddenly as it had erupted. Silence and emptiness returned to the cañons, and the yarns about wild Indians which had burgeoned once again lost credibility. For the Yahi band itself the ten successive years of raiding were the first and the resistive phase of their last retreat. The Yahi tried to make a life on Mill Creek, to maintain a living space which took in upper Mill and Deer creeks with the ridges, meadows, and smaller streams between; and as the pressure from white encroachment grew unbearably constricting, to fill their emptying baskets from the intrusive and second grade but available food of the white man: his flour and grain and sheep. They failed. And so began the last retreat to Deer Creek.

There were, it is believed, only five Yahi left to make the withdrawal from Mill Creek to Deer Creek, each step of which was a surrender of another piece of heartland, of oak stand, meadow land, fishing place, and upland hunting ground. There remained to them when they at last put down their baskets only two separate but closely adjacent tracts of land on the south side of Deer Creek cañon, which they might with some reason call their own and occupy with relative security. Each tract was not more than half a mile wide and three miles long. The Yahi knew this country intimately, having formerly lived in good village sites close to the creek. Indeed, Ishi was born in one of the old Deer Creek villages. The Yahi could not, in the 'nineties, retreat to any of these old sites, for they were too exposed to view from above and from the north side. Instead, they built two tiny villages above and below the confluence of Sulphur and Deer creeks. The Speegle homestead and ranch were on Sulphur Creek, only a short distance from the new villages, but no one except the Yahi themselves ever entered the thickets of the cañon, which were a surer protection to them than remoteness itself. The sites were chosen for their invisibility and it might be said for their improbability, and because they were where the long and always risky trip to the creek could be made all the way to the water's edge under a screen of laurel. A grizzly bear, or bears, had at one time a den on the site of the larger of the new villages, hence its name, *Wowunupo mu tetna*, Grizzly Bear's Hiding Place.

The site of Wowunupo is a narrow ledge or trough five hundred or more feet above the creek, the only place where even the simplest of shelters could imaginably be built anywhere on the steep cañon wall. Trees grow tall along this ledge, shading it and screening it from below and from the other side. From the ledge to the rim of the cañon, another two hundred feet, is bare cliff, sheer and impassable, which provided the village with a sheltered rear wall and perfect protection from above.

None of the trees and only part of the scrub growth were cleared within the village proper, so that it remained well camouflaged from all prospects. Only the faintest of narrow trails connected the houses, and these were for the most part under an overhead growth. The easternmost building was a tiny house whose framework was of poles lashed together and thatched with boughs of bay. It was shaped like the letter A, looking, with its cleverly arranged covering, very like a tree from the outside. Inside, the little house was partitioned to make two rooms, the larger and back one a storage room for baskets of food and other provisions and tools. The door of the house faced downstream.

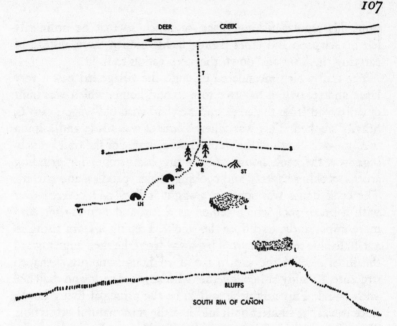

WOWUNUPO MU TETNA

L = loose rock slides. LH = living house. R = reservoir. SH = smoke house. ST = store house. S = surveyor's line. T = trail to creek. VT = village toilet.

Because of the shelflike setting, the village was laid out paralleling the creek. Downstream from the first house was a large digger pine in whose shade a rectangular "reservoir" had been dug, three by four feet in diameter and four feet deep. In winter this was kept packed full of snow as an additional source for water.

Beyond the reservoir, one trail led on through the village; another branched off to the creek, five hundred feet below. The trails were the very ones the bears had made and used when Wowunupo was a bear's den. Ishi found that by following the old grizzly trail he came out onto the creek at a good crossing, and that on the north side the fishing was exceptional. It became his regular fishing place, so much so that he ordinarily left his harpoon and other fishing tackle hidden there, instead of carrying them up and down the steep cañon trail.

The trail which meandered through the village led past a very large and sprawling bay tree to a second house, which was built of driftwood from the creek and overlaid with old wagon canvas, heavily smoked. This was where *charqui* was made and salmon was smoked. North of the smoke house, at one of the trail branchings, was the cook house, with a fireplace, stones for grinding acorns, cooking baskets, and cooking stones, paddles, and stirrers. The cook house was sunk in a slight hollow and covered over with a brush roof which served as a sun and rain shelter, and more importantly, to diffuse the smoke, keeping it from rising in a telltale blue spiral. One trail led away from the shelf edge toward the inner side of the site to the third house, another A-shaped structure, strongly lashed together with strips of bark, and thatched with laurel. This might be said to be the principal living house, since it was the tightest built and had the most natural protection. The original bear's den was a part of it. Here, although the space was cramped, there was a living area of sorts, and room for the five to sleep warm and dry when it was cold or stormy out of doors; and here were kept the coon and bearskin capes and the rabbitskin blankets.

Not far from the den house was a shaded and sheltered spot which was Ishi's workroom where he made his arrow and spear points. Enough obsidian and glass refuse from years of chipping accumulated there to fill one of the large carrying baskets of the Yahi. Here the village proper ended. A trail led off from the last house another fifty or more feet to the village toilet, a designated spot downstream.

Neither the swaying of a laurel branch, nor the soft ping of a bowstring at the instant of release, nor any other sound or movement betrayed that Wowunupo was occupied. The moons of fog and snow, of renewal, of heat and harvest, came and went. With the first of the harvest moons, the five hidden ones made a stealthy trek to Waganupa, a difficult and risky expedition, but it brought them relief from the breathless heat of the cañon as well as hope of filling their baskets on the mountain. No one ever saw them go or come.

The leaves of the calendar on the kitchen wall in the Speegle ranch house were discarded one by one, and the old calendar replaced twelve times. Still living in Bear's Hiding Place were the long-together five: Ishi, his mother, his sister, who was perhaps a cousin in a sister relation to him and whether older or younger is not known, an old man, and a younger one, these last two not related to the others. Then the younger of these men died, and four were left: a man and woman become frail and old; and a second man and woman, able-bodied, strong, and well, but no longer young. Toward the end of the retreat the two old people must have stayed close to the larger and more comfortable of their two villages most of the time while Ishi and his sister-cousin went up and down creeks and hillsides, fishing, gathering, snaring, hunting, foraging.

Sometime late in 1906 a cabin at the Occidental Mine on upper Deer Creek was broken into and a dunnage bag taken. The incident revived rumors about wild Indians; none were seen, but the alarm had been sounded. Some months after this, two white men, a man named Polk and his partner, were camped at the Speegle ranch. Whether or not Polk saw any Indians his account does not make plain, but he heard someone at their "grub," and he and his partner hid under a bluff with their guns cocked. The pilferers took alarm, making a getaway into Deer Creek and out of sight downstream before Polk had a chance to get a shot at them, nor could his dog track them in the water. There can be little real doubt that it was Ishi and a companion, probably his sister: a hat which they dropped was picked up by Polk, who later gave it to the museum; it is patched with bits of hide and sewed with sinew. Characteristically, none of Polk's canned food had been touched; and if further evidence were needed, only Yahi made a highroad of a roaring, boulder-strewn stream.

Some months after Polk's adventure, the Oro Light and Power Company which was contemplating the building of a dam at the junction of Deer and Sulphur creeks, sent engineers there to survey for a flume. In the early evening of November 9, 1908, two engineers were walking back upstream toward their camp at the Speegle homestead. It so happened that they were moving quietly and without talking as they came out onto a sandbank alongside the creek. There before them on a rock in midstream stood a naked Indian fishing with a harpoon. The Indian was Ishi. The engineers remembered somewhat differently Ishi's behavior upon seeing them. One said that he gave a "vicious snarl" and brandished his harpoon threateningly. The other said that he motioned them emphatically back, saying over and over something which surely meant "Go away!" They went away as quickly as they could, excitedly reporting their encounter at camp where it was received with general disbelief: they were tenderfeet, they had been deceived by some trick of evening shadows, they had been listening to too many sheepherders' tales.

One person in camp listened closely to their story. This was Merle Apperson who knew the Yana country well—he was with the surveyors as guide—and who found credible the possibility that there were live Indians on Deer Creek. The next morning he went down the south side of the creek, turning away from the stream after a half mile or more and working up the steep cañon through thick brush. He was making fair progress when an arrow whizzed past, narrowly missing him. He took the pointed hint and turned back, his guess confirmed, and rejoined the crew which was clearing a flume line below Sulphur Creek and along Deer Creek, utilizing the very shelf on which Wowunupo was built. About ten o'clock the same morning, the crew walked directly into the village.

Its four residents had no doubt been observers of the alarming activity around Speegle's place and at the mouth of Sulphur Creek. With an old man who was weak and could not move quickly and an old woman who was bedridden, there was little they could do but watch and keep out of sight. Ishi and his sister must have arranged that in the event of discovery, she would try to escape with the old man who could still walk, while Ishi would remain with his mother.

Ishi was not seen that morning by any of the party of white people, but the old man supported by Ishi's sister were briefly glimpsed as the two of them left the village, half running through the brush toward the edge of the level shelf of land, and then were lost to sight as they dropped downhill. The brush in that part of the cañon was so dense and so impenetrable, that had the surveyors chosen a line even so little as ten or fifteen feet to the right or left, they might have bypassed the village none the wiser that it was there. As a frightened fawn or partridge "freezes" at the approach of an enemy, taking on the look of inanimate nature, the four Indians must have waited the passing of the whites. When they did not pass, the three who could, ran, after covering up the helpless old mother with blankets and hides that she might by chance go unnoticed.

The surveying party searched the village. Under a pile of skins and rags they found Ishi's mother. Her face was deeply wrinkled, her white hair was cropped close to her head in sign of mourning, she seemed to be partly paralyzed, and her swollen legs were wrapped with strips of buckskin. As the strange men uncovered her, she trembled with fear. They tried to talk to her, and, somewhat reassured, she made some response, but she understood no English. The only communication was when Mr. Apperson said sympathetically, "Muy malo?" pointing to her legs, and she repeated, "Malo. Malo." The men looked farther. They found acorns and dried salmon in baskets in the storage room. In the cook house beside the small hearth there was a fire drill as well as the usual complement of Yahi cooking utensils, and in the other houses there were arrow-flaking tools, a deer snare, bow, arrows, quivers, a two-pronged spear, baskets, moccasins, tanned hides, and a fur robe of wildcat pelts. The men gathered together every movable possession, even the food, and for some unfathomably callous reason took it all with them as souvenirs. Merle Apperson was not a party to the looting. He wanted instead to carry the old woman to camp, but the others demurred. He felt that it would be a friendly gesture to leave at least some gift or token behind, but he could find nothing in his own pockets which might serve, and no one else offered anything.

It was too late to return that day, but Apperson came back to Bear's Hiding Place early the next morning; it was much on his mind that a terrible wrong had been done there. The old woman was gone; there was no trace of any Indians, nor were there footprints or any other sign to show where they might have gone. He was sure that they could not be far away, and he and some of the surveyors searched upstream and down without coming on the faintest clue. It should be said that not only was Apperson much troubled by the episode and its outcome, but Robert Hackley, one of the surveyors, wrote to Waterman on September 5, 1911, while the papers were full of the finding of Ishi and of retellings of this earlier discovery of the village. Said Hackley, "The discredit of driving these harmless people from their home does not belong to the survey party altogether as some of the cattlemen [in the party] considered that they had a grievance on account of stolen goods and proceeded to take matters off our hands." Most of the property taken that fateful morning is now with the "Ishi" collection of the museum, easily contained within a single small exhibition case. It was nonetheless four peoples' total means of livelihood.

The story of the finding of the Indian village was in the papers. Kroeber and Waterman corresponded with the surveyors who had seen it and with anyone else whom they thought might by chance have any leads to the whereabouts of its dispersed inhabitants. The months passed without any sign of them, and in October of the next year, 1909, Waterman tried to find them. With an engineer, G. W. Hunt, and the son of Merle Apperson, he spent a month beating the brush and the faint trails of Deer Creek. He and his party found evidence in plenty of former occupation of the two villages of the retreat, but they turned up no faintest trace of living Indians. The villages looked as they did when Apperson visited them the morning after their discovery a year before, and as they looked in 1914 when Ishi returned for a brief visit. Neither Ishi nor any other person ever occupied them after the forced dispersal. (See Notes, p. 242f.)

Waterman returned to the museum after an arduous month of searching, with photographs of the villages and other evidence of a hidden Yahi life in the wilds of Deer Creek cañon, but with nothing to suggest that there were any Yahi alive in 1909. Nor were there stories of encounters or suspicions of any unseen Indian presence there until April 13, 1911. On that day a surveyor, H. H. Hume happened to notice a bundle hanging high in a live oak tree. On examination it proved to be several old barley sacks and pieces of canvas wrapped around a collection of curious objects. The cache, for so it was, contained tanned deerhides with the hair left on, a pair of much worn moccasins, little bundles of pine pitch, and pine needles whose sheathed ends all pointed neatly in one direction. There was also a bar of unused soap, a cylinder of "sweetened" charcoal about an inch wide and three inches in length, a few nails and screws tied separately in a rag, and a sharp piece of steel with an eyehole at the large end. The cache was probably Ishi's. It was found four months before Ishi turned up at the slaughter house.

After the morning of the invasion of Wowunupo neither Ishi nor anyone else ever saw his sister and the old man again. Ishi was convinced that they had not long survived. His sister ran one way, Ishi another, but had she not met death soon, she and Ishi would have managed to find each other, their knowledge of familiar places to look being a shared one. Ishi believed that his sister and the old man had either drowned—the Deer Creek crossing was treacherous and slippery—or that they had met some other violent death and been eaten thereafter by a bear or a mountain lion, else he would have come on some sign of them in all his searching for them. So he reasoned and so it would seem to be.

Ishi somehow managed to carry his mother out of reach of Apperson's best efforts to find her. Dr. Pope understood Ishi to have told him that he took his mother up Waganupa. Perhaps he did carry her in that direction, but it is most improbable that he could actually have taken her up the mountain or that the two of them could have lived there had he been able to go so far. It was then mid-November; Mount Lassen was snow-covered and food was even scarcer on the mountain than in the foothills. One of Ishi's early efforts to talk to Waterman involved a pantomime of a woman bending over a fire, throwing heated stones into the water in a cooking basket, and making acorn mush. "Pukka–pukka–pukka" it said as it cooked, Ishi crooking and withdrawing a finger to indicate the bursting bubbles of a cereal boiling and thickening. Waterman could only conjecture the meaning. Was Ishi relating something about his mother? Or was he trying to do no more than identify for Waterman the sex of the person he was talking about?

Ishi and his mother were together until her death which may have been within days of the breaking up of the village. After she was gone, he was without human companionship for the rest of the time, perhaps for almost all of it, from November, 1908 to August, 1911. That Ishi was wearing his hair burned short in sign of mourning in August, 1911, was evidence of a death or deaths in his family, but his mourning may well have been a prolonged one.

Ishi and his people are at the end of their last retreat: the dim trails of the dispersal fade into the chaparral a stone's throw from Wowunupo mu tetna.

The door of the jail cell stands open, Ishi is dressed in the clothes of "civilization," pants and shirt and coat anyway, not shoes as yet. In the near distance a train whistles for the Oroville station stop. The train will carry him into new hazards, new experiences, and new friendships.

 Part Two: MISTER ISHI

The ordeal of civilization began for Ishi at the door of the Oroville jail. It was a sunny September morning less than a week after he had strayed out of his own Stone Age Yahi world into a twentieth-century world. This happened by chance, during an abulia induced by starvation and grief, and was out of character, either personal or tribal, except that another Indian than Ishi would have lain down in his home shelter, passively waited for death, and so died. Ishi was sick of life, but his tribal heritage opposed to Indian quietism and fatalism a stubborn will to fight to the end. This kept him on his feet and moving, even after he ceased to know or to wonder where his feet were carrying him. They carried him, in due course, outside the jail and onto Main Street; and whether his feet had served him well or ill Ishi could not then have said.

Fearful and preoccupied with the new reality, Ishi started down Main Street, a myth already beginning to weave itself around him. It was a personal myth, powerful enough to replace the old one of the Yahi people as plunderers, murderers, and savages. From the moment he was locked up, the new myth took over, wavering at first in its direction, playing with imagined dangers and excitements if the prisoner was to be freed. But Sheriff Webber pooh-poohed these as nonsense; reporters arrived from Sacramento; and telegrams poured in from the University and the Department of the Interior; from private citizens and from newspapers all over the country. No one outside had paid Oroville any attention since the gold rush brought it into being, and left it a country town, where young orange groves braved the freezing tule fogs, and the sterile detritus of placer mining. Now it was a name on the lips of people across the land because of the naked old Indian locked up in jail downtown. He was spoken of as the Wild Man of Oroville. The professor who came on the train from San Francisco said he was a Stone Age Man, the last in America: the myth had found its permanent, romantic direction.

The jailors, and the Mexicans and Indians who were allowed to see Ishi, kept the townspeople informed of all that went on in the jail. When the women heard that Ishi refused to eat, they sent him specially prepared dishes to tempt his appetite. Clothes for him to wear to San Francisco were donated from private wardrobes, also a selection of shoes of different sizes. Ishi gratefully put on underwear, shirt, pants, and coat, but he shook his head to the shoes. He tried them on, but they were too large, too stiff; they tripped him, they kept him from the familiar, necessary contact with the earth by which he kept in balance and informed of what lay beneath each footfall and what might be expected ahead. Besides, the great toe must be free if it is to cling and grasp. His feet had carried him far, and must carry him farther. The shoes were returned to their owners.

Side by side, Ishi and Waterman walked from the jail to the railroad station. Women and children peered discreetly from windows or over picket fences to catch a glimpse of the Wild Man, and there were several men and older boys waiting on the platform to see him. They kept their distance, and they were quiet. There was probably a little fear mixed with curiosity in their quietness. Ishi was by way of becoming a hero to them, a man of myth and mystery to whom tales cling and grow. He remains so to this day.

The black face of the white man's Demon rushed toward the platform, pouring out clouds of sparks and smoke, and filling the ears with its hollow, moaning voice. Mill Creek and Deer Creek were within range of the sound of that voice; twice a day Ishi had heard it ever since he could remember, and he had watched the train hundreds of times as it snaked along below him, bellowing and belching. His mother had reassured him as a small boy when he was afraid of it, telling him that it was a Demon who followed white men wherever they went, but that Indians need have no fear of it; it never bothered them.

Today, Ishi wondered. He had not been so near it before; it was larger and noisier and speedier than he had realized. Would the Demon know that he was Indian? He was wearing white men's clothes, and his hair was short like theirs. It might be as well to watch from a little distance, from the shelter of a tree or bush, as he was accustomed to, at least until he made sure that his friend was correct in his assurance that the Demon always stayed in its own old tracks, and that it carried people safely from place to place. He stepped behind a cottonwood tree alongside the platform. The Demon drew up beside the station and came to a halt. Ishi saw that it was as his friend had said—it did not leave its tracks. The white men who should have the most reason to be afraid, showed no signs of uneasiness, rather they climbed in and out of it, and one of them sat in its head waving to those below. Ishi came back onto the platform, and made no objection to going aboard with Waterman. He had committed himself too far to turn back, nor did he wish to do so; where his new friend led he would follow.

During the trip, Ishi sat very quiet. He found the speed of the train exciting; also the view through the window of hills and fields and houses racing in and out of sight. He averted his eyes from the strangers in the car, blotting out their nearness by not looking directly at them. The Demon carried them rapidly down its old tracks and after some hours onto a ferry boat which took them, engine, cars, and passengers, across Carquinez Straits. Waterman pointed out to him that this was where the Sacramento and San Joaquin rivers join, flow into the bay, and out the Golden Gate to the ocean. Like all inland Indians, Ishi knew that such was the destination of the creeks and rivers of his home, but, again like other inlanders, he was vague about how the river journey was actually accomplished, for his informants had known of it only traditionally and at many removes from any one who had seen either river mouth or ocean. He was sorry to leave the train at the Oakland Mole, but ahead lay further wonders—another ferry trip, this time across the bay to San Francisco; and after that, a long ride in a trolley car to the Museum of Anthropology.

Arrived at the museum, Ishi had gone a longer way than the miles which separated him from Deer Creek cañon. It was eleven o'clock in the evening of Labor Day, September 4, 1911, when Ishi the Yahi completed a trip out of the Stone Age into the clang and glare of the Iron Age—a place of clocks and hours and a calendar; of money and labor and pay; of government and authority; of newspapers and business. Now he, too, was a modern man, a city dweller with a street address.

Chapter 7
ISHI'S NEW WORLD

A museum has an almost cloistered remoteness from the active center of twentieth-century living, but this Ishi could not know. Most museums would make but sorry and unwelcoming homes, and that the one to which he was taken should so readily and literally have become home to a stone age man or to anyone else is a matter of a curious ordering and timing of certain events in the history of the developing University, and of a unique and personal twist which should be explained, since the museum became the secure shelter within which Ishi spent the rest of his life.

Anthropology was instituted at the University of California as a department and a museum associated with the department, by action of the Regents in September, 1901. The Regents would not have taken such action, at least not then, except for Phoebe Apperson Hearst, one of their number. Mrs. Hearst liked to surround herself with objects of beauty, and she liked acquiring and possessing them. At first her interests were purely personal, but after a time she began to think of founding a museum for the University, and ultimately leaving to it her personal collections. Toward this end she had already by 1899 made several contracts for extensive archaeological expeditions, and for the purchase of art objects from dealers where digging *in situ* was forbidden. Thus by 1901, collections coming from ancient Egypt, Peru, Greece, and Rome were piling up in packing boxes on the campus. It was suggested to her that she might like also to do something for her own state of California whose Indians and antiquities had been almost wholly neglected. This appealed to her increasingly, so that by the time of the actual, formal announcement of the department and museum, several appointments of young anthropologists to do linguistic and ethnographic field work in the state, and to make collections for the nascent museum had already been made.

By 1902 the storage problem was so acute that Mrs. Hearst had a corrugated-iron warehouse built on the Berkeley campus for the packing cases which continued to arrive from all over the world. The year 1903 saw the warehouse full to bursting, and the acquisition of the old Law School building on Parnassus Heights in San Francisco alongside the Medical School as the regular museum and the scene of the early activity of the department, other than actual classroom teaching which was in Berkeley. With the roomy, four-story building, there was space at last to begin to unpack the collections, catalogue them, and arrange them in trays or on ·shelves, where they were available to qualified people to study.

By 1911, two months after Ishi came to live there, the museum could be opened for the first time to public exhibition. It continued to be a part of San Francisco's cultural life until 1931, when the museum building was razed to be replaced by a new hospital wing. The collections were boxed and removed to Berkeley, there to be stored, some in an old brick building assigned for the purpose, some in the basement of the women's gymnasium. As these paragraphs are being written, the Art and Anthropology departments are moving into their new and permanent quarters on the Berkeley campus, facing Bancroft Way at College Avenue; into a modern, concrete building with proper storage for two-thirds of the present four hundred thousand and upwards of specimens there and in a near-by basement belonging to the museum, and for all archival material. There is as well an exhibition hall where, under a system of rotation of material exhibited, visitors may again see the remarkable and growing collections, and understand and participate in what Mrs. Hearst initiated and what has since been accomplished.

It should be explained that Mrs. Hearst, bitterly as she regretted

it, had to forego her project of building a museum. So heavy were
the demands on her that by 1908 she had brought to a close the
foreign and local expeditions, confining her contributions more
and more, until she was doing no more than paying the coal bill
for the museum and the salaries of two old family retainers whom
she had established there as guard and assistant respectively. Her
interest in the museum and in the people who had worked with
her in its beginnings never flagged. Up to her death, she held to
her dream.

And it was precisely because this dream was a woman's dream
with a quaint domestic touch that Ishi and others found the
museum to be a home as well.

The building being neither fire nor earthquake proof, two men
slept in, so that it was never left alone. The first two caretakers
were, as mentioned above, people whom Mrs. Hearst had known
for years, and for whose decent housing she assumed a certain
responsibility. There were sufficient lighting, bath, kitchen, and
bedroom facilities, and the museum was kept warm at all times.
This "coziness," with its accompanying independence of cheap
restaurants and rooming houses, made for good cheer among
those who regularly or occasionally cooked or slept there. The
staff was composed of men of various origin and temperament,
but chosen for character and for a steady dependability. Each in
his own way was loyal to Mrs. Hearst and to Professor Kroeber
and protective of the specimens, which they guarded jealously
and handled carefully.

On the ground floor there was even a small room, occupied
frequently by Indians who came for a few days or a few weeks
to get acquainted, to be linguistic informants, perhaps merely as
guests, as Professor Kroeber and others in the field had been
guests of their house or village. It was a comfortable arrangement
for them; they added color and variety to the serene round of life
of a preparator or assistant, under whose chaperonage they became acquainted with the city. So it was that when Ishi arrived,
Indian guests were a normal part of museum living, and his own

sense of strangeness was made less acute through his new acquaintances' feeling of ease and accustomedness. They were merely more interested in his coming than in that of a "civilized" red man, and somewhat more particular to try to make him feel at home, but he fitted a slot already made, with the difference that instead of being a transient visitor he became a permanent member of the group.

The morning after Ishi's arrival at the museum he and Professor A. L. Kroeber, who would become his Big *Chiep* (Ishi pronounced *f* as *p*), met and a friendship was born of their meeting. Of Ishi then and in succeeding days when the ordeal by fear and strangeness was most acute, Kroeber says that the first impression of him was of his gentleness, and of a timidity and fear kept under severe control. Ishi started at the slightest sudden sound. The boom of a cannon fired in artillery practice at the Presidio several miles away brought him up from his chair. A stranger, the hearty type, burst into the room where Ishi was talking with Kroeber, grabbed Ishi's hand and pumped hand and arm up and down in vigorous greeting. When released, Ishi stood, his arm frozen in the air for several seconds.

One curious, patient gesture which never entirely left Ishi was characteristic of him in those days—a raising high of his mobile, arched eyebrows. It was an expression of wonder, but also of ignorance, of incomprehension, like our shrugging of the shoulders. It was his one sign, for he seemed afraid to use his limbs freely at that time. He was, even when perfectly at ease, little given to gestures. He sometimes used pantomime effectively when he wished to explain or demonstrate, but never profusely nor with any marked or instinctive ability.

His shyness at first was acute. When he first met Kroeber, he said a phrase to him in English, one Waterman had taught him, then blushed as though he had presumed, or committed a *faux pas*. A blush, coming with a painful intensity, caused his face to mantle and cloud. He continued to blush easily even after he was no longer fearful and tense, covering his blushes with a deprecatory smile or a laugh and the placing of the fingers of one hand over his mouth, in that universal gesture of embarrassment.

Deeper than shyness and fear was Ishi's awareness that he was alone, not as the unfriendly or too introverted or misanthropic are alone, for he was none of these. To be sure, he would sit, unbored, dreamy, and withdrawn into his own mystic center, but only if there was nothing to do, no one to talk to or to work with. He much preferred companionship, and he smiled readily, his smile beginning in the eyes and traveling from eyes to mouth. He was interested, concerned, amused, or delighted, as the case might be, with everything and everyone he knew and understood.

His aloneness was not that of temperament but of cultural chance, and one early evidence of his sophisticated intelligence was his awareness of this. He felt himself so different, so distinct, that to regard himself or to have others regard him as "one of them" was not to be thought of. "I am one; you are others; this is in the inevitable nature of things," is an English approximation of his judgment on himself. It was a harsh judgment, arousing in his friends compassion, then respect. He was fearful and timid at first, but never unobservant, nor did his fear paralyze his thinking as it paralyzed his gesturing. He faced the areas of his total ignorance, of the disparity of content between Yahi culture and white, and the knowledge that he could not begin from so far behind and come abreast. He would not try to. He would and did adapt as one of goodwill and breeding must adapt to one's host in dress, in the forms of greeting and leavetaking, in the use of knife and fork at table; these and other conventions of simple etiquette. Judgments and decisions he left to those who knew better than he could hope or presume to know.

Meanwhile, he remained himself—a well-born Yahi, never unmindful of the code his mother and uncle had taught him. It might be conjectured that this position of aloofness and aloneness would have driven him into a depression, but such was not the case: Ishi had kept his morale through grief and an absolute solitariness; the impact of civilization could not budge it. Beneath the shyness and the reserve, he remained possessed of natural, temperamental, and unimpaired outgoingness and interest in people and phenomena, which he was able, day by day, to express ever more spontaneously, as the museum home became more and more *his* home.

His self-respect and pride no doubt prevented Ishi from acquiring a more rapid and facile command of English—he was reluctant to use a word or phrase until he was fairly sure of it—just as they hampered an easy fellowship with people he knew only slightly. But these character traits seemed not to have seriously cut him off from the people and activities he really valued, and they did serve to discourage even the least perceptive white person from the benevolent superiority of the civilized to the primitive, of the first-class citizen to the second class. Many people, after a while, laughed with Ishi. He was no king's jester: no one ever laughed at him.

In this there is much that will be recognized by those readers who have known undisrupted Indians of whatever place or tribe. What was somewhat atypical in Ishi was his un-Indian volatility, which seems to have been a Yahi trait, suggesting kinship with the Eskimos' expressive temperament and with the Mohave Indians on the Colorado River. These Indians are also volatile, friendly, and smile easily, and share with the Yahi a willingness to fight, and against great odds.

Personal identity for man in modern Western civilization resides first of all in the family name to which he is born. At birth, or within a few days after, there is added the personal name bestowed by the parents, confirmed by the religious rite of baptism, and made legal and official by its formal recording in the books of the county clerk along with the family name and the exact place and time of birth; and to be changed only by permission of a court of law. It is both a public name and the name by which the individual is known to his family and friends. He may also have a private name, a nickname known only to family and intimates, and this name may be one or successive names, transient or persisting, or there may be none such at all.

Before dismissing the Yana naming custom as merely quaint, it should be recalled that our own custom is not, in its completeness, of great age. A personal name continued to do for the ordinary and obscure person in Europe even into the eighteenth century, and on all levels in mediaeval Europe. John, son of James was usually sufficient label. If further identification was added, it was likely to be the name of the parents' village, or else a reference to some personal peculiarity, such as "Harold the Bluetooth." The Greeks did not have family names. Pre-commune China continued into the twentieth century under a system older and more widespread than our own, that of clan identification by which a baby is born into the clan of his father. This clan becomes his own lifetime clan, with strict taboo against marrying within his clan however numerous and scattered its membership. Sooner or later, someone in the family gives the new baby a personal, private name or nickname, perhaps more than one. This, too, was the Yana practice.

The stranger whom the dogs held at bay outside the slaughter house was nameless; his jail name became "The Wild Man of Oroville." The present account of him has come to the beginning of his second day at the museum, and by sequential logic it should have kept him nameless to this point. But, to modern ears it is hopelessly artificial to speak of the "One from Bear's Den," or "Deer Creek Cañon Man," while the designation "Wild Man" jangles the sensibilities with its crudity and its inappropriateness.

Reporters demanded to know his name, refusing to accept Kroeber's word that the question was in the circumstances unmannerly and futile. Batwi intervened, engaging to persuade the wild man to tell his name—a shocking gaucherie on Batwi's part. The wild man, saving his brother Yana's face, said that he had been alone so long that he had had no one to give him a name—a polite fiction, of course. A California Indian almost never speaks his own name, using it but rarely with those who already know it, and he would never tell it in reply to a direct question.

The reporters felt, not unnaturally, that they were being given "the runaround." Batwi lost caste with his fellow Yana without being of service to the whites; the museum people were themselves saying they must have something by which to call the Yahi, except just that. Kroeber felt more pushed than did his nameless friend who remained relatively detached not understanding most of what was said, and standing quietly by Indian custom so far as he did understand. Said Kroeber, "Very well. He shall be known as *Ishi*." He regretted that he was unable to think of a more distinctive name, but it was not inappropriate, meaning "man" in Yana, and hence not of the private or nickname category. Thus it was that the last of the Yahi was christened Ishi, and in historic fact, *became* Ishi.

He *never* revealed his own, private, Yahi name. It was as though it had been consumed in the funeral pyre of the last of his loved ones. He accepted the new name, answering to it un-reluctantly. But once it was bestowed it took on enough of his true name's mystic identification with himself, his soul, whatever inner essence of a man it is which a name shares, that he was never again heard to pronounce it.

Ishi now had a name and an address. Before his status was further fitted to the mold of modern, industrial man, there was a clamoring outside the museum walls for the wild man who was felt now to belong to San Francisco as he had for some days belonged to Oroville. Giving him a name merely made it easier to ask for him, and a museum is not a jail nor was there any wish to make it seem to be such.

Mountebanks and showmen are part of the human condition. The distance their message reaches and the tools of its transmittal change with time and place, but not their business which has always been to inform, to exaggerate, to advertise, to tell the world what the world wants to hear. For the human condition is often drab, or disappointing, when it is not desperate. It is good then to listen to the beating of the drums, to feel the blood leap to the increasing tempo of the message, to surrender for awhile to illusion and fantasy, to follow wherever the drums may lead. They may lead to the give-away of a television program, or of a potlatch; to the county fair or to the feast celebrating a young girl's first coming of age; to orgy by way of revivalist's tent or ancient nature worship; or it may be the voice of the barker, falsetto and arresting, which entices the listeners to pay to see what waits behind drawn curtains—be it freak, belly dancer, hypnotist, or wild man from Borneo, or better yet, from Mount Lassen.

Ishi's arrival in San Francisco was quiet and private, coming as it did before the days of klieg lights and microphones. But the newspapers announced that he was come; reporters, motion picture companies, and entrepreneurs of carnival, circus, and vaudeville specialty acts were as avid on the trail of novelty as they and their radio and television brothers are today. The candid camera as an uncandid tool waited upon the future. The reporters brought to the museum on Parnassus Heights their clumsy box cameras and were followed by private persons, men, women, and children with their Brownie and Graflex cameras. The wild man had aroused a city's imagination.

The museum was overrun with mountebanks and plain and simple exploiters with their offers. There were the impresarios of the large vaudeville circuits—Pantages and Orpheum—one of whom had the imagination to offer to "take over" both Kroeber and Ishi, to promote them as a two-man act under a billing of "educational" and "edifying." A cut below were those who wanted to "borrow" Ishi for a "showing," or as an "exhibit"; and below them, those who were ready to carry Ishi off to be part of a traveling carnival. And then there were the hard-bitten and unsavory tribe who operate narrow dives like peep shows on lower Market Street, calculated to catch the lonely sailor on liberty and the drifter with a nickel or a dime to pay to have a look at the well-illuminated painting of a nude woman, or at the highly realistic figure of a head hunter in the round and in the buff. For a few weeks, at least, a live wild man might have been expected to be worth as much as two bits to see.

It was on Ishi's second day in San Francisco that the American Phonograph Company proposed making records by and about him, the bonus to be a gold-mold master record from the Edison Company. No commercial recordings were made, then or later. What was done instead to preserve the sound of his voice and his language is not without interest as a microcosmic example of the plodding, slipping back, and now and then rushing forward nature of the growth of the science of man.

The museum owned, as of this writing it still owns, several machines for making voice recordings, some of them going back to the early 1900's. Most of the songs, texts, and myths in the record library were taken on these old phonographs which made a wax impression on a cylinder, accurate in its reproduction, but bulky to store, easily broken, and wearing out from many playings. All the Yana language recordings, Ishi's and Batwi's, were made in this way. During four decades the ghost of Ishi's voice lay gathering dust in its waxen grooves along with the ghosts of other Indian voices whose languages are departed with their one-time speakers to the Land of the Dead.

When the cylinders were resurrected from their dusty graves in 1957 as part of a present renaissance of linguistic study in the University, it was found that not one of the several machines which could take the old-fashioned cylinders was whole. Parts were missing, and, being long since obsolete, were irreplaceable. A reproducer had given out; a sapphire needle was cracked. It seemed that the voices were silenced forever, but a talented music and linguistic student, James Hatch, made the rounds of San Francisco's *aficionados* of old records. From them he learned how the machines were put together and how to operate them, and from this knowledge he rehabilitated a single machine from the several cripples. What followed was an exciting rescue. One by one, with Kroeber sitting by to identify languages or tribes or rituals, and to choose between better and worse renditions of a song, a prayer, or a text, Hatch transferred the best of the old, so nearly lost voices, Ishi's amongst them, to permanent tape recordings. The neat, compact stack of metal boxes containing these tapes are samplings, some large, some small, of twenty-nine California languages from a hundred and twenty-five wax cylinders, enough for a modern-day linguist's highly expert and exact analysis and synthesis; supplementing them as he can with the old vocabulary lists of travelers or *padres,* when there is nothing more; with the notebooks of earlier ethnologists and linguists, and with his own field notes if, as in some cases, the language is still spoken today.

Motion pictures were a novelty in 1911, a time of many small, hopeful enterprises dedicated to celebrating on the screen such subjects as "art" or "education" or the "ethnic view." Some declared their goal to be quite simply "inspirational." As the industry solidified into big business, the fringe companies along with their fringe objectives were absorbed into the few dominating producers of entertainment; or they disappeared altogether.

The museum files, beginning with Ishi's first week, have many requests from such small companies then operating independently in and out of San Francisco. They were anxious to get Ishi into a picture, any sort of a picture. Some of the less reputable clamored to be allowed to make a short film to be shown as a curtain raiser to Ishi's personal appearance on the same stage. Such requests used the word "exhibit," and referred to his being "shown."

The museum owned only still cameras, and the staff was anxious to have action pictures of Ishi, but it was three years before an arrangement could be arrived at which met its terms: one copy to be given to the University; and no part of the film to be used in another film, for example, dubbed into a story, or otherwise shown except as received and passed by the museum staff. It was the California Motion Picture Corporation which finally made 1,500 feet of finished film. The company no longer exists, and the copy of the film which was duly deposited with the University was found upon opening its container after many years of dead storage to have undergone chemical change, and to have melted into a single glutinous mass. It may have been kept, as were some manuscripts, in the basement of one of the University buildings where steam pipes run overhead creating an almost airless chamber with a temperature of 80 degrees or more. Damage and loss of property of intrinsic or historic value through wrong storage and lack of custodial care is a sad waste. Moreover, with old films, it can be dangerous. There is the faint hope that somewhere, sometime, a copy of the Ishi film may be found intact in some library of ethnic and educational films. If so, it should be sent to a film-processing specialist to open, since long-sealed films sometimes explode upon first contact with the air.

The film was good: let us hope an unspoiled copy turns up. It showed Ishi entering, leaving, and repairing his "house," a Yana summer shelter which he had built on the museum grounds. It recorded the complete process of fire making with a fire drill; the fashioning of an arrow point, breaking a block of obsidian, and the chipping and flaking and finishing processes; stringing a bow, aiming it, and shooting at target for height and for speed. It showed Ishi placing a shell ornament in his nose; putting on a native net cap; drying his hair and cutting it by burning. It included a closeup of his lip movements when speaking and singing in Yana; it showed him doing janitorial work; counting on his fingers; and working a multigraph. There were two more close-ups: one of Ishi's hands which were uncalloused and straight fingered; and one of his flashing, friendly smile.

Would-be exploiters and showmen soon dropped off, but a problem remained. Ishi was an attraction, something Waterman and Kroeber had somehow not taken into account until the reality threatened to disrupt all normal activities of the museum. How to cope with the friendly crowd? It could not be put off as could the exploiters. It meant no harm to Ishi, and asked nothing for itself but to be allowed to see, and if possible to shake hands with, to touch, to "know" the last wild man in America.

The crowd could not imagine that it was something fearful

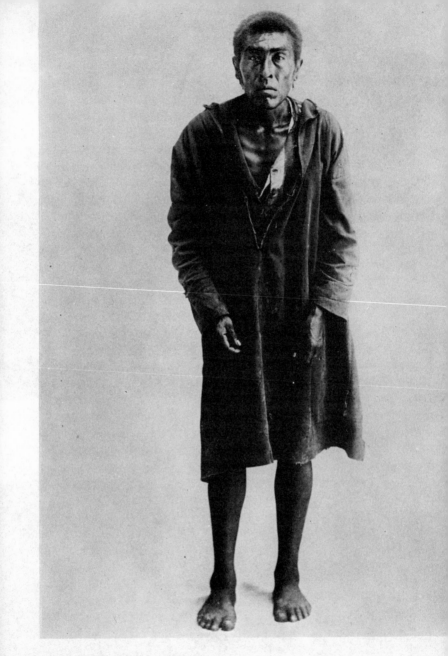

ISHI, AUGUST 29, 1911

YAHI COUNTRY,
THE MOUNT LASSEN FOOTHILLS

PACK TRAIN LEAVING THE CAÑON, 1914

ISHI'S OTTER-SKIN
QUIVER

WOMAN'S MOCCASIN
FROM WOWUNUPO

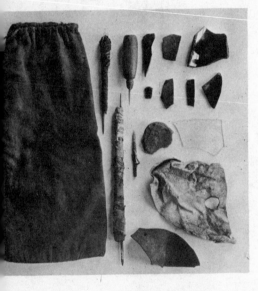

ISHI'S ARROW-MAKING KIT

TOGGLES FOR
A SALMON HARPOON

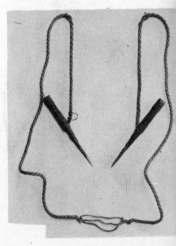

TWO-PRONGED WOODEN SALMON HARPOON

DEER SNARE
MADE OF HEMP FIBERS

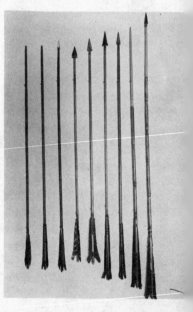

ARROWS MADE BY ISHI

ISHI'S BOWS
OF HICKORY, ASH, AND YEW

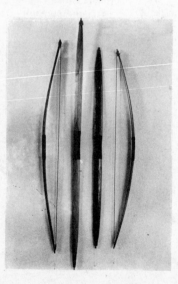

DEER-HEAD DECOY

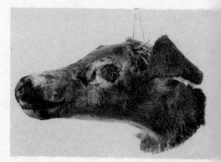

AFFILIATED COLLEGES, 1912
LEFT, DENTISTRY AND PHARMACY; CENTER, HOSPITAL; RIGHT, MUSEUM

PROFESSOR A. L. KROEBER

JUAN DOLORES

ISHI AND SAM BATWI
AT THE ORPHEUM THEATER

STRAIGHTENING DRILL

FIRE MAKING.
BLOWING SPARK IN TINDER

HEATING DRILL

ADZING JUNIPER WOOD FOR BOW

SHOOTING FROM KNEELING POSITION

SHOOTING
DIRECTLY AHEAD

STANDING POSITION

CALLING RABBITS

PREPARING TO HARPOON SALMON

BINDING HARPOON POINT TO SHAFT

BINDING COMPLETED

ISHI SWIMMING IN DEER CREEK, 1914

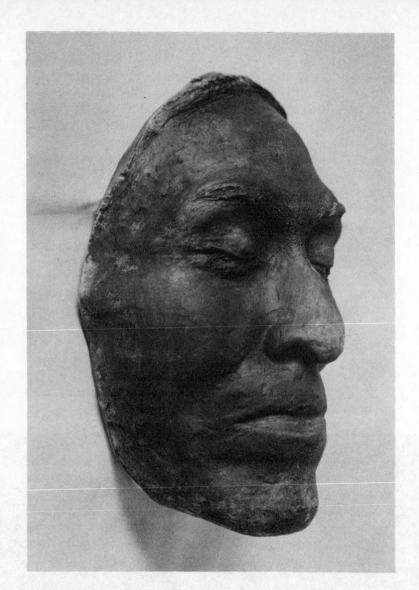

DEATH MASK

and monstrous to a man whose norm for "many people" was as the bucket a child brings to the shore to empty the sea of its waters. Ishi could recall from his earliest memories one occasion, possibly two, when "many" of his people came together to gather acorns in the fall. There may have been forty or fifty of them. He knew for some years a world which numbered twelve or fourteen souls, but the world he had known longest and most accustomedly numbered five until it came to number only himself. He knew that in the old days the acorn-gathering encampments were several times as large as the one he remembered, and he knew that former neighbors in the valley belonged to tribes more numerous than his own, but none of these people had he ever beheld.

A lone white man had been, until a few days back, a signal of mortal danger. He was becoming fairly at ease with his friends in the museum, and concealing his sudden fears from them as best he could, but the crowding around of half a dozen people made his limbs become rigid; and his first closeup of a group of perhaps eighty or a hundred people left his faculties paralyzed. With time, he came to realize that crowds were not intrinsically menacing, and his early terrible fear abated, but not his dislike of people in numbers such that the individual becomes lost in the faceless throng. He never liked strangers to come too close or to touch him. He learned to suffer the handshake as a custom universal to the white man and of friendly intent, and to acknowledge a proferred hand promptly and with courtesy. He never himself initiated a handshake.

No dream, no wildest nightmare, prefigured for Ishi a city crowd, its clamor, its endless hurrying past to be endlessly replaced by others of its kind, face indistinguishable from face. It was like a spring salmon run, one fish leaping sightlessly beyond or over another, and he disliked the sweaty smell of people in numbers. It suggested to him the odor of old deer hide.

A complication in dealing with Ishi's crowd phobia was that his coming preceded by only a few weeks the first opening of the museum to the public. Three floors of exhibition of art, archaeology, and ethnology from more or less all over the world were out on shelves and stands, labeled and lighted. New, formal blue uniforms were ready for the guards who would act also as guides to museum visitors. It was anticipated that hundreds of school children and adult San Franciscans would come, like what they saw, and come again. The state University was younger then. Except as a practical aid in agriculture it had not yet interpenetrated and become part of California's way of life as it has with its and the state's growth and maturity. The museum staff felt a duty to a public it hoped to make its own, as well as to Ishi. The problem was how to do right by both. Waterman remarked gloomily to Kroeber that the only solution he saw was to put Ishi in an exhibition case during visiting hours, where people could see him but would at least be prevented from touching him.

Even before the public opening there loomed only days away a reception to nearly a thousand invited guests. Benjamin Ide Wheeler, president of the University, would be at the head of the receiving line with Mrs. Hearst beside him. Regents, personal friends of Mrs. Hearst, perhaps the governor, friends of the University, art patrons, artists, people representing the Academy of Sciences and distant and foreign museums and academies would be there, many of them would wish and indeed expect to see Ishi. What should Ishi's role in the reception be? Emaciated and weak as he was from the near starvation of his last months in the hills, he could scarcely be expected to stand in the receiving line, to face the stares of hundreds of strange and curious however friendly faces. His clothes would pass muster, to be sure, and he was possessed of a sense for correctness and neatness of personal appearance, but his small perfect feet were bare. And his English vocabulary was limited to a very few words.

It was suggested that Ishi might be in one of the smaller exhibition rooms for as much of the long party as he wanted to take part in, in this limited and quiet way, and to this Ishi agreed. He was excited about the party which as he understood it was to be on the sensible lines of an Indian house warming to which you invited your friends for a feast, an exchange of news and gossip, and some singing and dancing. There was, to be sure, no singing and dancing at the reception, but there were refreshments, and there were the exhibition cases of interesting objects to be pointed out and explained and exclaimed over. Ishi stayed for the whole long party, hovering observantly in the background. From time to time Kroeber left the receiving line to bring a Regent, an artist, some person who had asked specially to meet him, to Ishi. There followed a formal introduction, after which Mister Ishi and the guest shook hands. Kroeber was particular to pronounce the visitor's name distinctly, Ishi repeating it with great exactness and a disarming smile. He appeared to feel no serious constraint or strain during this party in his own home, and to be intrigued by the people he met and their remarkable names.

Ishi's pleasure in the repetition of peoples' names was surely in part amusement with their strange sounds, but there may well have been an added fillip in saying aloud and as it were promiscuously, personal names which by Yana custom could not thus be bandied about. He may have thought the names to be really circumlocutions such as his people were accustomed to use, nicknames with unimaginably funny meanings and associations, as Yana common or nicknames are likely to have. Whatever the reason, he was curious about personal and family names, his first, and if need be, repeated question about a newcomer being, *Achi djeyauna?*, "What is his name?" He repeated a name until he had memorized it, and he was careful to associate name and person.

The formula for the reception satisfied a considerable number of people and gave pleasure to Ishi without imposing on his strength or sensibilities, and suggested the pattern for his public "coming out." For this event, the museum made simultaneous announcements in the city newspapers to the effect that Professor Kroeber and the wild Indian Ishi would be at the museum on Sunday afternoons, between two and four thirty for the next several weeks, to receive visitors who wished to meet them. In order to insure an ethnic spread as broad as San Francisco's, the notice appeared in all the city's daily and weekly papers, which included the *Chinese Free Press,* the *Japanese American,* the Danish *San Francisco Demokrat, L'Italia, La France Californien,* and the German weekly the *New San Franciscan,* besides the English language newspapers, and the *Argonaut* magazine.

As announced, Kroeber and Ishi were in one of the large, upstairs rooms of the museum on Sunday afternoons. If there were few visitors, there were personal introductions and conversations, as at the reception. The numbers were usually too great for this, in which case Ishi was introduced as to an audience, Kroeber talked briefly, keeping it informal, answering questions, and translating Ishi's answers. Usually Ishi demonstrated stringing a bow, or he made fire with the fire drill, or he turned out a chipped arrowhead while the visitors watched. The chipping became the favorite demonstration because Ishi would afterward graciously present the finished arrowhead to someone in the audience. Soon the demand for Ishi-made arrowheads became burdensome to him, and they were given only to school or museum collections.

At times other than these Sunday afternoons, Ishi might or might not be in sight. Sometimes he could be seen working at a bow or chipping glass or obsidian, but that was a matter of his choice. He came and went freely about his own business, or sat out in the sun watching whatever was going on on the Heights, when he was not doing linguistic or ethnographic work with Waterman or Kroeber. He always had a friendly smile and a wave of the hand for anyone who spoke to him.

Ishi began to look forward to the Sunday afternoons. They were in his own home, the Chiep was with him, and, more and more, individuals emerged from the faceless throng. There were those who came again and again, and became, as it were, his friends and neighbors. He began to distinguish nationalities and professions. "Dutchman" was an early favorite. Why, it is hard to say. Perhaps because German-speaking people were more likely

than those of other tongue to talk to Kroeber in their own language, thus setting themselves apart from other whites. "Chinaman" was another; he recognized a racial difference between
Orientals and whites, although the Chinese gentleman whom
Ishi singled out was a newspaper editor dressed in conventional
Western clothes and speaking an accented but perfect English.
Nonetheless, Ishi said of him that he was *yana,* not *saltu. Yana*
means a person, a human being; or many persons, all of the
people. Yana is used in English translation as a proper noun—
the name of a people and a nation. Such transfer of a common
noun to the proper noun category occurs over and over again
in English tribal nomenclature for California Indians, through
the chance that the commonest initial inquiry of a white traveler
made to a strange Indian took the form, "Who are you?", to
which the usual Indian answer was, "I am a person." What else
was he to answer? It was a rude question, whether rudely meant
or not. One did not say one's name, certainly not to a stranger.
One belonged to the people. One was a person.

As for *saltu,* Ishi's name for the white race, it means a being of
another order, a non-human, a pre-human, or a spirit. It is often
translated as meaning ghost, but this is not, strictly speaking,
correct. There are other words for ghost and for soul. All Indians
tend to have a word like *saltu* that has been used, anciently, for a
different and special category of being and which fits the need
for a word to designate the white race. There attaches to *saltu*
neither the denigration usual to our use of the word "native," or
"primitive," nor does it imply a superior being. It is denotative
of difference, as of a separate phylum.

Ishi's recognition of the Chinese editor as *yana,* human, sent
discreet academic chuckles echoing down museum corridors, it
being an *ad hoc* corroboration of the anthropological theory of the
Mongoloid origin of the American Indian. Ishi, however, examined his Chinese acquaintance more particularly, and went
on to note distinguishing racial characteristics which Indians lack,

such as the epicanthic fold. With two fingers he then delicately pushed up the outer corners of his own eyes when saying "Chinaman."

A fireman, a military man in uniform, and above all, a mounted policeman impressed Ishi even more than did the Chinese editor. With such a horse, and such trappings, the policeman must surely be a great chiep, and Ishi practiced long, until he could say to his satisfaction, *bahleeceman*. The friendly crowd was beginning to fragment for him, to individuate, to lose some of its robot terror.

Ishi did not venture off Parnassus Heights alone until he had been in the city some time, but he went to various places with one person or another. His first such expedition was on the day after his arrival. Waterman took him across the bay to Berkeley where he saw the campus of the University and had dinner with the Waterman's and their two children—his first dinner at a white man's table in a white man's home. He was there many times later, and of this first time Waterman reported only that Ishi so closely watched his hostess, imitating her in her choice of fork or spoon, in her use of a napkin, and in the amount of food she put on her plate, that his exactly similar motions appeared to be simultaneous with hers.

Anyone who has had California Indians as house guests will recognize this as very "Indian." Customs differed from tribe to tribe, but a strict etiquette of eating was observed by all of them. The shift to new food and a different way of serving it seems to be adroitly managed when the principle and habit of conventional behavior "at table" is already ingrained.

The following Sunday afternoon, Ishi was taken for an automobile ride through Golden Gate Park and to the ocean beach. The ocean is something every inland Indian has heard of, and has some sort of picture of in his mind. They speak of the ocean even when, like Ishi, they have never seen it, and it is likely to figure in myths and tales. Ishi was looking forward to seeing it, but when the car stopped on the bluff above the Cliff House, giving onto a wide view of ocean, surf, and beach, Ishi's breath drew in, not because of the great rolling Pacific, but because of the thousands of people who covered the beach below and spilled over into the surf—a Sunday afternoon crowd on a rare warm September day. He said over and over softly, half-whisperingly, *Hansi saltu, hansi saltu!* Many white people, many white people! He had not known so many people could inhabit the earth at one time; the shock of sheer numbers obliterated every other impression. Kroeber thought to distract him by pointing out some of the taller office buildings as a less disturbing wonder to him. Ishi looked at them appraisingly, but without being greatly impressed, since, unlike his inexperience in estimating population figures, he had an adequate measuring rod for the height of a building. He had lived until now in the shadow of Waganupa and in sight of Mount Shasta and between the sheer walls of Deer Creek cañon. The vertical walls of a city are indeed puny, scarce worthy of comment, by comparison.

As the automobile was driven up and down and across the park, the group of University buildings of which the museum was one repeatedly came into view, and each time this happened a smile relaxed Ishi's otherwise tense features, and he said in a tone of happy recognition, *Wo-wi!* "My house, my home!" He pointed out each junction with roads already traveled or perhaps merely crossed, and the various landmarks—a tree, a boulder, or a statue —by means of which he was already committing to memory the pattern of the park.

On one of the less frequented roads, the noise of the car disturbed a flock of quail. The quail brought Ishi to his feet to follow their movements as long as they were in sight. He called softly to them, *Chikakatee, chikakatee!* The sight of the familiar top-knotted gray birds in these strange surroundings gave him intense pleasure. The quail and the swarming beach crowds were the two memorable, emotion-filled moments of the three-hour drive, the surprise and satisfaction of the one more or less ameliorating the shock and perturbation of the other.

The next week a newspaper reporter in search of a story, in-

vited Ishi to go to one of the theaters featuring a vaudeville show.
When the invitation was explained to him, Ishi said he would like
to go if Kroeber went too, and so it was arranged. The reporter
wrote a story of the evening, but as he imagined it should have
been, not as it was in fact.

They sat in box seats which commanded as good a view of the
audience as of the stage. During the whole of the first two long
acts Ishi looked exclusively at the audience: here again as at the
beach were the saltu, packed like dried salmon in a storage
basket, unbelievably many of them, and of far more interest than
the two actors who were doing something incomprehensible on
the stage. Batwi was of the party also, and Batwi prodded and
insisted until Ishi turned his attention to the performance.

A punster-rhymster was holding forth with rhymed repartee
of the moment, such as "And sitting in the box you see/ The
Indian from the universitee." Whenever the audience laughed,
Ishi smiled or laughed, in automatic response to its laughter.
Through the rough, custard-pie humor of the next act he remained attentive but grave. There followed an acrobatic display
and a performance of tumbling, both of which failed to excite his
interest. In yet another act he did not catch the very visible cues
by which direct physical sex appeal was communicated to the
Caucasian audience.

When an actor or an episode on stage was called to his notice,
he smiled politely but embarrassedly, watching more closely the
gestures of the person speaking to him than what was being
pointed out. Not a single act caught his imagination or roused
his interest, but he had studied the audience minutely, and he
was ready to talk about it on the way home. Batwi would not
listen or interpret; he insisted upon telling Ishi about the show.
Perhaps it was from Batwi that the reporter got his story?

Vaudeville is considered very simple theatrical fare, of appeal
to children and to the unsophisticated. It may, however, be the
least communicating theater to the uninitiate.

Would not a concert or an opera, outlandish in its sounds no doubt, have communicated something to Ishi? It would seem that the human voice raised in song however strange would have had kinship to Ishi's own love of song. Or the sonority and force of formal verse drama might have carried over to him some overtone of ritual tension. Unless, as is possible, the sea of faces, so many and so near, would have blocked entrance to any other sensation. Ishi's first theater was, all in all, his own most Stone Age and aboriginal performance.

Ishi now was possessed of an official name and address; the first excitement of his coming was over in the museum; the un-directed curiosity of the friendly crowd was appeased; the worst of his ordeal by fear was lived through; and his native crafts were matter for wide and respectful interest. Both inside and outside the museum Ishi was regarded as a permanent part of it. It was November, and high time for settling into the new routines; time to face up to the problem of support for Ishi.

Ishi required little, but, first of all, he must eat. As long as Batwi was in the city, he and Ishi ate at a small, close-by boarding house. After Batwi left, Kroeber or Waterman bought enough extra food for him to make breakfast and lunch in the museum kitchen. They took him home or to a restaurant for dinner, or he might eat at the hospital, next door, or back at the boarding house. They saw to it that he had a little spending money for tobacco, or ice cream or candy. His laundry went into the museum bag. Modest as was the sum which would cover food, such clothes as he would need from time to time, carfare, and an occasional cinema—twenty-five dollars a month would do it, was their estimate—neither of Ishi's friends could afford that sum or even part of it, month after month. Nor could the University be asked to "give" it, its rules of finance, sensibly enough, prohibiting anyone from being paid or given food and lodging except in return for services. He was indeed performing a service in his Sunday demonstrations, but the staff feeling was strong against his losing his "amateur" status. However, Ishi was already helping the janitor and the preparators at their varied tasks, because he liked the work and the sociability. It was decided to regularize his continuing presence in the museum by having him appointed an assistant janitor with a monthly wage.

This was the more easily done since there were no professional janitors in the museum, in keeping with Mrs. Hearst's expressed desire that only people whom the staff knew well and who were an integral part of it should have access to museum and collections. One or another of the guards put in extra time and drew extra pay for doing the janitorial work, and it was arranged with the comptroller's office to have Ishi appointed a janitorial assistant at a salary of twenty-five dollars a month.

He spent a couple of hours a day on exhibition days cleaning up the litter left by visitors, particularly the classes of school children. After a few days' practice, he bustled about in the early morning, handling broom, duster, and mop like an old hand, using great care toward cases and specimens. He was good with his hands, and there was about this job as about everything he did what Kroeber calls a "willing gentleness." He was most grateful for the work, having observed that everyone in the white man's world had a regular job for which they received a regular wage. And he was pleased to have the *mahnee,* which permitted him to pay for his own food and whatever else he-wanted, instead of having it given to him. He was a proud person, to whom economic independence meant a great deal. Ishi now had a name, an address, and economic status, his name appearing on the University pay roll from this time.

A minor difficulty came up about how the payment was to be made. The University pays only by check, and the museum was fifteen miles from the comptroller's office. Kroeber was not Ishi's legal guardian nor did he wish to be. Instead of coping with the legal tangle of having checks for Ishi made out to someone else, he decided to teach Ishi to write his name so he could endorse his own checks. To this end, he wrote out in black ink on white paper the name Ishi, making the four letters as simple as possible, well rounded and continuous, then gave Ishi this pattern, along with some tracing paper, suggesting he practice tracing it, and explaining why this was desirable. Ishi could scarcely have been expected to grasp the mechanism of banking, but he did understand that if he learned to make this peculiar winding mark on paper, it would in time be converted into money; this cause and effect chain intrigued him very much.

For the next week he spent ten or fifteen minutes each day tracing the signature, and after many repetitions, he was able to make a fair facsimile of it from memory. (His signature is reproduced on page 238 of this book.) He practiced some more, perfecting his writing, until the first check arrived. Proudly he endorsed it on the back, "Ishi." A storekeeper at the foot of the Heights who knew him cashed his check, and Ishi received twenty-five dollars in silver money. This might be said to have marked his entrance into full citizenship at least as regards economic status. The question of political citizenship and voting rights did not come up, and it seemed as well not to raise it.

Ishi did not worry about the safety of his money, keeping some of it in his pockets, and some in a box beside his bed; but this was not thought by the others to be a good idea. There was a museum safe in which manuscripts were kept along with the gold specimens, when they were not on special exhibit, gold being the great tempter and corrupter even of visitors to an ethnographic museum. Kroeber offered to keep Ishi's money, except for small amounts, in the safe. He showed him how the safe was operated, and explained that only he and E. N. Gifford, the new curator, knew the combination and could open it.

Ishi had many times made a cache of valuables of one sort or another—food, arrows, tools, and the like—burying them under a pile of rocks or hanging them high in a tree. He was pleased to learn about the white man's cache, and to put his silver there. He saw his money wrapped and stored, his own name plainly written on the outside of the package. The safe was closed. He twirled the combination, and, trying to open it, saw that the box would not open. He was immensely satisfied; his treasure was now both well hidden and accessible whenever he wanted to get to it.

All four Yana dialects used a single counting system with almost identical numeral names. Early in their work with Ishi, Waterman and Kroeber asked him to count for them in Yahi, which he did willingly enough: *baiyu, uhmitsi, bulmitsi, daumi, djiman, baimami, uhmami, bulmami, daumima, hadjad;* the same words as in the other Yana dialects except for some consonantal changes. But unlike the others which continued from ten to higher numbers and multiples of higher numbers, Ishi's counting stopped with the numeral *hadjad,* "ten." When he was asked to continue, he would say, "No more. That's all." Here seemed to be an astonishing culture loss, not before encountered in California. The two ethnographers mentioned it in print and on the lecture platform, rationalizing it as owing in all probability to the decades of decimation and hiding; perhaps in the shrunken and meagre life there had been little occasion to count or to think in numbers higher than ten.

To make it as easy as possible for Ishi to become familiar with a complex new number system and particularly so that he could learn to make change, the money from his salary check was converted into half dollars for him. The pieces of silver of identical size pleased him, and he soon discovered that an empty cannister which had held a film roll was a good container for them. Forty half dollars just filled it, and when it would take no more, Ishi screwed the lid on tight and brought his first cache of the white man's treasure, which he called *twen-y dahlah,* to be deposited in the safe. There were more empty canisters, because someone was always taking pictures of Ishi; soon a second one was brought, full of treasure, to be laid beside the first, and then a third, for Ishi was saving about half his salary!

From time to time, if it was foggy or rainy out of doors, or after his work was finished, Ishi would come to the office and ask to see his money. Upon being handed it from the safe, he would go to the big table in the center of the room, open the cans, take the half dollars out, and spread them over the table—a king in his counting room.

It was one of the counting-room days. From his desk in the same room, Kroeber watched as Ishi absorbedly spread out his money, restacked it in piles, and divided some of the piles into half stacks which he fingered as if he were counting them. The stacks looked to be the height of the forty pieces which filled one container. Kroeber joined Ishi at the table. "How much? How much money?" he asked, pointing to a full stack. Ishi answered at once and correctly: *daumistsa,* "forty." "The half stack?" Ishi replied: *uhsiwai,* "twenty." Three half stacks he identified as *baimamikab,* "sixty"; and two full stacks as *bulmamikab,* "eighty." The questions and answers went on, but it was already obvious that Ishi's numeral vocabulary and his knowledge of the full Yana counting system were undiminished.

The system was quinary, that is to say there were basic numeral names up to five, and from five to ten there were additions to these, with further additions from ten to twenty. When twenty was reached, it became a new unit as one hundred is with us, the twenties or scores being given names not built on the smaller numeral names.

Why had Ishi said "No more" at ten? Counting in the abstract was something he was not accustomed to do. He probably found it trying, and surely he found it pointless. Counting is for counting something tangible such as beads or treasure or the number of quivers in a case, or the number of arrowheads finished, or the numbers of geese in flight, or salmon in a catch. Abstract numbers did not interest him as such, nor did they figure in philosophy in the Yana world view. Ishi's interrogators knew this, as they knew also that the questionnaire form of putting a query may be expected every so often to yield misinformation, since the presumptions from which it arises may be unknown or meaningless to the person being questioned. They were disconcerted to be caught out using it. That their culpability should have come to light as the wild man was engaged in counting his civilized money in quite the manner of a bank teller was particularly humiliating. Thus, step by step, Ishi began his solitary penetration into the wilds of civilization while his friends made some groping progress into the Yahi world.

Chapter 8
LIFE IN A MUSEUM

An immigrant to America in 1911, even though he was solitary and without knowledge of English, and facing a way of life drastically unlike anything he had known at home, could look forward nonetheless to identifying himself with a nuclear group of his own nationality and speech, often to being with relatives or friends from his own home village or district. For Ishi, there was no such buffer against loneliness and strangeness. This made him, to a degree far beyond that of the outlander, dependent upon the people he chanced first to meet, and particularly upon the sort of friends he succeeded in making during his first days of contact. Indeed, had the slaughter house been at some distance from Oroville, or had Ishi's wanderings carried him to a lonely prospector's cabin or to a remote ranch wherein dwelt Digger-haters—and there were some left in the hills—he might actually have met the violent end he at first anticipated.

Sheriff Webber, Undersheriff White, the townspeople of Oroville, and the Indian Service were friendly and concerned to do what was best for him, but their best would have been to send him to a reservation, probably to Round Valley. On any reservation there would have been the inevitable total language barrier, and in Round Valley there would have been as well Ishi's strong and sensitive sense of difference from those surviving Indians of the Pit and Sacramento River drainages, his ancestral friends and enemies, but soft men who had made their peace with the invaders, or whose fathers had, leaving the Yana to fight alone.

Ishi's solitariness in confronting a new life meant that his earliest friendships determined where he lived and how; his social and intellectual milieu; what he did; what he was shielded from; and what he was encouraged to experience. Almost everything that happened to him in the five years following his first conversation with Waterman flowed from that conversation. In Ishi's despairing retreat from a life which had become no longer bearable, he was as a stone skipped randomly across the surface of a quiet pond. He might have died from starvation or violence and disappeared without trace, the world none the wiser. But he did not die. Rather, quiet riffles of contact and influence formed round him in widening circles, carrying him to foreign and unimagined shores. The innermost of these circles was composed of three men who became Ishi's closest friends for the rest of his brief life.

Thomas Talbot Waterman, the first white man to converse with him however haltingly in Yana, was Ishi's first friend. The two men liked and understood one another, a warm relation of equals developed from the acquaintance between an old man, as Ishi seemed to Waterman, and a brash but lovable young man, as Waterman seemed to Ishi. Waterman initiated and shared Ishi's first train trip, his first view of San Francisco, and his introduction to his future home in the museum. Waterman's was the first private home to which Ishi went as a dinner guest to sit at a white man's table with his wife and children. Later, for three months in the summer of 1915, when the linguist Sapir worked daily with him in Berkeley, Ishi lived with the Watermans. Mrs. Waterman and the children were only less fond of him than was Waterman, who complained that his wife and daughter held Ishi's amiability and neatness up to the *pater familias* as a desirable example for him to follow.

Waterman had first thought to study for the ministry. By the time Ishi knew him this early plan had been superseded, and he was an instructor in anthropology preparatory to taking a doctorate in the subject. There remained with Waterman from his earlier bent a scholar's knowledge of Hebrew, Latin, and Greek, and an informed historical and social view to which was added an original and winning personality. He was friendly and curious, sensitive, perceptive, and impulsive. Ishi gave him love and loyalty, responding to Waterman's moods and sometime extravagances, amused or bemused or entertained by him, as was Waterman by Ishi. It was Waterman who set the tone of Ishi's entrance into the modern world. Two close friends were added, but neither replaced Waterman in Ishi's affections.

Sam Batwi, the interpreter, whose father had been a Central Yana, his mother half Southern Yana and half Maidu by way of a full-Maidu maternal grandmother, might have been expected to become one of the inner circle, but such was not the case. He went with Ishi and Waterman to San Francisco, remaining there for three weeks or so. Waterman and Kroeber undoubtedly benefited by having him there to hasten their progress in speaking Yana. But he was an unsympathetic person at best, and particularly exasperating to Ishi. Batwi regarded Ishi as an ignorant country cousin whom he was hired to initiate into the mysteries of the white man's ways. To Ishi, Batwi was a renegade who had gone along with the expectably cowardly Maidu, a renegade who defiled the beloved language which they shared by his barbarities of syntax and accent, and who, worst of all perhaps, had grown a beard in imitation of the whites. Beards belonged to white men; no self-respecting Yahi would permit beard hairs tó be seen on his face. Certain it was no one ever caught Ishi with an unplucked mustache or trace of beard. Batwi, in short, was everything a proper Yana was not: he was of mixed blood, a person without standing amongst his own kind, a *poseur,* a "phony" white man. And with each passing day the beard became more and more the symbol of Ishi's irritation.

Ishi was a conservative whose forebears had been men and women of rectitude; whose father and grandfather and uncles had carried with dignity and restraint the responsibilities of being principal men of their villages. Ishi's own manners were good; Batwi's smacked of the crudity of the frontier town, which was what he knew best and which, by the custom of the time, he knew from its least enlightened citizens, except for his work with Sapir and with an ethnologist or two, briefly, and late in his life.

It may well be that upon first meeting, Ishi and Batwi recognized that they were from different strata of Yana society, Batwi's the less well regarded, and that Batwi met this mutual recognition of status difference with braggadocio in the face of Ishi's inexperience in the white man's world. The two were in any case hopelessly uncongenial, and everyone in the museum was relieved when Batwi went home. Ishi and one of the museum preparators escorted him to the depot, Ishi watching his departure on the train-demon with real satisfaction: his wish was to learn his new world from its own natives, and from people of standing and character. He would repay their time and trouble—he would instruct them in knowledge of the pure Yahi tongue, and proper Yahi behavior. And so it was.

Ishi's second friend was Alfred Kroeber. Nine years Waterman's senior, he was twelve or fourteen years younger than Ishi. But he was the responsible head of the museum, and in charge of the teaching and research programs in anthropology. He was, in other words, the headman of Ishi's village, the *mudjaúpa,* or chief, the person to whom one took one's questions, to whom one turned in uncertainty and trouble, the one to say Yes or No to all requests. Requests came rarely from Ishi; they were usually from outsiders who wished Ishi to do something or to go someplace with them. It was Kroeber who set the limits to which he might venture from Parnassus Heights, limits which widened as his English vocabulary increased, and as he came to know the nearer parts of the city. It was Kroeber who shepherded Ishi's occasional public appearances; who prevented the merely curious or the bad-intentioned from getting to him.

Beyond all this, wherein Ishi's role was that of the acquiescent and the dependent, there were areas of fact and feeling which they both regarded as important on which to base a man-to-man friendship; and there were sufficiently varied situations which they both found amusing, or grotesque, or intriguing, to leaven the time they spent in each other's company. Each man increased his control of the other's language; each shrewdly measured the other's culture, finding it worthy of further study. The relation was one of respect and trust and abiding affection, each for the other. Ishi never asked Kroeber, as he sometimes asked Pope, whether he was an Indian. It would have been an idle question. Kroeber *understood*. The Yana world view was a subject to be gone into comfortably and knowledgeably with him, and all things Yana became near and natural and worthy and living once more, as Ishi and this friend of his talked about them, such being the special *Geist* of the born ethnologist.

Ishi made many subtle distinctions. He adopted the white man's habit of calling people freely by their names, except for Waterman and Kroeber. He spoke *of* Waterman to others by name, Watamany was his pronunciation, but he did not use his name when speaking *to* Waterman. When speaking *to* Kroeber, he said "you," English, or *ai'numa*, "you," formal address in Yana. As will be seen, Ishi did not shrink from hierarchy. A village had first of all a chief, its *mudjaúpa*, whose seat was at farthest remove from the smoke hole entrance, whether in his own or another's home, or in the men's house. Below the chief, other men sat also according to the respect due them. A bastard's, a *wataurisi's*, was the seat of least honor—closest to the entrance way and the ladder. *Wataurisi* is translated literally, "sits-at-the-foot-of-the-ladder." Ishi was sure of his own native worth and position had there been a Yana society, and he coolly and amicably ranked people in white society. There was the matter of unplucked hair on the face. Waterman wore a mustache, Kroeber wore mustache and beard. Hirsute grotesquerie Ishi accepted almost as a badge of the white man. It was logical that the younger man should have only a mustache, and that the elder, the headman, should have mustache and beard.

This book contains, newly garnered from Kroeber—the only one of Ishi's three friends alive in 1959—some fond or amusing

memories and solid blocks of fact. What Ishi gave to Kroeber
that belongs to the world of learning has long since been committed to print or is in the museum files. For the rest, the
world of friendship is a private world, lived through and when
one of the two friends dies, put aside, not to be dragged forth for
later parade. Kroeber seems to find it somewhat depressing and
uncongenial to recall the often painful, and always poignant
memories attaching to Ishi. He reacts rather as did Ishi himself
when a question directed to him carried him back into his too-
laden and private past.

It was not until the autumn of 1912, a year after Ishi's coming
to the museum, that Saxton Pope completed the inner circle of his
intimates. Dr. Pope, an age-mate of Kroeber, had been recently
appointed to the teaching staff of the University's medical school
which was next door to the museum on Parnassus Heights. (The
hospital and medical school are still there.) Pope had not yet
been inside the museum nor had he met Waterman or Kroeber.
He knew Ishi slightly as a patient who came now and then to
the hospital for examination or treatment. This doctor-patient acquaintance might have remained that and nothing more had not
Pope one day glanced out a window which opened onto the flat
of ground behind the museum and seen Ishi there absorbedly
fashioning a bow. He joined Ishi outside where he could observe
him closely, and got Ishi to show him his shooting stance, his hold,
and method of release. Watching, he became filled with a desire
to learn from one who had lived by bow and arrow the technique
and the folklore of archery pursued not as a pastime but as a way
of life. That same afternoon found the two of them practicing on
the open grass at the edge of Sutro Forest; and so began Pope's
mastery of the art of the bow. Archery, hunting big game with
bow and arrow, and perfecting his knowledge, performance, and
form, particularly in the classic British school of shooting, was the
passion of Pope's later years. Theirs—Ishi's and Pope's—was a congenial and fruitful conjunction of temperaments and interests.

It would be difficult, truly, to say which of the two meant the most to the other.

In view of the later closeness of the group, and of Kroeber's and Pope's continuing friendship after Ishi's death, it is somewhat surprising—it even surprises Kroeber now—to discover by way of old interoffice memoranda that Waterman at first regarded Pope's interest in Ishi as a schoolboy sort of fancy, and that he and Kroeber had to be won over from an initially grudging and partial faith in him. But there was no resisting his sincerity, his enthusiasm, and his unembarrassed romanticism. Ishi came to believe that his friend Popey, as he called him, was quite the brightest, the least predictable, and the most fascinating person in the world. He liked him very, very much. Moreover, he discovered that Pope was an excellent *kuwi,* that is to say, a powerful shaman or doctor—Ishi was referring not to Pope's skill in surgery but in sleight of hand, which Pope had learned originally to entertain his own children, and which he now found the open sesame to Ishi's confidence.

At last Popey had his wish: a true aborigine was his friend. He and Ishi spent hours together, week after week, month after month. Together, they spoke a pidgin Yana-English all their own. They shot Ishi's bows and English bows. They tried out the bows in the museum's collection that were not too fragile from age and dryness, matching the performance of bow against bow. They lived in a happy communion in the Robin Hood world where man dominates the denizens of wood and stream and prairie by means of his skill with the swift and soundless bow.

Outside, but barely outside the circle of Ishi's three close friends stood Edward Gifford, who came to the museum as its assistant curator the year after Ishi was established there as a resident and part-time helper. Gifford probably saw more of Ishi at least during museum hours than did the others; certain it was he carried the brunt of responsibility for him during the last months of Ishi's life. Gifford was newly married when they first became acquainted; when Gifford took Ishi home with him for the weekend, he was the first of many Indian friends whom the Giffords would have as visitors in the years to come. Mrs. Gifford recalls now that she was somewhat apprehensive when Ishi took his first tub bath in her home. The sound of generous splashing prepared her to find a bathroom awash, but no, the floor was dry, the tub was clean, and the towels neatly folded on their rack.

Ishi was, as is explained later, shy and distant with white women. Mrs. Gifford was a happy exception. He liked to walk with her in the hills where they sometimes found wild plants which Ishi knew and which they transplanted to the Gifford garden under their Yana names. Sometimes they sat on the ground quietly until quail and other birds came close to them. Ishi's ease with her stemmed, Mrs. Gifford believes, from her own interest in whatever they did—an interest as thoroughgoing as Ishi's own—and in her skill in imitating bird songs and calls. She is no doubt right, but it might be added by way of further explanation that Queen Salote of Tonga finds Delila Gifford a congenial and interesting companion and friend, as have many people of high and low estate, and of different languages, and of all degrees of skin pigmentation the world over.

Besides Gifford there were the museum guards and preparators and janitors. Between them and Ishi there was daily association. Two of the five or six employees cooked and ate some of their meals in the museum and one of the two men always slept in the building. There were strongly marked personalities and temperaments among these men, and between them and Ishi an odd, impinging, and lively *modus vivendi* developed.

Ishi became assistant to Poyser, the head janitor. The work was light, and to Ishi, interesting. The simple straw broom of modern manufacture is not far enough removed from the ubiquitous grass-bunch broom to have seemed at all special, but Poyser's array of mops, mop wringers, furniture polish, and above all, squeejees for cleaning windows were a wonder and a delight to his assistant.

Warburton, the head preparator, was an Englishman from Birmingham, stood five feet one in his shoes, was strong and muscular. He had been a rating in the British navy until he decided it was time to settle down, marry, and have a family, which he did in San Francisco. He was active, accurate, good with his hands. His h-less English and his wit abated not a jot during the many years which had passed since he last touched English soil.

Llewellyn Loud, a guard and assistant preparator, was as Welsh as his name, come by the way of Maine, which state acted only to make him more so: taciturn, stubborn, a man of few words. As might be expected, Warburton exhibited a humorously impatient city man's tolerance for the knobbly Welshman, who was in turn neither impressed nor influenced by anything Warburton or anyone else said.

Ishi added a dimension to each of their lives, as they did to his. Warburton took the same meticulous care of the museum and its specimens that the British navy had trained him to give to its ships and their fittings. Ishi respected tools: he was a maker of tools. Warburton's tool chest was as a treasure chest to one who understood well the tasks of sawing, boring, planing, and hammering. The wonder of the tools lay not in their functions which he knew, but in their variety and ease of use. Never before had Warburton had such a tractable and curious and teachable lieutenant. Ishi never tired of helping Worbinna, as he and after him others in the museum called him. Ishi probably wisely ignored Worbinna's English, as Worbinna did Ishi's Yana, leaving their understanding of one another to tool and touch until eventually Ishi's English vocabulary came to do for basic communication.

From Loud the Austere, whose museum name became Loudy under Ishi's liquid pronunciation, he learned a strictly Loudian form of marketing, cooking, and housekeeping. Loud was penurious in the extreme, getting satisfaction from pinching and saving and cutting corners. He introduced Ishi to a bakery which sold day-old bread and Ishi ever after bought his bread there. Loud took him to buy at the neighborhood stores where food was cut rate or cheap, and he taught him to cook a frugal meal like his own on the little gas stove in the museum. Kroeber protested some of those meals when he saw them, but Loud did Ishi no harm, on the contrary, he helped him to become independent of boarding house and restaurant. Ishi was after all expert at his own kind of housekeeping. He did not mind the stale bread, and he soon learned to select from among the strange foods those most congenial to his own tastes. Loud's austerity appealed to his own Yana understanding of asceticism, as did Loud's emphasis on savings. The morality and desirability of husbanding one's possessions was something he had learned early, and had practiced on Mill Creek and Deer Creek.

Loud is the person in the museum group on whom Ishi probably made the least impression. Loud's loyalties were to general principles rather than to people. He was no more silent with Ishi than with Warburton. When he spoke, it was likely to be a brief sermon on one or another of the world's injustices or evils. He had been narrowly Christian and had come first to the University to learn something about Africa where he hoped to go as a missionary. He stayed on, with a cautious sense, no doubt, that the archaeological specimens with which he worked in the museum were less intractable opponents of his will than would be sentient human beings. Gradually his earlier zeal to bring to heel those of heathen religious persuasion became diverted to a fervent socialism and to a protest against the wealthy, well-dressed, and, as he felt, intolerant sects within Christianity itself. Fortunately, Ishi understood Loudy as little as he did Worbinna, so the gloomy pronouncements and accounts of the evils of San Francisco's congregations neither touched Ishi, nor interfered with his and Loudy's amicable sharing of stove, utensils, and food, and a peaceful and comfortable, if rather odd, life side by side.

Ishi made friends also with Juan Dolores. Back in 1908, on a rainy winter night, a strange Indian had come to Kroeber's home in San Francisco. He introduced himself as Juan Dolores from Arizona, a Papago Indian. He had heard of Kroeber from a

Navaho Indian who was employed in a curio shop in the city, and had concluded that he would like to know him. Sitting before an open grate fire, an old-fashioned center table covered with a fringed tapestry between them, the two men talked. Kroeber noticed that as he talked, Juan fingered the fringe, and after a while he said to him, "Do you know how many fringes you are putting together in each bunch?" Juan had been serious and a touch reserved up to this question, which amused him, coming from a *gringo,* but which also pleased him, as being knowledgeable and perceptive. He answered, "Of course. Four. Always four." Four, the sacred number, the number of balance and beauty. Many years later, more than twenty in fact, Juan recalled this early conversation, and added that he had been noticing lately that Kroeber was arranging the burned matchsticks from his pipe lightings and relightings into neat piles, but with five to a pile, a regrettable number, five, said Juan.

No person was ever less "primitive" than Juan. To divide whatever was divisible into fours was one of many things he had learned and remembered from his grandfather's teachings. He loved his people, and respected what they taught him, what they believed. His mother and sister were devout Catholics, hence Juan's name. His father and elder brother were devout Papagos. Juan put the case for himself, "I am a devout nothing." In that phrase lies much of Juan's story, but that is, as the expression goes, another story, adumbrated here, because his and Ishi's paths crossed.

Juan would have found the eighteenth-century enlightenment a congenial milieu, gracing it with his ineradicable irony and his agnosticism, and his instinctive preference for the intellectual and the sophisticated. He found himself, with such a mind and such feelings, a desert Indian of the twentieth century, forced to make what sense he could of his life. He brought to the making a better linguistic equipment than do most white Americans. He was trilingual, speaking and writing English, Spanish, and Papago. The Papago he learned to write phonetically from Kroeber, and his work on that language became the single intellectual achievement which was of any satisfaction to himself. His only scholastic degree was from Hampton Institute, a school founded for Indians and Negroes, attended largely by Negroes, and rating educationally at about the level of a technical high school. Clearly, his education did not go far enough for him to live by it. He lived by his skill in handling horses, most particularly a six-horse team on a construction job. This work paid well, and he could always have a job when he wanted it. Handling horses was a real satisfaction to him, but the people and surroundings of construction camps were rough and dreary and uncongenial.

As he said, he should have stayed in the East after his graduation from Hampton. The prejudice against Indians is less than in the West, and his teachers could have helped him to go on to further education. But he was homesick for the desert and for his own people. He came home for the summer vacation, and what with the financial help he could give his family, and the fatalism which was deep seated in him, he stayed in the West.

When he had some money saved from teamstering, Juan would spend a few weeks or months and, finally when he was older, several years at the museum. The pay was inadequate as were all academic salaries of the time, but he liked the work and the people. The University did what it could for him, financing his linguistic studies from time to time, and at least once sending him to spend a year in Papago land, recording. There he collected tales, prayers, and songs from the old men of his tribe who spoke only Papago, and who knew the myths and rites in all their fullness.

This was how he came to know Ishi. He wrote to Kroeber early in November, 1911, asking if quarters were available in the museum, and if he might come for a visit. Kroeber replied, "Your quarters are always at your disposal, though you may have to share [them] with our wild Indian." Juan answered that he had read the newspaper accounts of the wild Indian, and added, "I think I will have to run away and hide some place in the mountains of Arizona, and when you find me we will tell [President] Taft or somebody that they have to make a treaty with me. I think that will be the only way I can get some good place to stay the rest of my life. Goodbye. Your friend Juan Dolores."

Juan nonetheless came, and stayed until April, 1912. He lived at the museum where he divided his time between writing parts of the Papago language, and giving a series of brief lectures or talks to museum visitors on one aspect or another of the exhibits. Two letters from him, coming a year later from Nevada where he was working, speak very differently of Ishi. They are to Kroeber, and the earlier one says, "My friend Ishi is well I hope, and has by this time learned a few more words of the English language. Maybe he is a better cook than I am, and enjoys himself by eating the food which he knows is well cooked." The later one says, "I received the pictures you sent to me, and was very glad to look at my friend Ishi. Just now, I can see that Ishi is in a better place than this place where I am today. Should any accident happen to him I am sure he will be well taken care of." Juan's brother had had a serious accident, hence the association of Ishi with an accident.

Ishi and Juan began their relation with reserve, but they became fast friends, each considering the other to be a proper Indian, a person of manners, sensibility, and dignity. Juan could shoot a bow, but he was no match for Ishi, and he watched with respect while Ishi turned out a perfect obsidian arrow point with Stone Age tools, something Juan could not do at all; he had never before seen it done. Ishi was the better of the two at any task requiring deftness and precision of hand operation. Juan's hands were misshapen from heavy work, the joints enlarged, the fingers stiffened; Ishi's hands were without any injury, muscular and sure of touch, as the ideal sculptor's hand is supposed to be.

Juan, for his part, was adept and adaptable in language, so that he understood Ishi's limited English interlarded with Yana words and concepts nearly as well as did Kroeber. He probably increased

Ishi's English vocabulary considerably, but if so, it happened by way of whatever they were doing together. He knew San Francisco, its restaurants, cinemas, parks, and entertainment places, and he had many friends and acquaintances—Indians of different tribes, Mexicans, and Caucasians. He took Ishi with him to places and occasions which he thought Ishi might enjoy and of which he was sure Kroeber would approve. In retrospect, it seems good that Ishi had at least this one friend from his own race who was also of the modern world. It must have made it all a little less strange, less foreign. And their relation, the things they did together, the places they went, the people they met, must have meant something different to Ishi from the people and places he saw with his white friends. The pity is that Juan was at the museum so briefly in those years.

The list of Ishi's intimate friends closes with Juan. He made other friends: visitors to the museum, hospital personnel, and patients. His acquaintances were limited for the most part to people who lived on Parnassus Heights or who came there more or less regularly. The time was too brief to allow for a widening of his circle beyond the museum and "Popey's House"—the hospital. Popey gave him free run there, and more or less of what he did there is known, but not who his favorite people were, nor what they and Ishi meant to each other.

One or another of Ishi's friends was always near him during his San Francisco years. They and the museum, or the hospital when he was sick, shielded and cushioned him from a terrifyingly large, crowded, and complex world. There were nonetheless many and curious contacts, meetings, and impressions from outside, none of which can now be reconstructed whole. There is a beginning of one in a letter, a reference to another in a memorandum which happened to be preserved, and there are the discontinuous recollections of people who knew him. These fragments are like the shards of a pottery vessel which the archaeologist assembles to suggest so far as he can some image of the whole.

Food and clothing, friends and sociability, work and special interests are ingredients of life in a museum as of all living. Ishi's adjustment to his new world, some of it, was not more extreme than that of other travelers to foreign and unknown parts of the world today.

It was to be expected that dressing and undressing might be awkward and onerous to one who had had only to adjust a G-string, or if it was cold, to slip a cape over his shoulders. But Ishi took to clothes, except as said before, to shoes. He held out against shoes for several months. When asked if he would not like a pair to wear when he went outside he said, "I see the ground is stone here. Walking on that all the time, I would wear out shoes, but my feet will never wear out." Perhaps it was Juan Dolores who persuaded him to shoes. Anyway, he was wearing them by mid-winter.

A letter from Juan to Kroeber written in June, 1912, when Kroeber was away briefly and Juan was again at the museum, has to do in part with shoes and feet. Juan writes, "I suppose you have heard that my friend Ishi has been sick. For three days he lay in bed, and I was afraid that if he stayed another day, he would never get up again. Yesterday, I saw him making a spear point. He was finding fault with his materials. Something was too small or too short, anyhow he said, *Chi'kita, chi'kita!* This morning I saw him doing his work again, so I guess he is well. Poyser was scrubbing the floor and Ishi carried the water for him. While Poyser scrubbed Ishi was sitting on the bench laughing at his partner because he was barefooted. When he found Poyser's tracks on the floor he was very much amused. I think Ishi was thinking that footprints are funny looking marks. More than this, he was reminded of the time when he used to go barefooted. I think he also got the idea the proper way to scrub the floor is to go barefooted." Juan never went barefoot except perhaps as a young child. At home he wore the high, close-buttoned moccasin of the desert, and away from home, shoes. Hence a further interpretation of Ishi's amusement over Poyser's tracks which did not occur to Juan may have been the deformity which every shod foot undergoes to greater or less degree and which must have appeared most strange to Ishi.

Getting into and out of a suit coat or topcoat he found unhandy at first, whereas a single demonstration was all he needed to learn to tie a four-in-hand cravat, since he was used to knotting and tying cords of hemp and hide. Pockets he appreciated; within three days of having them he had them filled, and with the usual male miscellany. With the clothes went the code: Ishi, to whom nakedness had been the normal and unmarked state, refused to have his picture taken except when he was fully dressed. Pictures of him in native undress had to await his return visit to the Lassen foothills.

On Seventh Avenue between Golden Gate Park and Judah Street at the foot of the Heights there was a block of small shops where Ishi made most of his purchases, at first with Loudy, then alone. The street was his shopping center, its tradespeople his acquaintances and friends with whom he learned to do his own marketing and errands, and even to undertake certain purchases for Loudy. He was greeted by name by the grocer, the baker, the tobacconist, the cobbler, all of whom were ready to pass as much of the time of day with him as his limited English permitted. He searched out the day's best buys like a thrifty housewife and, like her, something bright and strange was sure to attract him. "How-muchee?" he then wanted to know. "Too-muchee" he might decide, and pass on. Or again, he might buy, if it was something irresistible such as a penny whistle or a kaleidoscope.

How such objects were made, how they functioned, intrigued him deeply. A childish interest? No doubt. But how is it something so small as a penny whistle makes so shrill and carrying a blast? And who was the genius who made the first kaleidoscope?

Ishi enjoyed riding on streetcars and ferries. A favorite trip was to go from the museum in San Francisco to the University in Berkeley, which took an hour and a half each way including a trolley ride to the Ferry Building, a boat trip across the bay, and a train ride from the Oakland Mole to the end of the line, a block from the campus. He enjoyed the walk across campus, past the Library and North and South Halls, along Strawberry Creek, and through Faculty Glade to the tin Anthropology building and his friend Watamany there. On the return trip, he took the number 6 or number 17 trolley at the Ferry Building, either one of which brought him close to the museum. Having once memorized the look of these numbers, he never mistook them.

Golden Gate Park was only three blocks from the museum. Pope and Ishi went to the park for their archery practice. Occasionally Ishi went there alone: he followed the park's meandering paths, and came close to animals and birds with his noiseless tread, or he sat still, watching the captive herd of buffalo, learning the look and ways of these strange and surprising creatures.

The street on which he shopped, the street car which passed the museum entrance, Golden Gate Park which lay in full view from the museum, became Ishi's new world. Looking down over city and park, he could follow with his eyes the circle of his world's boundaries—the limit of its extent and its invisible borders. Kroeber says that Ishi could no doubt have mapped it accurately, as he mapped his old Yana world.

When Ishi came home from shopping, his market basket contained such food as bread, jelly, honey, tea—and later, coffee—sugar, canned salmon or fresh, salt pork, beef to broil or stew, sardines, dry cheese—not soft cheese—potatoes, beans, rice, dried and fresh and canned fruit, and a choice of fresh vegetables.

What did Ishi like for dinner? Beef or fish roasted, baked or broiled. Potatoes boiled in their jackets and eaten dry; or rice or another cereal, plain. A vegetable. He liked all vegetables whether raw, baked, roasted, or boiled (but see below cook Ishi's word on boiling); and all fruit, raw, or dried, or canned; canned peaches were a favorite. Bread he ate plain. He thought well of honey, also of candy. Jelly tasted to him a little like manzanita berries. He liked ice cream; an ice cream soda best of all.

Ishi considered tea the white man's best drink, since it was clear like water. Clarity, according to him, was a desirable quality in all liquids, including meat broths. Coffee, by its nature cloudy, was not a proper liquid, but since everybody drank it, Ishi learned to do so, after a time.

Whisky was clear, but no good. *Whisky-tee crazy aunatee die man,* whisky is crazy fire; causes death. Ishi knew this, he had seen its effects on others early in his civilized life. Some of the ladies of the W.C.T.U. came to interview him, probably thinking of the ravages of whisky amongst Indians. They need not have worried. He barely tasted it, once, when some ill-advised person offered him a drink.

Beer was a medicine, to be taken only in small quantity diluted with sugar and water. Milk was for babies. Ishi began to put condensed milk in his coffee on seeing Loudy do so, but when he learned that it was merely another form of milk, he took his coffee black with sugar. Ishi ate no butter, for butter ruins the singing voice. Soft-cooked eggs cause head colds, therefore he ate only hard-boiled eggs. He disliked custards, blanc mange, and other puddings, and thickened soups and gravies. Soup should be clear like tea, and meats and vegetables should not be disguised by murky sauces. There is a discernible pattern of dislikes for the cloudy, the too smooth, and the too soft, despite Ishi's fondness for his staple food, acorn mush, a dish of indubitably glutinous texture; and for a mixture of flavors and textures of foods which he preferred cooked separately, in clear broth or water.

The white man's stove he found good for roasting and broiling as in his own earth oven or open-fire cooking, but he considered that the modern stove ruined boiled food. Said Ishi, "White man puts good food in pot full of boiling water. Leaves a long time. Food cooks too fast, too long. Meat spoiled. Vegetables spoiled. The right way is to cook like acorn mush. Put cold water in basket. Place hot rocks in water till it bubbles. Add acorn meal. It cooks *pukka-pukka*. Then it is done. Same way, make deer stew. Or rabbit stew. Cook *pukka-pukka*. Not too long. Meat firm, broth clear, vegetables good, not soft and coming apart."

There were the gadgets, tools, and amenities of civilization which impressed Ishi as desirable or ingenious or delightful, as there were those which left him indifferent or which he rejected.

Ishi and his people built winter houses against rain and cold, summer houses against heat, and storage houses. He found the houses of civilization good. They gave protection against both heat and cold, were comfortable, and provided much space for storing food and clothes and tools. He liked chairs and beds and tables and chests and towels and blankets. Running water and flush toilets were not only good, they were very, very clever, as were electric lights, switches, and gas stoves. The telephone was amusing, but less intriguing and genuinely interesting than the penny whistle and the kaleidoscope. Matches were one of civilization's true delights, rated far above gas and electricity.

Someone gave Ishi a watch, which he wore and kept wound but not set. He could "tell time" after his own system. He knew midday, and any hour which was pointed out, keeping his appointments punctually and without strain by some sun sense plus his simplified reading of the museum and hospital clocks. His own watch was an article of pride and beauty to be worn with chain and pendant, not a thing of utility.

Automobiles interested Ishi far less than trolley cars. He could watch trolley cars endlessly. They ran on tracks like the train-demon, their gongs were superior to automobile horns, and they were equipped with air brakes which released a cloud of sand and dust with a satisfying "phoosh" whenever the brakes were applied.

To see Harry Fowler take off from Golden Gate Park on a flight across the continent was an event, in 1911, exciting and novel enough to draw a crowd to the park, Waterman and Ishi among them, Ishi the coolest of the lot. He was most interested when the propeller blades began to whir and the engine started with a roar. But when the plane rose, circling over their heads, he nodded in its direction, asking, *Saltu?* "White man up there?" He raised his eyebrows at the funny ways of the civilized: a building is not so much compared with a mountain, and an aeroplane is not so much of a performer in the air as the hawk or the eagle. Birds fly so high in the air that you cannot follow their flight, animals run on the ground more swiftly than man, and fish swim in the sea and rivers, the salmon climbing rapids no boat can make. The white man showed his true cleverness when he harnessed a demon to metal tracks.

Even in a house there was something which ran on its own tracks: the roller shade. The first time Waterman snapped a shade up, Ishi did not know where it had gone. When he found where it was, and that he too could make it obey his will, he was charmed. The sheer pleasure of putting a shade up or down remained one of life's surprises never to be taken quite for granted.

Banking, money, and wages were good, as were savings. Ishi looked forward to the day when he could buy a horse and wagon, his ideal of the ultimate in worldly possessions.

The tools he liked and learned to use skilfully were the hammer, saw, hatchet, knife. He rarely used level or square, being accustomed to measure according to some body dimension such as a palm's breadth, or the length from finger tip to elbow. He was accurate for close-range heights and distances through his experience in hunting at close range, a nice calculation being ancillary to netting or snaring or shooting his prey. Longer distances were measured not by paces, but most naturally to him by the length of time it took him to cover the distance; if a very long one, by the number of "sleeps" or days. He rarely used a plane, a draw knife, an augur, or a chisel. A small bench vise, on the other hand, he took to at once, substituting it for his big toe to hold whatever he was working on. Glue he rated next to matches, as one of the white man's important inventions. He kept a pot of glue in his work kit for feathering arrows, cementing bindings, joining sinews for bow strings and for attaching the backing to a bow.

Door knobs, safety pins, and typewriters he regarded with quiet hilarity. If memory or record served to add to this somewhat gnomic threesome, we might come on the source of the hilarity. Certain it is he enjoyed them beyond their functional, useful roles. They carried an odd and added dimension of significance, much as we use old Chinese charcoal irons as ash trays, and discarded cartwheels as candelabra, finding them pleasing in themselves, and being indifferent to their original, native values.

Looking back at Ishi's other choices, some pattern emerges. The seventh wonder is not so wonder-filled as was the first. The train, which belonged also, in a way, to his old life, sufficiently stood for the inventions of civilization that were beyond his technological experience. For the rest, he preferred what he could relate to: a sawmill, a carpenter building a house, a cabinetmaker mending a chair, a tool or toy which he could hold in his hands and judge and admire with a craftsman's critical appreciation.

Ishi's public did not tire of its Stone Age Man. He was settled in a contented routine, which was, however, neither dull nor uninterrupted, to judge by the fragments which flutter out from the museum files, carrying with them hints of unexpected impingements.

Amongst them are "Fannie's" letters. Someone unknown to Ishi or the museum—one of the medical students, perhaps—must have run a "personal" in the lovelorn column of a St. Louis newspaper, using Ishi's name, for on November 6, 1911, he received this letter, "Seeing the add. in the paper that Ishi the Aborgine is in search of a wife I thought I would answer. I will exchange Photos if willing. Send Photo by first mail. [Signed] Miss Fannie . . . 1143 . . . Street, St. Louis Mo. [Original spelling and punctuation kept.] This letter must have been answered, because there is a reply ten days later, "Mr. Ishi: Dear sir: Hear is my Photo Graph which you asked for in your letter it is not a very Good one but I hope you will be pleased with it. As you wanted to know of my circimstances I am a widow. And I am working for a salary. And I have a Goodeal of Realstate at My Mother's Death. And if you wish to investigate you are perfectly welcome to call and do so. I remain Your truly Miss Fannie . . ."

The last word we have on Fannie is a telegram which would seem to have been in answer to one from the museum. It comes from the *Post Dispatch* of St. Louis, Missouri, and says, "Will you kindly wire at our expense text of St. Louis woman's proposal to Ishi and any information you may have regarding her. We will be glad to investigate matter for you."

There are requests, a good many of these, to have Ishi interpret "charm" stones, but none of the stones belonged to his people or closely related ones, and he knew no more of their esoteric meaning than did their present possessors. And there are letters, even today, asking for a picture of Ishi, and coming from places as wide apart as Lone Pine, California, and Birmingham, England.

There are many requests for Kroeber to repeat a lecture, "Ishi, the last of the Yanas," at evening parent-teacher meetings at schools, or before lodges, usually with a discreet postscript expressing the hope that Mr. Ishi will be with him. The Academy of Sciences in San Francisco, in announcing such a lecture, adds that "Ishi will present himself to the audience."

There are many invitations, which belong more or less in one of three categories of social occasion—fiesta, club activity, or private party. One fiesta invitation suggests how well the young Ishi myth was thriving back in his home country: Kroeber and Ishi are invited to be the "honored guests" at a "Fiesta Arborea" at Chico, in the Sacramento Valley, the hotel and traveling expenses to be paid by the fiesta committee, "in as much as he [Ishi] is from this section it would add greatly to have him." The letter is careful to say that whereas Yana basketry and other crafts will be featured in the exhibitions, the committee wishes Ishi to come solely as a guest, not as a performer.

The club invitations follow somewhat the pattern of one to Kroeber from the Local Walk Committee of the Sierra Club, which says in part, "A party of fifty or more of the Sierra Club will start from the Baker Street entrance of the park on a seven mile walk by way of Buena Vista Park and Sutro Forest to the Anthropological Museum. If convenient to you, you will confer great pleasure upon the Sierrans by joining their party, bringing Mr. Ishi if possible. The pleasure of meeting Mr. Ishi will be long remembered. Trusting that you and he will be free to join us in our ramble through the woods, I remain . . ." The personal invitations range from dinner in a private home to engraved cards to consular receptions.

That Ishi was active in the pursuit of his old crafts is apparent from the numbers and occasional urgency of requests from the museum staff for materials to be brought or sent in from the hill country, such as sacks of acorns, bundles of buckeye for fire sticks, hazel shoots for arrows, and willow and alder for building and repairing the summer shelter which Ishi had put up on the museum grounds; his project to build a winter or earth house as well was never realized. He knew what he wanted in these materials. Black oak was once sent in place of buckeye. The sender is told, "Ishi says do not send black oak. Black oak is of no use for any purpose." Kroeber was in Quincy, and sent from there some mock orange and, as he thought, several kinds of pine. Gifford writes him, "Ishi says that the white flowered mock orange is not good for arrows and that the pine needles you sent are of one species only. Ishi was very much tickled with the postal you sent him"—even though he evidently had some reservations about the pine needles.

People heard Ishi speak in Yana and some of them picked up a word or a meaning which set their imaginations to finding similarities. That the likenesses were random made them no less convincing to those who wished to believe in their significance, as in the letter which follows:

At one time I was matron of the Japanese Woman's home in San Francisco. Therein I learned two of the alphabets and to speak some to the women. Therefor am much interested in the aborigines of the continents. I believe in heredity and environment. Therefor think the Japanese and Indian are the same. Many words are alike etc. I offer these words as a suggestion to you and with your knowledge and power to investigate, give the Japanese word and its meaning.

Isehi = A stone.
Yana = A weir or basket to take fish.
Nogi or *Noji* = Pertaining to agriculture.
O ha yo = Good morning.
Yuba = A kind of food made of bean.
oro-oro = here and there, little by little.
Hobo = all about, everywhere.

My father assisted in placing the flag on South Butte, Sutter Co. July 4, 1861. I am respectivatly [*sic*] a native daughter. [Signed.]

Here is another letter.

"In Genesis the woman is called Iska and the man Ish. Did Ishi by mistake get the feminine title?"

People wished to be told all about Ishi. Some of them retold his story to local home papers, with odd comments of their own, as in the one which concludes: "He [Ishi] shows characteristics of great kindness and has a well developed head, although absolutely ignorant." Affection for him and concern that he be well cared for and happy are aspects of much of the correspondence, as in this letter:

"I cannot tell you how pleased I am with the arrowpoint [Ishi's]. I prize it more than words can express. I have been deeply interested in every item relating to Ishi and many times have 'God blessed' you all for the kind and considerate treatment that has been given him."

Because Ishi was often asked if he wished to return to his old home, many letters came to the museum protesting this possibility. The example given is typical of the earnestness of these protestations, and of an appreciation both of Ishi and of the museum:

Professor Kroeber. Dear sir, At a visit at the Affiliated Colleges on Sunday past I heard you say about the Indian that you ask him if he wanted to go back again. Would that not be as cruel to turn that poor fellow loose as the history of poor Ishi the last forty years and can't the city keep one lone Indian and he ought to be right at home in so splendid collection of Relics as are in the college of which I believe half of the people have no knowledge and would visit more if they did. Respectfully, [Signed.]

There were those to whom Ishi was Rousseau's unspoiled savage. One such writes, "It would be too bad if one of his child-like nature should be treated as one of ourselves." Then there were those who feared lest he fall into evil, particularly that of drink, while yet others fretted over the state of his soul. Ishi could be drastically reassuring. About whisky he did not *say*, "It makes me sick," but he pantomimed the words, a gesture which was convincing, since he reserved it to express an extreme disgust. Few things called it forth, drunkenness was one, and the sight of an adolescent boy wearing a mustache was another. As to his soul, a lady one day asked him, "Do you believe in God?" Ishi answered "Sure Mike!" Some of his English was learned from the boys who hung around him, watching him make bows and arrows, or talking to him for the perfect pleasure of knowing a real Indian.

Ishi's human appeal seems to have been a universal one, his history more interesting and bizarre in the face of his friendliness and a characteristic quiet élan. On the other hand he touched lightly if at all the imagination of the artist during his brief museum years. A woman requested permission to make a medallion of Ishi, but this seems to have come to nothing. The Public Museum of Oakland, California, now owns the only bust that was ever made of him, a plaster cast made by F. H. Frolich. Ishi was photographed so frequently and so variously that he became expert on matters of lighting, posing, and exposure, but so far as the record shows, no art photographer ever asked to have Ishi sit for him, nor did any portrait painter. Photographs of him were bought or made to be treasured as mementos along with family pictures and camera records of a holiday or an excursion.

Neither does he seem to have been memorialized in fiction. There is one request from a man then living in Stirling City,

California, for the Yana words, "I know," "Come," "Come on and see," and "No money," with an explanation of a story he is writing "in which Ishi comes to the rescue in proving an identity which was of great moral value to a sturdy pioneer of this locality." The Yana words were supplied him, but whether or not the story was written, the record does not indicate. Stirling City is in the upper Sacramento Valley not far from Yana country, and the projected plot indicates considerable growth of the myth only six months after Ishi's departure to the city.

Perhaps the one person who could be said to have seen Ishi with an artist's eyes and to have exploited the aesthetic possibilities in his features and in the finish of certain of his expert and stylized motions in archery and in handling the long spear was Dr. Pope. Both as physician and as artist he found Ishi's hands and feet perfect functional examples of what human hands and feet should be and should be able to do. He made casts of the feet and took close-up photographs of the hands. Ishi's death mask also was his loving handiwork.

Popey's house—the hospital—was next door to the museum. Ishi had made friends there even before he knew Dr. Pope; he went over so regularly that whenever he was wanted and could not be found in the museum, the hospital became the first place to look for him.

He might be in the kitchen. He liked to see what was cooking in the oversize cauldrons and pots and bake pans. Sometimes he ate there, finding the food not bad so long as he avoided the slimy, custardy, cloudy dishes the huge kitchen seemed to specialize in. Or he might be with the dietitian, watching her make up individual diet trays. Then there was the laundry. It was fun not only to watch the sheets and pillowslips whirling in the machine, the water and suds billowing from the wringer, and the finished flat pieces emerge from the mangle, but also to feed the washing into water, wringer, and mangle. The Chiep got very excited, however, when he found Ishi working the mangle, and said No. It seemed indeed a risky occupation for one uninitiated even in using the ordinary hand iron, much less machine tools of any sort.

But Ishi did not spend all his time with the cooks, the launderers, and the dietitians. Orderlies, nurses, students, and doctors all knew him. If one or more of them had time for a few minutes rest and a cup of coffee, Ishi sat with them, in silence if that was what they seemed to want, or he would sing them a song if they asked for it. Perhaps they would talk, a conversation compounded of gesture, Yahi, and English. These friends of his were not so quick at learning the proper sounds of Yahi as were Watamany and the Chiep. Often they understood the meaning of a word but could only approximate its pronunciation, in which case Ishi pronounced it their way so as not to embarrass them: they conversed, so to say, in pidgin Yahi. Ishi was not himself a kuwi, but he was knowledgeable about Yana medical practices, and whatever had to do with disease, its cause and cure, fascinated him.

The only surgical operation Ishi claimed to know how to perform was that of scarification for which a sharp flake of obsidian was used. The purpose of the operation was to strengthen the arms and legs of a hunter.

The hole through the septum of the nose served to hold a bone ornament, or, when Ishi had a cold, a twig of baywood or juniper became for the time a built-in inhalator of sorts.

A dog should never be allowed to lick a baby's hands or face, indeed, it is better not to have a dog play with a baby at all because he may give it a paralysis. [Commenting on this medical belief of Ishi's, Dr. Pope notes, in 1920, that Dr. R. H. Gibson of Fort Gibson, Alaska, reported the coincidence of poliomyelitis among the Tanana Indians and the occurrence of distemper in their dogs.]

Ishi's treatment for rattlesnake bite was to bind a toad or frog on the affected area. [Again reporting in 1920, Dr. Pope says, "This is interesting in the light of the experiments of Madame Phisalix of the Pasteur institute, who demonstrated the antidotal properties of salamandrin, an extract obtained from salamander skin, and the natural immunity that the salamander has to viper venom. Macht and Able have obtained a similar powerful alkaloid from the toad *Bufo nigra,* called bufogin, which has some of the properties of strychnin and adrenalin. It has been used as an arrow poison by South American aborigines. Experiments which I conducted with salamandrin as an antidote to crotalin show that it has a pronounced protective and curative value in the immunization of guinea pigs and in their cure after being bitten by the rattlesnake. It is, however, too dangerous and potent a poison itself to be of any practical value."

Ishi did not consider it wholesome to sleep with the moon shining on his face; he covered his head completely when sleeping in the open. The Yana were within a much larger area of elaborate moon lore; as far away as the Klamath River, the Yurok considered the winter moons to be bastards born out of wedlock and hence the moons to which a bastard should pray; whereas the summer moons, contrary to the feeling of our own lyric and romantic poetry, are the family moons, the respectable ones.

Ishi knew many medicinal plants, their names, their uses, where to find them, and when to gather them, but he put little faith in them: it is old women who administer and believe in herbs and poultices and drugs, said Mr. Ishi.

For curing, something more than old wives' tales and remedies is needed, namely, a doctor learned and skilled in the practice of his art. The serious ills of the body come from the magic passage into some part of it of "pains" which are evil and of deadly potency, to be overcome only by a magic more powerful than their own. Not just anyone knows or can practice such magic. The successful doctor serves an apprenticeship of fasting and prayer, resulting in a vision and trance, perhaps repeated ones, followed by long devotion to learning complicated and demanding rituals and routines, before he is able to remove a pain. Beyond this special knowledge, he must have the "gift," the temperament for curing. He will be rewarded and honored, once he can work cures, but he must not be venal if he would succeed, and he must resist the ever present temptation to sell out, to kill instead of cure, which his competence in magic puts it in his power to do.

A doctor uses smoke and ashes, blowing them ceremonially in a set order toward the east, the west, the south, the north, over the patient's body, sometimes into it. He passes burning coals through himself, sometimes through the patient. He sucks out the pain or pains, which turn into bits of obsidian or thorns or spines or even a bee's stingers when he has removed them, or when, as sometimes happens, he is able to pluck them out of the air where they are floating threateningly around the sick person. So soon as he has recovered a pain, he deposits it in a container made of a bird's trachea or of a piece of a large artery, seals the ends with pitch, and takes into his charge the now powerless pain, that it may do no more harm.

Many of the patients at the hospital had heard of Ishi; some of them had already met him at the museum. It lightened a long day for them to have the quiet, affable Indian look in on them, and, encouraged to do so by Dr. Pope, he took to making brief but frequent visits to the wards, most often to the women's wards. With hands folded before him he went from one bed to another as might a visiting physician, stopping for a few moments at each bed. If the patient was asleep or too sick to notice him, he looked into her face concernedly, but said nothing; if she was awake and responsive, he smiled and said some words in Yahi, and waved to her upon leaving.

Ishi observed correctly that there were in the hospital more men than women patients, and commented on this often enough to indicate that he would have expected the opposite. Ethnographers have not, so far as the writer knows, covered the point as such. It is perhaps implied in the changing sex ratios for age of death in our own society over the years, the conspicuously greater longevity of women being a phenomenon of our times. But Ishi was commenting, not on deaths, but on numbers of bed patients. In a Yana village on a normal day there would almost surely have been more women than men keeping to their beds. For six days each month—the ritual if not the actual length of her period—a woman was required to withdraw to a separate house and more or less to stay on her bed; there was the length of a moon's waxing and waning to be spent in retirement and rest following the birth of her baby, during which she was considered at most convalescent. In an environment where those not robust tended to sicken and die as babies or runabouts of two or three years of age, women probably suffered more temporarily disabling illnesses and were carried off more frequently by one or another of the sex-related deteriorative diseases than were men. Until the disabilities of old age, Yana men were probably in need of curing most often for a broken bone or other hunting injury, and for wounds suffered in a war raid.

Ishi felt quite sure that he knew the chief causes for men's sickening in civilization. They were, briefly, the excessive amount of time men spent cooped up in automobiles, in offices, and in their own houses. It is not a man's nature to be too much indoors, and especially within his own house with women constantly about. The white man seemed to him to have become excessively a victim to the ever present evil spirit, the Coyote doctor, as he called it. This could be due, in Ishi's opinion, to the white man's carelessness in failing to protect himself from the unwilled malignity and danger of the *sake mahale:* the woman whose moon period is upon her. The touch, the mere presence in the family house, of a woman during those days is a peril to any man. A woman should have her own separate house for her periods. Any blood is suspect of evil, but a woman's is positively known to bear a deadly power.

One day Ishi went, as usual, to the hospital, but seeing no one whom he knew, he wandered into a part of the building which was strange to him, down a long corridor, and through a door into the dissection room. No other living person was there, but there were several cadavers laid out on marble slabs, partly uncovered and in various stages of classroom dissection. This was a revolting and a terrifying experience to Ishi. All Indians know that it is not good to have a dead person's body around, that it is contaminating and dangerous. The body is touched as little as possible after death, and whoever undertakes to dress and prepare it, is ritually decontaminated before he rejoins his family. To the Yahi especially, as to all Indians practicing cremation, the extended handling of the body and its continued presence among the living is perilous both to the living and to the dead. The flames of the funeral pyre, which accomplish cleanly and at once the reduction to inert matter of the corruptible body, are also the beneficent flames which release the incorrupt and indestructible soul for its journey to the Land of the Dead.

Ishi knew that in his new home there were housed the mummified bodies of Egyptians and Peruvians as well as the skulls and other bones of many, many Indians. He did not like this, and he was careful to put nothing of his own in the rooms which held human remains. But these bones unlike the bodies on the dissection tables had at least received decent burial upon their death; their souls had been freed to go to their proper home. And some powerful magic was obviously at work in the museum because the skeletal material was cleaned and classified and handled by Worbinna and Loudy, and other people, all of whom continued to remain in good health and unbewitched.

Pope lured Ishi away from memory of the horror of dissection into the fascination of surgical healing of the living human body. He took him upstairs to the surgery where he let him handle and examine the paraphernalia of the white man's curing ceremonies, the intricately curved knives, the small scissors, the fine saws, and the needles of many sizes and uses. He encouraged him to look through the glass-paneled door as often as he wished until he had a clear idea of operating technique. Then he put a white coat and spectator's mask on him and took him into the operating room where, from the visitor's stand, he could see everything that happened.

Ishi watched closely and asked relevant questions. His knowledge of skinning, eviscerating, and dressing deer and bear as well as small game gave him much knowledge of the internal makeup of man. The physical act of surgery interested him without troubling him, but he was not able so easily to resolve the moral and ethical questions raised when one person, even a doctor, presumes to cut into another human body and to remove parts of it. The effects of anaesthesia troubled him almost more than the effrontery of human surgery: to induce sleep is to cause the soul to leave the body. This is a serious thing not to be lightly regarded or undertaken. The competence of the anaesthetist becomes then of more moment than that of the surgeon, for he who has the power to make the soul leave the body for a time must have the power to cause it to return before death results from soul loss. He must be a skilled man, indeed, and a good man; his power puts in his way the temptation to mischievous witchcraft.

Ishi watched Pope operate many, many times. Some operations he considered unnecessary, such as a tonsillectomy. Tonsillitis could be cured, he said, by rubbing honey on the outside of the throat and neck, then blowing ashes delicately over the inside of the throat from a quill or hollow reed. Operations for diseases or morbid conditions unknown to him before were more likely to be accepted by him as legitimate. He watched Pope remove a diseased kidney. This operation excited him very much, most particularly the methods used to prevent hemorrhage. He could not believe that recovery was possible, and enquired daily until the patient was well. From that day, Ishi recognized in Popey the born kuwi, one who had the gift and the skills for becoming a great Yana doctor, that is if only he would fast and observe strict taboo and receive the necessary, powerful vision.

Chapter 9
THE CRAFTSMAN

Visitors continued to keep the museum turnstile click-
ing, registering numbers far above the staff's most sanguine expec-
tations—there were more than a thousand of them who watched
Ishi at work on a single autumnal afternoon. Because he was in
his own home, because he had a function toward these visitors,
and, finally, because many of them came again and again, and
all were in a sense his friends, Ishi was not put off by their numbers. His audience was indeed various. It included children who
were reading *The Last of the Mohicans,* Mark Twain, and the
history of the wars and migrations of their own land and people;
boys especially who were acquiring a first skill with bow, sling,
or shotgun. There were men and women in their middle years,
mostly family groups these were, whose span of interest was less
than that of the youngsters. Then there were the old who, like
the young, were ready to sit, timeless as Ishi, following with
fascinated absorption whatever he did. Perhaps the sense of
history is more immediate and acute when we are at the threshold
of full adult participation in life, and again when we approach its
close, with time to reassess, to contemplate, and to commit ourselves once more to life's eternal verities.

It would seem to be so. In any case, Ishi's "public" was a serious
minded and a devoted one, of whatever age, aware with differing
degrees of consciousness and articulateness that when Ishi fashioned a tool or weapon under their eyes, or made fire with his
primitive fire drill, they were seeing in actuality the reënactment
of man's oldest and fundamental skills; so reads the story of
archaeology. Watching Ishi at work, the long road of history,

lost in the darkness of remoteness, became illumined and its distances telescoped, for man is the world's craftsman, the maker of tools, and what one man fashions with his two hands is not strange to another man's appreciation and understanding.

Ishi busied himself almost from his first day at the museum, with adding to its collections spears, and bows and arrows newly made there by him. He had of course brought nothing with him, and it became quickly obvious that the supplies of obsidian, flint, mountain juniper, and deer sinew in the museum were inadequate to his industry, to the public appetite for watching him at work, and to his own quiet insistence that the materials he used be the *right* grade of glass or stone, or of the proper species of tree: one of its near relatives would not do.

Ishi was kept supplied with raw material of the quality and sort he wanted. Some of this he collected himself on trips with one or another of his white friends to Marin County, or to the near-by Coast Range country easily accessible to San Francisco. For the rest, the museum correspondence suggests that whenever any one went into the field for whatever purpose, he was commissioned to bring or send back to Ishi fresh supplies of the materials he needed; and that when there was no one going out, a rancher or a surveyor in the Lassen country would receive a polite but sometimes pressing request for a special kind of wood to be shipped collect to the museum, as promptly as possible. There clings to these letters some sense that the supply was barely keeping up with the demand.

The use of the fire drill could be demonstrated indoors and before an audience; shooting with bow and arrow could not be done indoors; and fishing with the harpoon had to wait upon trips to rivers of some size.

Stone toolmaking and fire making are as old as man himself, and Ishi used the same materials to fashion the same tools that Stone Age man used the world over. He was accustomed to use as a hammerstone a waterworn boulder of heavy stone of a size and shape to fit the hand well. This is perhaps man's first and

simplest tool. For a supplementary prying and splitting imple-
ment, Ishi used a blunt-ended piece of strong bone. This he placed
against the boulder from which he wished to remove pieces without breaking the whole. By letting the bone receive the blow from
the hammerstone, he was able to remove flake after flake, and if
he so wished, to fashion the core into a tool.

Although he did not do this at the museum, Ishi knew how
to grind down and fashion the basaltic rock of Lassen into manos,
mortars, or pestles which women used for pounding and grinding
acorns and seeds. For his own use, he made wood-hafted scrapers
and knives of bone, obsidian, or chert, and he kept at hand some
sharp cutting blades, unhafted, of obsidian or occasionally of
chalcedony, an assortment of picking stones, and an anvil for
grinding paint. His kit, accumulated within a few weeks of his
coming to the museum, resembled closely the tools and treasures
which he had been accustomed to own: bone awls of different
sizes, bone and antler flakers small and large, bone harpoon
points, scrapers, and pendants and beads made of clam, abalone,
and Olivella shells.

He used, so long as he was in his own country, heavy baskets
for food storage made of pine roots, and finely woven, pitch-lined
cooking baskets, and baskets of various grasses, put to a hundred
uses. He did not make baskets in the museum, this being women's
work, but he did make rope from native hemp or milkweed, very
strong this was for use in climbing cliffs. He also made a lighter
rope, as well as string and thread of thin deer sinew; string intended for use in sewing or for bowstrings was as fine as many
strippings of it through the teeth could make it. Ishi was known
to sigh over this job, for threadmaking was not only tedious, it
was woman's work as much as was basketmaking. On the other
hand, every painstaking step having to do with hunting, and
including the manufacture of spear, harpoon, bow and arrow,
net, and snare, must be done by a man and away from women
and girls, the dark female principle being inimical to all that
pertains to war and the hunt.

Ishi's larger stone utensils were all basaltic. With other people, they may be granitic. They must in any case be stone of the sort which, when worked, grinds down, becoming smoother with working and use. Such stone will never give a knife edge and hence has never been used for edged tools and weapons, which are always made of one of the silicates of which flint is by far the commonest and most widely spread over the earth's surface. Tool-makers, when they could get it, preferred to flint the pure glass, obsidian, formed within the earth, darkly opaque and structure-less. Flint or obsidian or one or another of their associates such as chert and chalcedony are the necessary materials for the blade, the point, the thin, sharp, delicately made and dangerously pene-trating tool or weapon. California has enormous quantities of obsidian in the Shasta, Clear Lake, Napa Valley, and Mono Lake and perhaps other areas, enough that all California Indians were able customarily to use it rather than flint; those tribes who did not have it acquired it by trade. Obsidian was Ishi's favorite ma-terial for demonstration at the museum, although he made arrow points there also of flint, of agate, of plate glass, of the brown glass of beer bottles, and the blue of milk of magnesia bottles. As a final irony of the Time of Concealment, Ishi was cut off from trade to north and south, and Yana country has no obsidian or flint. Painstakingly and silently, Ishi had visited the length of Lassen Trail, every campsite of emigrant, hunter, or camper up and down Mill and Deer creeks, and the cabin middens and ranch dumps of whatever dwellings he could reach by night and return from by night, combing them for the discarded bottles they were likely to contain. Once back home, he shaped at his leisure the pieces of glass into his ammunition.

The museum audience never saw the first step in the making of an obsidian tool, the division or breaking up of the original ob-sidian mass, usually a boulder the size of a small loaf of bread, but very heavy for its size. To begin the manufacture of a large spear point or knife blade, Ishi used his blunt-end bone tool, placing it where, when struck with the hammerstone, it would trim off a large piece without shattering the whole boulder. To get smaller pieces for arrowpoints, he struck the obsidian mass directly with the hammerstone. Both techniques sent slivers of glass flying in all directions. It is a dangerous step, and Ishi was relieved when this part was done.

This first blow struck, the rest of the flint or glassworking could be done before an audience, there being no further danger from flying pieces except to the worker himself. For the actual shaping of the arrow or spear point, Ishi used a flint flaker, probably the first toolmaking tool, the original ancestor of all manufacturing machinery. It consisted of a straight wooden handle, exactly the length of the distance from Ishi's elbow to his extended middle finger, the handle tipped with a piece of deer antler neither too sharp nor too blunt. The butt of the handle he held against his ribs with his elbow, to give steadiness and a fulcrum. The right hand grasped the other end of the scraper, close to its point, while in the left hand, protected with a double piece of buckskin, was held the sliver of obsidian selected for finishing, a piece two to four inches long, one to one and a half inches wide and about a quarter of an inch thick, the fingers keeping it vertical to the flaker in its longer dimension. Ishi now began the "pressure finishing," pressing upon the lower edge of the unworked piece evenly and with increasing force downward and outward, in a scarcely perceptible motion. For a moment, nothing visible happened, then, with an almost inaudible click, a minute fragment of obsidian would detach itself and drop off. The fracture was semilunar in shape, thinning to a fine edge and varying in size from a sixteenth to a half inch in diameter. In this manner, he dislodged flake after flake, applying pressure at adjacent points and turning the piece from side to side, establishing the basic outline of the weapon.

As the work progressed, the first large flakes gave way to smaller and smaller ones, the opposite faces being alternately worked and a sharp eye kept for nicety of form and for taking advantage of the natural shape whenever possible. As the arrow or spear head developed under his hand into a graceful acute angle, he changed to a finer flaking tool so that in the finishing and notching, he would not break off the stem and so ruin it.

If, as occasionally happened, a small piece of glass flew into one of his eyes during the flaking, Ishi at once pulled down the lower lid of the eye with his left forefinger, while, with the right hand he slapped himself vigorously on the top of the head. This method seemed to dislodge the glass fragment. To finish an arrow point he went back over its edge again and again until the once smooth cutting lines were finely serrated, becoming sharper and sharper, the direction of flaking being from point to base.

He made arrow and spear points of different sizes and proportions, depending upon the game which they were intended to bring down, but they were always at the extreme of delicacy and sharpness for their particular size and purpose. Ishi completed the flaking and notching of one usually in about thirty minutes. He admitted that it was fatiguing work. The rapid, low click click of falling flakes is best accomplished with no change in position and with a regularly maintained rhythm; and it is exacting work, so much pressure, no more, no less, to give the symmetrical elegance desired, with only enough of a quick turn of the wrist of the flaking hand to insure an ever more finely and sharply serrated edge. (Among the illustrations are several showing Ishi at work, his tools, and his finished arrow points.)

The fire drill is ancestor not only to the flint and steel method of fire making, and to matches, but to all the many seemingly simple but tricky devices by which man has bedeviled and aided his fellow men with invention after invention. Waterman, instructed and aided by an amused Ishi, actually "made fire" in Ishi's drill. Enthusiastic as always, he announced to his class in Berkeley that no one, man or woman, who could not repeat his success need expect a passing grade in a course with him. Then, brashly, he undertook to demonstrate before his interested and ultimately applauding audience in the old chemistry lecture hall on the campus, how it was to be done. Ishi was not there, and the operation did not go so well without him. Waterman's own temperature rose, he removed coat and vest, working with a will, but a tantalizing thin wisp of smoke was his only reward. The new course requirement died as did the unborn spark at the bottom of Ishi's fire drill.

There persists the hopeful myth about rubbing two sticks together and so "making sparks." No fire was ever made so. There also is the belief that the secret of fire making rests within the peculiar qualities of certain kinds of wood. The facts of fire making with a drill are at once simpler than the fantasy and more inexorable. No manufactured object could be less complicated than Ishi's fire drill, which consists of a lower and an upper piece: a woman piece and a man piece, as he symbolized them. The hearth or lower piece is a flat slab of wood which should be somewhat softer than the wood of the shaft or twirler. Willow or cedar make good hearths, if seasoned and dry and not too old and brittle. One or more sockets are bored or gouged out with an obsidian knife to the depth of a quarter inch or so, and notched at one side. The notch leads into a shallow channel cut from the socket to the edge of the hearth.

The drill, or upper piece, is an ordinary round stick of a size to fit the hearth socket, about the length of an arrow shaft, but larger at one end. Ishi preferred buckeye for his drills, but sage brush, poison oak, or indeed any fairly hard wood will answer equally well. The making of fire with this drill rests upon the principle of concentration in one small spot, for only so can the human arm twirl fast and long enough to produce sufficient friction between hearth and drill to convert moving wood into heat.

When ready to begin drilling, Ishi first strewed tinder—usually dried moss, or thistledown, or finely shredded inner bark of willow—along the notch and channel of the hearth and on the ground where the channel led off the board. He then squatted, holding the ends of the hearth steady against the ground with his toes, or he might occasionally kneel on the hearth to hold it.

Next, he placed the drill upright, the larger end in one of the sockets, grasped it between the palms of his open hands as they were pressed together and then rubbed back and forth in opposite directions. With each motion the drill was forced to rotate, first to right, then to left. His hands at the same time were bearing downward, pressing the revolving stick into the socket. Small particles of wood were ground off the sides of the socket, becoming fine sawdust or wood powder which began to turn brown, to smoke a little, to turn darker and darker to charcoal, and to smoke in good earnest, at the same time being forced by the accumulating mass out of the socket into the notch, along the channel, and so off the edge of the hearth. Ishi, at this point, worked faster and faster as he approached his goal, keeping the stick twirling furiously until a tiny spark suddenly glowed within the charred and powdered wood. The effective spark formed, not in the bottom of the socket where it would be quenched by an excess of wood dust, but just outside, in the notch, from whence it traveled, spreading down the channel and onto the pile of tinder on the ground. Once this was alight, he added a small bunch of grass to it, and some coarser shavings; he blew gently on the young flame, and fire was "made."

Considerable strength and much skill are needed to achieve this result, however. The drill must be firmly and continuously pressed into the hearth—strength and coördination are both needed for this. On the other hand, too heavy a pressure at the outset will exhaust the operator's strength, so that when the crucial moment comes and the spark is nearly at hand, there is no reserve for the added push. Also, as the hands bear down on the drill, they gradually slip downward along it, until, just before the hearth is touched by them, the palms must be quickly raised to the upper end of the stick. The drill actually stands still at this time, which means that the change of hand position must be done so deftly and rapidly that the heated contact point does not cool. If the hands are shifted as the spark is about to appear, the moment of no motion may prove disastrous. This is probably what happened when Waterman attempted to demonstrate the drill.

The whole process calls for manual tact of a kind that only experience can teach. The fire must be coaxed out of the unwilling wood—coaxed and nursed. Haste, violence of motion rather than strength, continuity and rhythm will accomplish nothing, nor will indifference, lassitude, or a moment's let-up. Ishi's patience, perseverance, and delicate control were precisely the requisite qualities.

Could Ishi, overtaken away from his hut by a heavy rain, have made a fire to shelter himself? Without his drill it is scarcely possible. Wet trees and dripping branches will not twirl into fire any more than soaked matches will strike. Under the shelter of an overhanging rock he might have succeeded in whittling dry suitable pieces out of the heart of a tree. But since he actually lived in the wilderness, this was probably rarely if ever necessary, for as the careful hunter keeps his matches dry in a strip of oilskin, Ishi, when traveling in rainy weather, carried his drill and tinder protected in a covering of buckskin, dry and ready for use the moment shelter was reached.

It has seemed worthwhile to describe in some detail how Ishi worked flint and obsidian and used the fire drill, since these are crafts no longer practiced, except by an occasional archaeologist who trains himself to one of them, to prove that he, too, can do it, or to demonstrate to himself how, precisely, it was done. It is a motivation similar to that of the textile expert who will usually not offer a definitive analysis of a prehistoric textile until he can himself repeat and demonstrate its weave and stitch.

Ishi fished much as did other Stone Age peoples. Unlike shooting with the bow and arrow, which in the modern world has been declassed to the status of a game, men fish today with tackle and technique unchanged in their essentials since Stone Age times. The weir, seine, fish hook, line, rod, and harpoon are of immemorial antiquity. Ishi's mode of fishing followed the pattern of river and creek fishing wherever salmon run. He knew how to use fish poison, the weir, the seine, and net, but he abjured their use because they were visible evidence to others, or left traces. He took trout and small fish with a hair snare, or with a hook, and he may have used a dip net. For salmon, he used the conventional salmon harpoon, a thrusting not a throwing weapon, double-pronged, the prongs made of bone or horn and carrying detachable "horned" toggles, with a length of attached line for playing the fish.

Ishi, like all expert wielders of the harpoon, sometimes used it as though it were a spear. His quiver, for example, which is in the museum, is made from the whole skin of an otter; the head has four holes, indicating where the prong points entered, went through, and emerged. Ishi preferred to harpoon from a rock in midstream; he saw clearly down into the water there, and was poised for a surer thrust than was possible from the creek bank.

A fisherman today, fishing along Mill or Deer creeks will have lines of nylon, toggles of steel, and complex flies; but he could without serious disadvantagement, exchange his own for Ishi's fishing kit, and come in with a good day's catch (carried in one of Ishi's baskets), as Ishi could have used modern tackle with a minimum of instruction. Perhaps creek and river continue to draw young and old to their quiet pools to fish because it is restful and healing to reënact an age old craft. No other occupation or activity today brings modern man so close to his Stone Age ancestors.

By contrast, Ishi the hunter, and modern man the hunter, shared neither weapons, techniques, nor attitudes. Modern man hunts for sport, and he is wasteful of the game he takes, his need being not for the animal which he has killed, but to engage briefly and violently in the act of killing. Ishi hunted to live, used each hock and hair of the animal he killed, and lived in proximity to, and knowledge of, all animal life. American Indian mythology which has it that people were animals before they were people, recognizes, in however literalistic a fashion, man's biological continuity with all animal life, a system of belief which precludes the taking of life except with respect for it in the taking.

An archer may be expected to shoot well, or at least with some control of technique, and to be aware at once of the importance of form, and of any shortcomings in his performance, for the bow is not a weapon which lends itself to use by the careless and the ignorant as does its modern replacement, the gun. At some period in history the bow has been the weapon of war and the chase on all continents and inhabited islands of the world excepting only Australia and the Archipelago of Polynesia. There have been specializations of form, material, method of holding, and of arrow release, but everywhere mastery of the bow has been regarded as an art, difficult, honorable, and rewarding. And everywhere and in all eras its manufacture and use have been hedged about with protocol and taboo beyond the formality and etiquette necessary to the proper practice of archery.

So it was with Ishi and the Yahi. Ishi's friends in the museum learned from him to shoot his bow, and observed how he made bows and arrows; and they hunted with him. Ishi was a formidable hunter: he decoyed his game, coaxing it ever nearer, operating always at close quarters and with endless patience and resourcefulness. It was as hunter that Ishi was wholly the skilled artisan and artist. In the museum Ishi, falling in with the spirit of scientific experimentation, made and tested bows of many kinds of wood. But the bows by which he lived were made of mountain juniper. He chose first the tree, and then the branch from which a new bow should come. After this considered choice, the branch was cut off and the bow roughly blocked out. Even in this semi-emerged state the bow was possessed of a face and a back, and was so placed whether lying or standing as to respect these separate parts or properties: the face was the top of the bow and was at that end of the branch which had been closest to the mother trunk in life; the sapwood was always at the back of the bow.

Ishi fashioned a bow to the person who was to shoot it: there must be a certain proportion between the height of the archer and the length of his bow, and between the size of his hand and the thickness of his bow. The bow's length was the distance from the right hip joint to the left finger tips, measured with the person standing erect and extending the left arm forward in a straight line from the shoulder—a distance of four feet and two inches for Ishi. The greatest width and thickness of the bow is at either side of the hand grip. The width should be that of four fingers for a powerful bow; three fingers for a light hunting bow.

To participate in the cycle of manufacture of a bow as Ishi made it was to journey back into Neolithic human history with Yahi overtones. Once blocked out, the bow-to-be was placed for seasoning where it would be constantly warm and damp. During this time it lay horizontally face up, the top of the bow at the head of its bed. Indeed, the bow was laid, carried, and shot face up—else the arrow would not go true to its mark. For making the bow proper, the whole array of flint and obsidian knives and scrapers in Ishi's tool cache, was used. The final finishing was done with sandstone. Ishi's bows have an elegantly recurved line at the ends of the limbs. So symmetrical are they that it is surprising to learn how simply he achieved these curves: first, by working the end to be recurved back and forth over a heated stone until the wood was pliable, then by pressing it against the curve of his bent knee, protected with a pad of buckskin, and holding it there with a steady pressure until the wood was entirely cool, by which time the curve was "fixed."

To get the sinew needed for backing and for the bowstring itself, Ishi stripped the long tendons from the hind legs and the finer tendons from the shanks of deer. To "tease" these out, soak, chew, and work them was a tortuously slow process. When ready for use the long tendons had become flat parchment-like strips, thin and even, which were glued to the back of the bow, strip after strip to build up the bow's resilience and strength; the glue was obtained by boiling salmon skin. The smaller shank tendons

Ishi shredded by pulling them through and through his teeth until they were of the fineness of silk thread, which he then spun into a continuous string.

Before the bow was strung, it was again laid carefully in the sun and allowed to season for days or weeks. Then came the final smoothing and finishing, and the stringing.

To string the bow, the first fastening was made around the nock of the face or upper limb. Here is Pope's description of how Ishi did the actual bracing: "He [Ishi], seated himself, placing the upper nock behind his left heel, the belly [of the bow] toward him, the handle against his right knee, the lower limb upward in his left hand. In this position he bent the bow and fastened the string about the nock" [of the lower limb]. When all parts were in correct relation: length, thickness, and backing, Ishi's bow at full draw described a perfect arc—Ishi's ideal—and when drawn to twenty-five inches pulled or "weighed" forty pounds.

Although Ishi usually was content to wrap his bow in a piece of buckskin for a covering, he considered a mountain lion tail the truly correct bow cover. He was particular that when his bow was not in use it should lie and not stand. Standing, it continued to work, to sweat, and to become weak. Ishi's way of testing whether or not a bow was in good health and strength was to snap its string with his fingers: a healthy bow responded by giving a high, musical note. If the note was dull or dead in tone, the bow was no good, or it had been contaminated. Perhaps a woman had touched it. Ishi would lightly snap the string of his bow; the musical note would follow; then he might put the bow to his lips, and tapping the string, coax from it a plaintive melodious song to accompany an old Yahi tale. He loved his bow as he loved nothing else he owned.

He preferred the thin, straight stems of hazel to other wood for arrow shafts. As when making a bow, the arrows also were seasoned lying face up. It was Ishi's custom to make arrows in groups of five—five were carried through the various steps of manufacture together, and only when they were completed and laid aside to season, might another five be commenced. The hazel stick which was to become an arrow was first peeled of its bark, then any irregularities were straightened by the process of rolling over heated stones, after which it was smoothed with sandstone, and given a final polishing by rolling back and forth across the thigh, a technique reminiscent of the hand polishing of fine furniture in which the body oil contributes its finish, applied by hand friction. Arrows were made to measure—the distance from the base of the breast bone to the extended index finger with the left arm stretched along the arrow shaft in shooting position—twenty-nine inches for Ishi.

Some, although by no means all, of Ishi's arrows were made with a foreshaft of heavier wood, about eight inches long. In order to fit the two parts of such an arrow together, Ishi used a piece of bone ground to a sharp point which he placed upright on the earth and held in position with his feet. Onto this he set the main shaft, perpendicularly, rotating it between the open palms of his hands until a tapered hole an inch or more in depth had been drilled out. He then cut a spindle at the end of the fore-shaft to fit the hole, and secured it in the hole with resin or glue.

Although Ishi usually painted his arrows using a simple two-color ring design, much less interest attached to decorating than to feathering them. The preferred feathers were eagle, but he used buzzard, blue jay, and others. He mounted the feathers in sets of three, each set from a single wing—a custom generally observed by good bowmen everywhere. The angle of feathers to shaft affects the flight of an arrow. Ishi feathered at an angle of less than ninety degrees, that is, he mounted the feathers so that they leaned sideways away from the perpendicular, which is the more usual angle. The result in flight was that his arrows left the bow with a better spin and greater accuracy at close range, which was what he wanted, not the greater speed and distance which his method sacrificed.

The quiver which Ishi used until it was taken from Wowunupo the day of the dispersal is now in the museum. It is made of a whole otter skin, fur outside, and is large enough to carry Ishi's bow as well as arrows. He wore it slung over the left shoulder, hanging down his back.

Wearing only a buckskin breechclout, bow and arrows in the quiver on his back, Ishi would set off from camp or village to hunt. He moved noiselessly through the brush until he came to a likely looking clearing. Here he might stop, take his bow from the quiver, test the string and readjust the bracing if that was needed to have it ready for use, and tuck several arrows into his right armpit where they would not interfere with shooting, but would be instantly available. If he smelled or heard any game closeby, he waited concealed from full view by rocks or a bush. He would wait for hours if need be, his principle being not to look for surer or bigger game, but rather never to give up a prospect once sighted or suspected. As a hunter it was his business to be aware of the presence of an animal before that animal was alerted to him. Sight, hearing, smell, all his senses seemed to contribute to this initial advantage of spotting an unsuspecting quarry.

Perhaps it was a rabbit he had seen or smelled. If so, he would remain hidden, but make a kissing sound with two fingers pressed against his lips: the soft, plaintive cry of a rabbit in distress. While the inevitable rabbits drew near in response to this call, it was well for the hidden hunter to be prepared for more exciting game. A wildcat, mountain lion, coyote, or bear might also respond to this apparent invitation to an easy kill. In Ishi's repertory were also the different quail calls, the gray squirrel's squeak, the honk of wild geese, and many other bird and animal voices. He sometimes shot small game and birds from very nearby—a rabbit at five yards—or from as far away as forty yards. He shot birds in flight and animals running, but he preferred the still shot at close range. Because he was careful at all times to stay downwind from his prey, and because the bow is a silent weapon, animals were not alarmed even by an arrow which narrowly missed them.

He lured them to him through rousing either their curiosity or their concern by means of his imitations, making sitting targets of them. The extent of simple curiosity in birds and mammals, which primitive hunters exploit to their profit, is not available to the hunter of gun-shy game—the explosion of a gun introduces a terror which paralyzes other reactions and emotions. Ishi, or any solitary hunter with the bow, brings no seeming strangeness to the forest scene, being himself an enemy within the usual animal understanding of the concept, as is the skunk to the quail, the coyote to the rabbit, or the mountain lion to the deer.

Ishi took no aspect of hunting lightly, nor did he ever touch his bow except with respect and ceremony. To the hunting of deer was added some further measure of formality. Ishi ate no fish and used no tobacco during the day and night preceding a deer hunt, extending the time of abstention to three days and nights if that were at all possible. In a Yahi village, there would have been added sexual abstentions, of course. On the morning of the hunt, he bathed—in his old home he would have sweated himself—washed out his mouth carefully, and went on his way without eating: he would eat only after the hunt at the end of the day. Up and down his arms and legs he would have made fresh, shallow scarifications, with a sharp chip of obsidian, to strengthen his limbs. Through all the ceremonial preparation run two strains: the practical, which seeks to reduce to a minimum the special odors attaching to man so that the game will not suspect his presence; and the magico-moral, which seeks to channel the libido totally toward the hunt.

Whether he hunted in company or alone, Ishi preferred the tactic of lure and ambush to that of stalking or the chase. Crouched behind an artificially made cairn of rocks or behind or within a clump of bush close to where he had smelled or sighted or suspected the presence of deer, he would wait. He might imitate the whimper of a faun by sucking on a madrone leaf folded between his lips. This was sure to bring out one or several does, uneasy for the safety of their young. Or he might put over his own head a stuffed deer's head, usually with antlers attached. Showing only the head over the top of rocks or bush, he would move it about, cock it, simulate the nibbling of a leaf, and toss it. This device would bring a fullgrown doe or buck deer within a few yards of him. Whether the deer believed the decoy to be really one of their own species, or whether they regarded it as a strange and new forest creature, it is not possible to say with certainty. They were in any case curious and interested, wary, but not afraid. They might let an arrow or two whizz past; Ishi could expect to have opportunity to get the range and make a perfect hit before the deer, one or several, took alarm.

A grizzly bear is not game that a lone man armed with only bow and arrow seeks out. The Yahi hunted a grizzly if it was hibernating and only if there were several men together, enough to surround it with a circle of burning brush before it was fully awake. Even so, the shooting to be effective had to be close range. They shot into the open mouth if possible; small, sharp-penetrating points were the most likely to induce hemorrhaging. If a bear charged, a man tried to defend himself with a firebrand while his companions closed in with their bows and arrows. A grizzly bear hunt, whether the hunters were Yahi or white, seems from most descriptions to have been like a bull fight in that the kill comes only after the bear has been weakened through fatigue and loss of blood. Ishi killed single-handed at least one cinnamon bear—which is also the black or small bear of the West. He did not talk much about how he did it, but it was clear that he had been charged by the bear. Fortunately, before it closed with him, he had had time to get in one shot which penetrated the heart region. For the *coup de grâce* he used a short obsidian-bladed spear of the kind which he ordinarily carried hung handily on his belt or tucked into his breechclout. The skin of Ishi's bear helped to keep him and his companions warm in Wowunupo until the looting of the village; curiously, after some years, the same skin was given to the museum.

For the toxophilist the most interesting thing about Ishi is his shooting of the bow. An archer today knows the classic shooting stances, the different kinds of bows, and the historic methods of arrow release. These are technical matters, understood within the difficult language of a special vocabulary. The pictures of Ishi shooting his bow are more graphic of his method of handling bow and arrow than are words to the uninitiate. Briefly, the peculiarities of Ishi's shooting were, first, that he preferred to

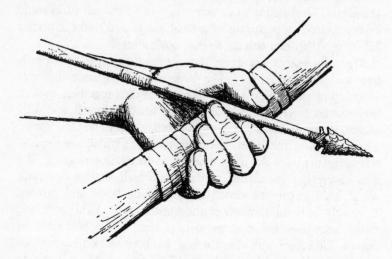

shoot from a crouching position. This was a matter of tribal custom and tied to the particular hunting practice of the Yana: a hunter, hidden and crouching behind scant cover, could scarcely hope to make a kill after luring game to himself if he then had to stand up before he could shoot. The crouch was not a cramped or disadvantageous position for shooting a bow no larger than Ishi's when held as he held it—diagonally across the front of the body, the face of the bow higher than the other limb and to the left. We might say that Ishi shot from the hip because of the bow position. Actually the string was drawn at cheek level.

Besides the characteristic crouch and hold, another unusual feature of Ishi's shooting was that at the instant of the arrow's release, the fingers relaxed, allowing the bow to revolve in his hand, until it turned over completely. To achieve this turn requires a steady hold so that the bow does not escape the hand, and a light touch, so that the revolution of the bow is not impeded. The rhythm of motion involved is comparable to the smooth and full follow-through of stroke after a tennis ball has been hit, or the completion of the arc described by a golf club and the motion of the pivot foot in a controlled but fully finished stroke.

Ishi's method of arrow release had this intriguing peculiarity: it was different from any previously described release, and remains to this day the only one of its kind to be found either in toxophilic or ethnographic literature. It was a seemingly Yahi, or rather a Yana, variant of the Mongolian or Asiatic release, which is one of the five great classes of arrow releases for the world, but one never otherwise reported for native America. The Mongolian release is expectably used for shooting the composite bow with the aid of a thumb ring, since it is the flexed thumb which accomplishes the pull, the fingers being used only to guide and support the arrow. Ishi used no thumb guard or ring, and his bow was a simple, not a composite one. His thumb became sore and swollen with prolonged target practice, but never in the course of hunting. Ishi drew the bow with the flexed right thumb as in the classic Mongolian release. The Yana variation was in one finger position: the tip of the middle finger was placed lightly against the thumbnail to steady and strengthen its hold.

The question is, how did it happen that the Yana shot their simple bow differently from all other bowmen, and that their arrow release, alone in America, is a variant of the Mongolian release? We do not know the answer. It could be that when Ishi's ancestors started on their long forgotten migratory wanderings out of Asia, they took with them the simple bow which they had become accustomed to shoot as Ishi shot his bow; and that this was in a time before the composite bow and the thumb ring had yet been invented. Such historical reconstruction carries us back into prehistory, and to a dry land crossing from Asia to America. It is speculation, admittedly, but it points toward the same presumptions of ancientness which cling to much that we know of the Yana and that an analysis of Ishi's language also suggests, as we have seen.

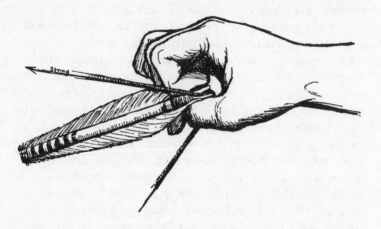

We *know* the history of the Yana only at that last moment before its extinction, when it was become meagre and flickering. Perhaps the ancestral Yana were amongst the early arrivals on the new continent, and for them there was a world of discovery and variety, of hope and expanding horizons.

Ishi was a storyteller as well as a craftsman. Pope recalled that Ishi had, one time or another when they were together, told him some forty distinct tales, recalled from the body of oral literature, story, and myth of the Yana people. Unfortunately Pope did not record any of these tales except for discrete items of native Yana custom or belief as they might have reference to whatever he and Ishi had been doing at the time. Whatever Yahi language Waterman, Kroeber, and Sapir wrote phonetically from Ishi's dictation, or took on phonograph records looked first to vocabulary and grammar and is contained in the recently published *Yana Dictionary*.

We have a single fragment of a story from one of Waterman's notebooks that is indubitably in Ishi's own words, a story about Wood Duck Man.

Wood Duck Man, so Ishi told Waterman, was a young man, a man of substance, a great hunter so successful that the sun might rise, pass over the Sky World and lower toward the west while Wood Duck lay at ease on his rabbitskin pallet. He was unmarried but well served; his two sisters who lived with him obeyed his every wish and order. He hunted, he sang; and he remarked truly, "I believe many young women are talking about me, and thinking that they would like to marry me." To his sisters he said, "Be sure to fill with deer meat and salmon meat the baskets of all the young women who come to visit at my house."

Wood Duck Man was the dallying, not the marrying sort. As he had predicted, a series of eligible young women came to visit him, to display their charms, to spend a longer or a shorter time with him, depending upon his wishes. All were sent away—but always with full baskets.

Waterdog Woman came, and Waterbug Woman; Bat Woman, Fishhook Woman, and Chipmunk Woman and Shikepoke Woman. There were as well Flint Woman and Rainbow Woman and Mussel Woman and Abalone Woman. Her host complained of Fox Woman that she looked as if she had no eyes; of Skunk Woman that she was too smelly. Mountain Quail Woman was invited to sit down and make herself comfortable, but she too was sent home after a while.

Brown Bear Woman brought sweet-smelling herbs and roots, but even so, she was dismissed. Dentalium Woman was more determined. During the time she was with Duck Man the whole house shook and rang with their struggle, but he was able at last to throw her out.

Magnesite Woman was given beads as well as the usual deer and salmon meat. And to Morning Star Woman were given beads and abalone shell ornaments and food. Duck Man must have been greatly tempted by Morning Star.

Duck Man called to his sisters to take Blue Crane Woman away, but only after it was full daylight. [!] Of Beaver Woman he said, "Take her away. She talks Wintun." Turtle Woman fared no better than the others, but she was rather special in that she wore a skirt made of elkhide and came from the *Affiliated Colleges!*

This is probably only a fragment of the full story of Wood Duck Man and his amorous adventures. Ishi may have chosen to tell it to amuse his friend Watamany as a tale whose motivation would not tax too heavily the language barrier between them. The time of its telling was during the first weeks of Ishi's and Waterman's acquaintance, while Batwi was still at the museum. Waterman's notes give alternative forms for some of the words: Batwi's Central Yana, and Ishi's Yahi. It is a man's wish-fulfillment tale, the kind to be told to while away a long evening in the men's house when nothing serious was afoot. It would lend itself to adumbration or elaboration and change, accommodating its content to the imagination and mood of the teller and his audience. It retains, through the mutilation of translation, some faint suggestion of Ishi's delight in absurdity and *double entendre,* for, under Yana sex code, Wood Duck's behavior is the height of humorous exaggeration, suggesting perhaps *Innocents Abroad* in our literature. Like Mark Twain also, and unlike the endless and primitive Coyote story cycles, Wood Duck is neither monotonous nor scatological. He is, however, very Yana. Not for a moment does he equate Skunk Woman and Morning Star; and Dentalium Woman was so aggressive and unfeminine precisely because she was not a Yana woman. Dentalium was wealth, which meant power and the habit of having or getting one's way, but Yana country was without dentalium, and all that its people possessed was come by sparingly through trade with outsiders.

Turtle Woman, too, was an outlander, but an important one, and her skirt was of elkhide and her home at the Colleges, because Turtle had participated directly in the creation of the world of the Maidu, next-door neighbors to the Yahi.

The following three stories are also very Yana. They are in Sapir's *Yana Texts,* in Yana with interlinear translation as told to Sapir by Betty Brown. Departures from Sapir's englishing of the texts, as from Waterman's for Wood Duck, are limited to making the stories readily intelligible and to expressing them in language as idiomatic in its English as it was in the original Yana. They are included to offer some faint suggestion of the range of feeling and the imagery within the body of oral literature which was Ishi's heritage.

A DEATH

The husband and the wife were young, without experience. The wife was several moons along in her first pregnancy. She was not well, and both she and her husband were frightened. The husband spoke thus to a friend, saying of his wife, "She is going to have a child. She is not well. All day she cries, 'Go and bring my mother to me.' Wait by my wife, will you, while I go fetch my mother-in-law."

The wife's mother came to the young people's home. The husband told her, "I am afraid. I do not go out to hunt. I stay always at home, yet she keeps saying, 'You must not go away from me.' Also I fear that she eats too much, causing the child in her womb to grow large, and thus making the birth difficult."

"You are right," his mother-in-law answered him. "It seems as though she never listens to what I tell her. I say, 'Do not look back when you go outside. This is bad for your child. Do not eat too much,' I say, 'your child will grow too quickly.'" But the remonstrances of her husband and her mother merely made the young wife cry. "You should not keep on saying these words. I have no pains in my back," was all the answer she made.

It came time for her baby to be born. She said, "I am

sick." But four risings and settings of the sun occurred, and still the baby would not come.

The doctor was sent for. To him the girl's mother said, "I can do nothing more. I am exhausted and good for nothing. She never believes what I say. Young girls do not know anything. They must learn from the experience of the old. But this one here will not listen to me."

The doctor came, but he was reluctant to do anything. He said, "What use, pray, am I? I do not know how to treat such cases. *Hehé!* What to do with her! She is very dry—that much I see. Do you women press upon her belly gently to help her. I am afraid of this illness. I can only advise, I cannot treat it."

"Please give me water, water to drink," the young patient cried.

Said the doctor, "Let us try one more thing. Give her strong sticks to support her so she can get to her feet. So—now go all the way around the house."

"Alas! I shall die!" said the sick woman.

"Do as the doctor says," her mother said. "Do not be afraid. You must learn to do what you are told."

Weak as she was, the wife ran once and then a second time all the way around the earth-covered house. It was not yet daylight, and a fox barked as she ran—a bad omen. She collapsed against the supporting sticks.

"Oh, what have I done, what have I done to you, my daughter," the mother wailed, while the husband wandered off into the woods, weeping.

His mother-in-law called to him, "Go quickly! Up the mountain! Make a fire of spruce twigs and pine needles. Run all the way. And pray to the sacred fire." This is what a father does each day at dawn when his wife is about to give birth. And repeating the ancient, oft-used ritual, this young husband felt hopeful and joyful and was reassured that all would be well with his family when he went home. All day he gathered wood, kept up the sacred fire, ran, and prayed.

At midnight, he returned to his home. "The baby has come? My wife is well?" he asked his mother-in-law softly.

But the fox had spoken truly. The young wife was gasping for breath, her baby unborn. And so she died.

A YANA CURSE

Suwa! Se'galt! maya! May you make me happy!

May you have happen to yourself
That curse which you put on me!
May you die without warning sickness—
You who drank my blood.
May you and all who are dear to you perish!

Drink my blood!
May I not be sick!
May I know happiness! *Suwa!*

A MARRIAGE

The girl's mother was a widow. She found it hard to feed and care for the many needs of her children and the old ones who were dependent upon her. When a young man of the next village to hers, a man of good character and a good hunter, brought food and other gifts to her house indicating that he wished to marry her daughter, the mother was much pleased and relieved.

But her daughter, as is often the way of the young and pretty, acted coy and indifferent, saying to her suitor plainly, "I do not love you." For once, the mother showed impatience and distress. She said to the girl, "I like that young man. I wish him to become my son-in-law. Take him for your husband, else you shall not enter this house again!"

The girl wanted, really, to be urged, to be talked to in this way. The next time the young man spoke with her alone she said, "I love you very much. Let us go together, and tomorrow, if you like, we could be married. All your people must come here to visit us and stay the night, too. This I would like. However, I cannot say how my mother feels. Perhaps, who knows, she will be content to have you for a son-in-law?"

When the girl told her mother she had promised to marry the young man, her mother said, "I am glad. I am weary of finding food for all of you. When you are married, you shall go home with your husband and keep house for him, and after a while there will be one grandchild and soon another. Then, truly, I shall come to you in your home, and your husband will come to us in our home. If I am hungry, you will give me food. And as for me—when your husband brings down a deer, it is I who shall help to fetch it home. And when he spears salmon, it is I who shall help to fetch them home. Do you and your husband give food to me and my household, and I will pound acorns for you and come loaded with them to your home, and you will feel rejoiced, my daughter! When you see me coming, laden, you will feel rejoiced and you will in turn give freely to your own people. You are a good girl and your husband is a good man. There will be satisfaction and happiness between the households."

The young man said to his wife-to-be, "I will hunt and bring you much food and many hides that you may have a buckskin skirt and a rabbitskin blanket and full baskets of food. Nor shall I ever strike you or be rough to you. And I ask that you for your part use care that you do not become a scold as sometimes happens to a woman once she is married."

And the girl said to her husband-to-be, "Stay now with me in my house. When I have borne our first child, then we shall go to your home." The young man answered her, "Yes, I will stay in your house. But now, I must go hunting."

She looked at him dreamily, saying, "You and I shall grow old together. And at the last—I wonder—will it be I who dies first—or will it be you?"

Chapter 10
THE BRIGHTEST YEAR

The year was 1914. Spring was in the air, seeping through the windows into the museum workrooms and the classrooms of the Kuwi's house next door. Ishi's three friends were restless, the semester was nearing its close, the urge was to be out and away. But where? Somewhere together, and with Ishi, and where better than back to Yahi country, to Mill Creek and Deer Creek? Watamany, Popey, and the Chiep thought this a fine idea, and one sure to please Ishi. Ishi was less than enthusiastic when they asked him if he would like to go. Too many people had asked that question too often. He tried to reason with his friends: there were no houses on Mill Creek, no chairs, no beds, no food; it was cold and uncomfortable. How would they get into the cañons? There were no trails, and it was a long way from the train. Their answer was that they wished to be away from houses and chairs, that they would take blankets and food, and would hire horses to carry men and baggage. This last idea did not make the trip any more attractive to Ishi. True, he dreamed of owning a horse and wagon, but his actual experience of a horse had been as an animal to be brought down with bow and arrow, butchered, cooked, and eaten when hunger and the scarcity of deer and salmon had forced him to it. The idea of riding a horse was terrifying to him. But his three friends brushed aside all objections. Since they had set their hearts on going, he acquiesced, confiding to Worbinna in the museum, "That treep, a crazy aunatee treep!" He shook his head, he shrugged his eyebrows. Resigned to his friends' madness he was, but very, very unhappy.

It was not that he feared he might be left behind in his old home to resume the lonely vigil which his life there had become, for the Chiep had told him his home was, henceforth, the museum, and the Chiep never said untrue words. But—to go back! It would be like going to visit the Land of the Dead. The unquiet souls of his murdered people lingered there, some of them. To revisit Wowunupo mu tetna where the engineers had surprised him would be to relive the terrible fright, and his sister's flight in one direction and his own in another, never to find trace of her after that day. He would have much preferred not to go, but he made no further objection, merely protesting one gratuitous risk in getting ready such a dubious expedition. The cooking utensils, blankets, tools, and gear for the trip were collected from Popey's home, from Berkeley, and from the museum, packed, and then stored against departure in the old-bones room of the museum. To put them there, of all places, was to invite trouble, as Ishi told Popey plainly. The outraged spirits of those desecrated bones would enter the gear and food, making the trip trebly hazardous. Popey listened. He pointed out to Ishi that he was aware of this risk and had already taken measures against it. Each article was tightly sealed in a can, or was enclosed and buckled or locked in a case or bag; his, the Kuwi's, magic was strong against any spirit's breaking or opening locks or seals or buckles. The Kuwi's magic was potent; Ishi could only hope potent enough to keep the contamination of that room, into which he himself never went, from penetrating the seals and buckles.

He packed his own best bows and quivers and arrows, his fire drill, his harpoon—tools made with loving care in the museum, and demonstrated there with pride. He was accustomed to seeing them on exhibit in museum cases, to having people look at them behind glass, but he had not thought he would be using them seriously, nor that he would be showing his new friends his old home. The smell of the pines on the slopes of Waganupa, the taste of fresh salmon and deer, the feel of the cañon trails against bare feet, filled his senses, nostalgic, sweet, familiar. To breast again the rapids of Deer Creek! To thrust a spear, to aim a bow, not for an audience or for "sport," but to get food for himself and his companions! The old memories flooded in, confounding doubt and fear with desire until by the time of departure, Ishi was the most excited member of the party.

Before Ishi's deer could be brought down, there were authorizations required; such as the somewhat unusual *permiso* from the Fish and Game Commission which reads:

> To whom it may concern: In accordance with law permission is hereby granted to the Department of Anthropology of the University of California, acting through and by its agents, Dr. A. L. Kroeber, Dr. T. T. Waterman and Dr. S. T. Pope, to take for scientific purposes one male deer at any time and in such manner as the gentlemen mentioned above may select. This permit also authorizes the transportation and possession of such deer as may be killed under its authority and its subsequent use or exhibition. In the event of shipment, this permit must accompany the animal or its parts and will exempt it from seizure in this state. By Order of the Board.

The trip was also cleared through the University. A memorandum from Waterman to Kroeber hints at the far from frivolous reasons there were for pressing Ishi to make the trip, and throws an oblique but bright light on the personalities of the party. Waterman says,

> I think the three of us, working in cordial cooperation for a summer could do the ethnography, ethnobotany, ethnogeography and ethno-everything else of the Southern Yana [Yahi] up brown. [Then, speaking of Pope,] A Doctor and an instructor in surgery is after all no fool, if he does take up archery. I feel that this man [Pope] is made to order for us. I'd like to milk him dry. He could get Ishi's names for plants a great deal better than I could. He knows more about it and would probably have more industry. He could pick up such information without fatiguing Ishi. You can't lure the man with funds. His time is worth $2.50 per twenty

minutes for office calls, if he wants to earn money. I think the chance to shoot a deer with bow and arrow in aboriginal company and the opportunity to publish are the only bait we have for him. To preserve my standing with Ishi I should like to get him over to Berkeley a good bit this spring, and get to be able to talk with him. I will try to make some plans to have him at my house. [Lengthy reference to Pope.] When I said Pope understands Ishi I meant emotionally, not necessarily linguistically. He has made firm friends with Ishi and they understand each other in that sense. They've got a good bit in common . . .

Came the month of May, and the Yahi expedition got under way. It included Dr. Pope; his eldest son, Saxton Jr. who was then eleven years old, tall for his age, and with a mop of blond hair; Ishi, moonfaced and round of body, this being the period of his best health and greatest weight, his black hair worn long in Yahi style; and the two professors, one with a somewhat dramatic mustache, the other bearded. Passengers and trainmen alike peered curiously into the drawing room which the expedition occupied. Bow cases, specimen boxes, quivers full of arrows, notebooks, and battered tin cooking pots filled every free space. Two sleeping bags lay opened out on the floor, for there was regular sleeping room for only three people. Ishi looked forward to the train trip this time, being by now a veteran traveler of trolleys and commuting trains. The pullman car was, however, new. He and young Saxton together investigated the pull-down, pull-out, and turn-over beds, the ingenious wall lights, the porter's bell, and the private toilet facilities of the compartment. Ishi chose to sleep in the upper berth; its position and ladder made it the most exotic and interesting of the various possibilities. His friends put their shoes outside the door for polishing. Ishi demurred, saying that he had polished his own shoes before leaving the museum. It was late before lights were out and sleep took over in the crowded compartment. And it was very early next morning when the expedition, loaded with gear, left the train at Vina. As he stepped from the train, Ishi bestowed a twenty-five cent tip on the surprised porter with all the careless aplomb of a traveling salesman.

Vina is situated in the valley, where Deer Creek flows into the Sacramento River. Here they were met by Mr. Apperson whose son had been with Waterman in 1909 on his fruitless search for Ishi and his companions. Apperson was a rancher who knew the Lassen country well, having run stock in the hills for many years. He supplied the saddle and pack animals for the present party and he and his son went along as guides. Richard Gernon, the surveyor quoted earlier in the book, said of Apperson that he "tells a fine tale of this trip" and well he might. If it were possible to recover his version of his month with the Yahi expedition it would no doubt enliven the present somewhat pedestrian account which comes from Pope and the professors to whom there was nothing strange or remarkable in what they did during that May or in how they did it.

The Appersons were cordial to Ishi, genuinely pleased to have him back in his "own" country, Ishi remaining reserved toward them for the first few days. Apperson may never have seen Ishi, or known that it was he who had tried to shoot an arrow into him in 1908, but Ishi had seen him and his son and his herders and cowboys many times, himself hidden; he had almost surely raided his store houses or those of his friends more than once, and perhaps in a desperate hour had killed a sheep, a cow, or a horse belonging to him. Ishi was scrupulous in his honesty and in his respect for other peoples' property. He understood in May, 1914, as he could not have in August, 1911, that as the white man saw it, he and his people had taken what was not theirs to dispose of. He would never forget the robbers and killers, white men, who had wiped his own people from the face of the earth. Their deeds remained incontrovertible, tragic truth, but Ishi had meanwhile learned many other truths concerning white men, their values, and their complex ways. Confronted with the Appersons and other ranchers who "owned" and were living on old Yahi ground, Ishi was inclined at first to expect the worst from them, and with his newly learned sophistication, to feel as well some shame for having himself once robbed and pillaged. It is not in Indian puritanism any more than in Anglo-Saxon, to mitigate one's own guilt because it is less than another's. But the strain and mistrust passed. By temperament, and unlike most Indians, Ishi was the least suspicious of men. He found his old enemies to be of good will and, after the first days, he responded with his own natural friendliness.

At Vina, immediately the pack mules were loaded, Ishi had to make another drastic adjustment, that of riding a horse instead of hunting it. This new relation of rider and horse Ishi left largely to the horse, sitting his mount solidly and stolidly, as remote as a wool sack, his horse choosing whether the gait should be a walk or a jog trot. Leaving the valley, the party single filed into the hills, climbing amongst chaparral and rocks and boulders, and making camp where Sulphur Creek flows into Deer Creek. After some further inspection of the terrain it was decided to make this first stopping place a base camp, since it afforded an open level area of perhaps half an acre lightly timbered, some felled logs from an abandoned homestead, and good pasture for the horses.

Unlike many expeditions, the cooking, cleaning, dish washing, and other camp-policing routines were shared without strains and recriminations. They were experienced campers, all of them, in their separate ways, and they were having a very good time, also in their separate ways. They were in country as lonely and remote as when it was Ishi's country; the sun was benign, the evenings cool enough so that the supper fire might be prolonged into a night campfire. Ishi reverted to his native undress, wearing only a breechclout. His three friends and young Saxton, in romantic unison, also took to undress when in camp. Only Ishi remained entirely modest, wearing his breechclout even when swimming. He must have watched carefully over these unaccustomed wild men, for there seem to have been no outbreaks from poison oak, no cut and bruised feet, no painful sunburn. Perhaps the spirits of the ancient Yahi came to his aid in protecting these clever, good, but foolish friends of his.

They swam daily in the cold stream; they ate meat and fish which the hunters, Popey and Ishi, took with bow and arrow or spear and broiled on forked sticks before an open fire. They sat or lay around the fire singing to Popey's miniature guitar, or if the songs were Yahi, unaccompanied except by the rattle. Ishi taught Saxton Jr. to dance with him the simple stamping step of the Yahi circle dance to the rhythmic clapping of hands supplementing Ishi's song. And they all told stories. The formal stories, if Yahi, could be matched by Watamany and the Chiep with tales from other Indians, and Popey and Ishi and the Appersons could swap yarns of hand-to-hand encounters with bears, of the dangers in bringing down an elk, and of fishing exploits.

This innocent Yahi *fête champêtre* has its own poignant place in the story of a man to whom life alloted no other days of such unclouded enjoyment. His capacity for gaiety was such that it bubbled up given the smallest opening. Ishi was quite literally the life of this party, and it was his own and his only party.

He and Popey failed to get a deer their first day of hunting. Ishi asked reprovingly, "Who smoke?" and invoked a no-smoking ban for two days because the odor of tobacco, a powerful and a sacred substance, clings to the breath and the body and alarms the deer. After two days of this and other properly observed taboos they got their deer, proving Ishi's point.

There was another occasion when matters got badly out of hand. Popey and the Chiep killed a rattlesnake and brought it proudly into camp. This was in itself wrong. One should be wary toward a rattlesnake, careful to step aside from its path or coiling place, leaving it to itself as the best assurance of reciprocation in kind. But, having foolishly killed it, they were compounding foolishness by insisting on cooking it, someone having told them that its flesh was as good as that of frog's legs. The Appersons and young Saxton sided with Ishi in refusing so much as to taste the cooked reptile, their acquiescent silence seconding his prognostications of trouble: in fact, Ishi expected those who had eaten the snake to die.

Rattlesnake proved to be tough and unrewarding fare, but there were no calamitous aftermaths from eating it. This could be explained only by the kuwi's truly strong power, and to Ishi's personal discretion in withdrawing from use the machete with which the rattler had been beheaded and sliced for cooking, as well as the contaminated frying pan in which it had been cooked.

Beyond the nonsense and high spirits, what, precisely, did the expedition do; what did it hope to accomplish? It was hoped that once Ishi was back in his own country, and over the first shock of revived and often terrible memories, he would be willing to take the party step by step over the whole of the intimately familiar, limited area; that they might come to understand and "feel" one Indian's world with something of the accuracy and fullness and intensity which ethnologists know that almost all Indians have felt for their homeland. Non-Indians also, it should perhaps be added, but not most North American whites. Our own Southerners who have this sense for the homeland, as have many New Englanders and occasional individuals elsewhere amongst us, run the risk of being regarded as "odd" and "introverted."

The expedition's hopes were more than fulfilled; Ishi's response was something more and different from anything his white friends could have expected. There were two streams of reaction both partly emotional and partly intellectual which contributed to this full-flooding response. One was the relief and release Ishi experienced in being able to demonstrate a complete reënactment instead of struggling to explain in broken English and half-comprehended Yana such things as the stalking of a deer, its evisceration and skinning, the spearing of a salmon, the techniques of rope climbing up and down perpendicular cañon walls, or of swimming in swift deep waters, and dozens of other everyday routines of Yahi living. The second response arose perhaps from this reliving and redoing of the familiar, but to the familiar an added dimension was born of the sudden comprehension of a sense of history, of the past not as nostalgia but as part of a living future. Through permanent, painstaking record, he, Ishi, and his annihilated tribe should live on. Technology, geography, religion, whatever he knew of the old life, he told to his friends, that the Yahi too should become part of the lengthening, elaborating parade which is the story of mankind.

Each day, something was added to his friends' store of knowledge of life during the concealment. Each day, they went to a new place. They went to the camp where the "smallest nation" was living in 1908 when the surveying party came unexpectedly upon it. This camp was downstream from the base camp no more than two or three miles, but between the two camps intervened the almost impenetrable chaparral of the California foothills. It was a long day's trip there and back, walking or crawling through and under the brush, clearing a way sometimes with machetes. This trip, and others like it, taught them not only how the five survivors had traveled between camps during their last confined years but also why no one had seen them. These trips necessitated crossing and recrossing Deer Creek many times. They used a rope to prevent a single person's being caught by one of the roaring stream's whirlpools and battered against the boulders which are as common to the stream beds there as to the dry land. Where the stream widened and quieted somewhat they swam it, Ishi piloting young Saxton through rough places by having him cling to his long hair.

Place names, the significance of a particular area, the favorite or customary hunting, fishing, and gathering and harvesting places, permanent and temporary living sites, the tiny villages, the caves, the hidden trails, the exact locale of a bear fight, a massacre, a close escape, all these became as real to the white men as they already were to Ishi. Here you swung down on a rope to the creek far below and returned to the bank above without risk of being seen; here were the ashes from a funeral pyre; in this cave were buried the bones of the ancestral dead, this a place no living Yahi in Ishi's time had ever disturbed. The memories crowded one on another—here and here and here—the ordinary day-to-day comings and goings, the route of the last retreat, and the agony and chaos of the dispersal.

The expedition went for a week to Mill Creek exploring and making camp at different places, learning a little of the Yahi terrain as it had been when Ishi's people had been free to range widely. When it rained, Ishi led his companions to a shallow cave which overhangs Mill Creek, the same one that the five survivors had used many times when they, too, had been overtaken by night or a sudden storm. The cave consists of a more or less level rock ledge from four to eight feet wide and protected from the south by an arching roof. Here the present party, much as had the earlier ones, made a fire, cooked, ate, slept, and talked or sang, dry and comfortable until the rain stopped, some two days later. Popey's entire repertoire of songs was called for, but especially Ishi's favorites, which were a dramatic rendition of "Gunga Din" and "Mandalay." The talk was likely to be of heroes of old, of the world above—the sky world and its people—and of life after death. Ishi and Popey seemed to be in agreement that the land of the dead was peopled with strong hunters, and included the bounding deer and the mighty bear.

In the Mill Creek country Ishi took the party to village sites which he had known from childhood, but which were already empty and abandoned when he was too young to know more than their names and who a few of their most important people had been. Daily, Ishi came on some forgotten place which would start a train of associative memories. There were the old deer licks, and the ambushes to which he had lured deer. One day the party was passing an unusually large boulder. Ishi stopped and scratched the ground with a toe. Yes, it was the right place! He began to dig in earnest and soon came on the bones of a bear's paw—here it was he had killed a bear one day and he and his people had eaten well on roasted bear haunch. Because they had stayed there for awhile, they had given the spot a name, *Wamo-*

loku, Bear's Claw Place, probably, and one of the claws was buried there in commemoration of the fight and the feast.

By the time both the month of May and the crazy-aunatee trip were drawing to a close, the expedition led by Ishi had covered a large part of Yahi ancestral territory, mapped it in detail, with village sites, trails, hidden brush shelters, and the smoke-lined

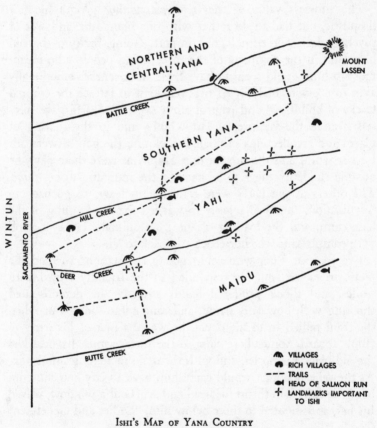

ISHI'S MAP OF YANA COUNTRY
This was Ishi's first attempt at map making drawn at the
Museum of Anthropology, about 1914.

caves occupied by the five survivors exactly located and named. On the maps were more than two hundred native place names, and in the notebooks an equal number or more of plants and herbs used by the Yana for food or medicine, and a minutely accurate record of ancient, old, and modern Yana village hunting and burial sites. There was as well a photographic record including pictures of Ishi hunting, fishing, swimming, and making fire, against a backdrop of Yana streams and hills and boulders.

The timeless value of the trip was neither geographic nor linguistic, but had to do rather with one man, Ishi, and was of psychological, not ethnological import. Going back to the old heartland in the company of the three living people who meant most to him would seem to have been an adventure emotionally akin to a psychoanalysis. At first reluctant to retrace the covered tracks of childhood and painful adult experience, Ishi gave himself over to the venture, at last wholly, and in the sharing of places and recollections succeeded in closing the gap between his former world and the present one. Happy as were these days, he became suddenly eager to be back in the museum, to be *home*. The others of the party were reluctant to leave, to go back to "civilization," but Ishi eagerly forwarded the dismantling of the base camp and the loading of the pack animals. He even took with complaisance the horseback trip back to Vina.

Everyone in Vina who could get to the station crowded the platform to see Ishi. He responded to the friendly crowd with smiles, and shook proffered hands amiably; he demonstrated shooting with bow and arrow, and sang some songs. But when the train pulled in to the depot, he was the first of his party to climb aboard. Somewhere close to the surface must have lurked the old black memories, and with them, an increasing uneasiness. As the wheels which would carry him back to city and museum began to turn, Ishi thrust his head and arms out a window, waved his hat, and shouted to those below him, "Ladies and Genelmen! Goodbye!"

During the homeward train ride, the four members of the

crazy-aunatee party made plans to repeat their trip in the fall when the acorns would be ripe for harvesting, and again in the spring, in the time of new clover and of the big salmon run. The day was the first of June, the year 1914. Their plan would be consumed in a conflagration which would become the First World War. The four friends could not know that never again would they be together in this carefree way; that for Ishi there was ahead but a scant year of enjoyment of his present radiant health. It is perhaps the moment to take stock of the wild man; to learn from those who knew him best what manner of man he was; to "place" him, and so fulfill as far as is possible the duty and goal of biography.

First of all, there is his official classification. Ishi, along with all other native American Indians within the borders of the United States, was considered a "ward" of the government. It follows that there should have been an official dossier on him. There was such. A brief exchange of letters illuminates the pigeon hole in Washington into which Ishi had been made to fit.

C. E. Kelsey was the Special Agent for California Indians for the Bureau of Indian Affairs with local headquarters in San Jose, California, where he also had a law practice. He it was who had sent the telegram which released Ishi from the Oroville jail and allowed him to go in Waterman's care to San Francisco. Two months after this telegram, Mr. Kelsey received a letter-directive instructing him to inform himself about Ishi. The letter was from a second assistant commissioner in the Department of the Interior, Office of Indian Affairs, subtitle, Education, Law, and Order, and sub-subtitle, *Wild Indians* [italics mine], and reads:

> It is difficult to form a clear idea as to the possibilities in this Indian as regards civilization, and from an industrial standpoint. As this Indian has been in the care of the authorities (at the museum) for some time, they have had opportunity to make observations and to gain some idea of his intelligence, and capacity for civilization. Make inquiry with special reference, first, to the possibility of training him to

conform, at least to a reasonable degree, to the customs of civilized life; and, second, as to the possibility of training him for the performance of simple manual labor. [Signed] 22nd. Assistant Commissioner.

Kelsey may be presumed to have despaired of putting this request into humanistic and realistic form, merely sending it on as it came to him. Kroeber's reply was brief:

"I beg to state that from the outset Ishi has conformed very willingly and to the full extent of his understanding, to the customs of civilized life."

Kelsey then came in person to the museum to see Ishi and to make plans for his future. He assured Ishi that he was free to go back to Deer Creek, or, if he did not wish to do that, to be taken to a reservation where he would be with other Indians, there to live under the care and at the expense of the United States Government. Ishi had been through all this before—in the Oroville jail. Aware that no pressure whatever was being exercised to persuade him to stay where he was, he indicated a prompt and unequivocal negative to Mr. Kelsey's proposals, answering him in Yahi as follows: "I will live like the white man for the remainder of my days. I wish to stay here where I now am. I will grow old in this house, and it is here I will die."

Kelsey, having done his official duty, recommended to the Bureau that it accept Ishi's decision and wish. His recommendation was followed, and there the Bureau rested until May, 1914. Mr. E. B. Merritt, Assistant Commissioner of Indian Affairs in Washington wrote directly to Kroeber:

The opinion was given [whose, the letter fails to state], that owing to his [Ishi's] advanced age—about sixty years or more—he was not likely to speak English with any degree of fluency: and that, owing to his previous manner of life, his mental development as far as understanding of our manner of life was concerned, was not beyond that of a six year old child.

Kroeber replied civilly, if briefly, to Assistant Commissioner Merritt's remarks:

Ishi has taken readily to civilization and has been self-supporting for over a year, serving as assistant janitor and general helper about the museum. His age appears to be between fifty and fifty-five, and he has learned English slowly, but succeeds in making himself understood. Every month is adding slowly to his command of the language. His ignorance of civilized life was complete, but his mental development was by no means stunted or sub-normal. He has picked up practical matters with the utmost quickness. He has been free to return to his old home and manner of living ever since being with us, but much prefers his present condition.

There is no record in the museum files of further interest in Ishi on the part of the Bureau.

Now for a nearer view of Ishi in 1914. Ishi was a man of middle stature, five feet eight inches tall, presumably born between 1860 and 1862, hence fifty-two to fifty-four years old in 1914. Pope could find no evidence of childhood disease, and Ishi did not remember having had any. Neither was there evidence of smallpox or of chicken pox; no glandular abnormality, no scars from boils or burns or injury.

Skin—light reddish bronze which darkened with sun exposure, fine in texture. *Hair*—black and straight, worn long over the ears, tied in a single brush down the back. *Musculature*—well developed with even distribution of subcutaneous fat. *Teeth*—all present, strong, no evidence of decay or pyorrhoea. Molars much worn but in good condition. *Eyes*—set straight, lids Caucasian in contour. (Eye and lid contour in many California Indians suggests a more Mongoloid form.) *Breath*—sweet and free from foetor, an Indian trait noted also by Stephen Powers when he traveled amongst and wrote about California Indians in 1877. *Body odor*—faintly musty. (Non-acid.) *Nose*—strong and wide. *Chest*—

full, normal. *Thighs and legs*—well-formed. Spring and leg action not that of one who in his youth had been a sprinter. Both habit and build made for endurance rather than speed. A tireless walker. *Hands*—medium small. Size 8 glove. Palms soft and pliable, fingers tapered, fingernails ovaloid in outline, texture excellent. *Feet*—broad and strong, toes straight and unspoiled, longitudinal and transverse arches perfect. Skin of sole thick but not rough. Toenails round in outline, strong, and short.

Pope preached a sermon about feet to each of his classes in medical school after he had examined Ishi's feet and taken casts of them. Indian scouts, hunters, and ethnographers who have traveled and lived with Indians in forest, desert, or plains have commented on how quietly they walk, without the snapping of twigs underfoot and the disturbance of dirt or sand and pebbles which happens when white men walk. Pope observed and described how Ishi actually walked:

He [Ishi] springs from the great toe which is wonderfully strong in its plantar flexion and abduction. His method of locomotion is that of rather short steps, each foot sliding along the ground as it touches. Neither the heel nor the ball of the foot seems to receive the jar of the step. The foot is placed in position cautiously, not slammed or jammed down. He progresses rather pigeon-toed, and approximates crossing the line of his progress each step.

Ishi had no history of venereal infection. He knew, in a vague and general way, that there were such diseases. He was free from sex perversion of any sort. Kroeber found that Ishi was reticent about any discussion of sex, blushing furiously if the subject came up. He did not question him about his personal sex life at all. Pope did, using a doctor's opportunity and privilege. Ishi had had very little if any actual experience in sex function; perhaps a little when he was barely pubescent. There were no women left in the tiny band whom he could have married or with whom he might have had a passing relation by the time he was grown.

There was only one young woman, and she was a sister or a cousin. In any case, she stood in a sister relation to him. He was much attached to her in what seems to have been a brother-sister bond made closer by their own youth, and the older ages of the other three in the group. There was certainly fondness and tenderness in their feeling for one another; there is not the slightest evidence for construing sex interest or experience to have been a part of it.

Toward all white women whom he met during his museum years, Ishi was friendly but reserved. He was a guest for dinner and overnight many times in his friends' homes, and he lived with the Watermans for three months. During these visits he never initiated conversation with his hostess, her daughters, mother, mother-in-law, or any women guests. When a woman spoke to him he answered courteously but without looking directly at her. This behavior, it must not be forgotten, was correct Yana etiquette, a proper showing of respect. How much of it was something more than that—a shyness born of sex starvation in a person who was reserved but not shy, generally speaking—it is impossible to say. Having accustomed himself to living without any sex life during his young years, there was, no doubt, little urge to change his ways in his late forties or early fifties, particularly among strangers.

Whether Juan Dolores talked to Ishi about women and sex, is not known. He probably did. And if he did, he undoubtedly said that Indians were well advised not to become interested in white women; that no Indian ever really understood a white woman, and that even if there was much love between them, the relation was doomed, the woman belonging to the advantaged civilization, the man to the disadvantaged. This Juan believed, even though, late in life, he was himself married for a few years to a Caucasian woman.

Continuing old Yana custom, Ishi bathed daily, and daily he plucked out any beard hairs which had sprouted overnight, using tweezers of split wood. No one ever saw him at this operation except by coming on him while he was engaged in his toilet in private. Daily he brushed and combed his long hair. He washed it frequently, drying it by a filliping and beating, using a flat basket paddle. In the hills, he would have put grease on it. Pope offered him bay rum, as a city substitute, but he declined it. In the hills, his bath would have been a sweat bath. The Yana used a solution made by heating the leaves and nuts of the bay tree until they were reduced to a semisolid state, and rubbed this solution on the body after a sweat bath. It acted as a soporific, "like whisky-tee" said Ishi. Ishi kept in his clothes box a bar of scented soap and a can of talcum powder, "lady powder" he called it. These were gifts that he treasured but never used.

Ishi was orderly by nature probably, and by old habit, certainly. His clothes, toilet articles, tools, treasures, all his possessions, stood neatly on shelves in his small room, or were folded in exact arrangements, or were wrapped in paper and stored in drawers. He worked wherever he chose to in the museum, and his was the sort of work to make chips or flakes or scraps and to create disorder. But he spread newspapers or a tarpaulin to work on, cleaning everything up when he was finished. In camp, his friends found that he cleaned fish or butchered a rabbit or a deer with deftness, leaving no messy and fly-attracting scraps about, and that his cooking and dishwashing were done more quickly and neatly than their own.

This easy competence and pleasure in well-ordered arrangements of the tools and possessions of living suggests the Japanese flair for raising mere orderliness to an aesthetic of orderliness. There is a temperamental, and possibly a kinaesthetic something in this trait not to be explained by poverty in the variety of things owned, or difficulty of replacement and consequent need to take good care of them. Poverty the world over does not, *per se,* make for orderliness or aesthetic satisfaction, nor for cleanliness nor pride nor even for care in handling the little one has. The aesthetic of order and arrangement would seem to be rather something inborn, deep-seated in the individual psyche. Some cultures turn this preference and capacity into an approved value: thus the Yana and the Japanese. We do not, nor do the Mohave, to name two different value systems.

Ishi enjoyed smoking, but was not a regular or confirmed smoker, going without tobacco for weeks sometimes. Tobacco was no novelty to him, the sacred pipe being a part of ritual and ceremony and prayer with his people. The no-smoking rule which held both in the museum and the hospital he regarded as reasonable: he may well have assumed that the taboo covered more esoteric hazards than those of fire. He believed tobacco to be bad for the young, not so much for reasons of health as of propriety. Amongst his acquaintances in the museum and adjoining buildings were a few who chewed tobacco. He enjoyed this pastime with the copious spitting which is part of it, but only when he was alone with one of his tobacco-chewing companions, and always out of doors. It would have seemed to Ishi a nest-fouling performance to engage in inside a house or shelter.

Ishi liked doing all kinds of things with other people. The young internes and medical students and orderlies at the hospital drew him into their games, some of which Popey knew of only afterward. None of them could match Ishi's skill in rope climbing, nor did any of them venture onto an upper window ledge of the hospital as Ishi occasionally did. Teetering there above them, laughing, and pretending to be about to accept their "dare" to jump, he clung with his bare feet to the man-made ledge as securely as he used to cling to the high ledges in Deer Creek cañon. He was not so good as the least good of his young friends at any sort of ball game, for he was not able to throw as far or with as much accuracy as they. To be good at throwing and catching, one must have learned it early in life. Although innocent of technique, Ishi made a respectable showing in informal boxing and wrestling, and he found a friendly scuffle great fun. He was expert in certain styles of swimming, using the side stroke except in rough water, where he changed to a modified breast stroke. He knew no overhand or other fancy strokes, and, unlike the

Yurok Indians, he did not dive. He was accustomed to slipping into a river at water level, but he could swim underwater with great skill and for long distances. He would walk, hunt, fish, or practice archery without fatigue all day. And he was a tireless and interested partner in any sort of work at all within his range, although Pope quaintly remarks that "Ishi was indifferent to the beauty of labor as an abstract concept. He never fully exerted himself, but apparently had unlimited endurance."

Whether it was play or work, Ishi preferred company to solitude; but not in order to compete or to excel or to demonstrate his own strength or skill. The impulse to any sort of exhibitionism was totally absent in him. He might well have found in Pope's "beauty of labor," as in the white man's strenuousness and competitiveness and wish to be first, some of the seeds of the display motive which he so shunned. This reticence may have accounted also for his strong distaste for acrobatics and tumbling, whether as participant or as audience.

Ishi was normally calm and equable of disposition, never vehement nor given to bursts of anger. He showed displeasure and on occasion some excitement when an unauthorized person touched or misplaced his belongings. He was scrupulous in never touching anything which was not his, and so watchful of museum property that he reproved Popey for picking up and putting into his pocket a museum pencil. On the other hand, nothing made him happier than to be able to give something. He would give away his arrow and spear points, even a bow which had taken many patient hours to make, or anything else from his little hoard. During the camping trip he enjoyed the role of host, cooking, ladling out, and sharing his bounty from a successful day's fishing or hunting.

Ishi was religious, his mysticism as spontaneous and unstrained as his smile. He believed according to Yana formula in the making and peopling of the world by gods and demigods, and in the taboos laid down by these Old Ones. He also believed in a Land of the Dead where the souls of Yana live out their shadow community existence. Christian doctrine interested him, and seemed to him to be for the most part reasonable and understandable. He held to the conviction that the White God would not care to have Indians in His home, for all Loudy told him to the contrary. It may have occurred to him that the souls of white men would fit but poorly into a round dance of Yana dead. If so, he was too polite to say so.

Perhaps it was as well Loudy did not become a missionary— he left Ishi with certain misconceptions about the story and teachings of the New Testament. When Ishi saw the cinema of the Passion Play, which moved him and which he found beautiful, he assumed that Christ was the "bad man" whose crucifixion was justified.

At ease with his friends, Ishi loved to joke, to be teased amiably and to tease in return. And he loved to talk. In telling a story, if it were long or involved or of considerable affect, he would perspire with the effort, his voice rising toward a falsetto of excitement. There is a letter from Kroeber to Sapir, written in the spring of 1915, which says, "You will find Ishi bursting with mythological, ethnological, tribal, and geographic information, which he is delighted to impart, but he may need a little training before he will dictate connected texts slowly enough for writing."

Needless to say, Ishi did not learn to read beyond recognition of no smoking and electric and billboard signs which were constants of San Francisco; the letters and numbers which identified the streetcars which he rode; newspaper titles; and his reading of a clock, however that was done by him. He enjoyed funny pictures, and had no difficulty in getting their "point." Perhaps funny pictures of forty years ago were more simply comic and less narrative than most of those today, less dependent upon words for communicating their meaning.

Ishi's "broken English" was much commented upon during his life at the museum—too much, perhaps. Kroeber says that none of the staff except Sapir, whose genius was for language and who knew Northern and Central Yana, pronounced Yahi as well, or used it as idiomatically, as Ishi used English; and he estimates that by 1914 Ishi commanded an English vocabulary of at least five or six hundred words. He of course understood many words which he did not himself use. Many Yana words end on a vowel sound like Italian words. The consonantal endings of English were sometimes troublesome to Ishi as they are to Italians, and he tended to naturalize them to the sound and speech pattern familiar to him as do Italians when speaking English. "How much?" for example under Italian and Yana vowel end preference may become *How mucha?*

Before giving any further approximations of Ishi's English pronunciation, it should be said that there is risk of a misconstrual of the person in such quotations—they tend to make Ishi sound quaint or childlike, whereas he was neither. A European refugee of Ishi's age and with no previous knowledge of English will in all likelihood attain a good mastery of English usage and vocabulary after four years here. Ishi's English vocabulary by comparison remained small and his usage relatively pidgin. But it should be understood that Ishi was simultaneously confronted with unfamiliar objects, activities, meanings, and concepts, as well as with a strange language. Book, bank, and dishpan are not difficult words to learn, you may say. But what of their difficulty if your long experience had not included the concept of writing so that you did not know what were the significances of marks on the pages of a book, much less their meaning, or if you did not know what money was, or what the purpose of a dishpan?

The phonetic writing of Yahi words has been simplified in this book, to preserve something of their flavor and rhythm without attempting to indicate the heavy aspirations and cracked consonants which so delighted Waterman, but which are vivid to the ear, not to the eye.

When Ishi said for "hat," *hatna,* he was, according to Yana usage, giving the word its complete, male-dialect form. Had the word "hat" occurred in Yana, the women would have said *hat,* the men *hatna.* Just so, "a sheep" was called *sheepna* by Ishi. The ending *ti* or *tee,* which is much quoted both by Waterman and by Pope, appearing at the end of such phrases as *How muchatee,* and such words as *watertee,* or "quail," *chikakatee,* is Yana for "it is"; "a quail it is," "how much is it?" etc. It is not, as would seem to one reading the words with no knowledge of Yana, a "primitivism" or a diminutive. In fact, "How muchee" was probably said to Ishi. Otherwise he would have continued to say, like the Italian, *how mucha,* or *how muchna?* It is well to be on guard against the pidgin English of a foreigner—he may have learned it from a native speaker.

Of interest are the words which are examples of sounds spoken at first hearing by Ishi without appreciable accent. "Sure" was one such, and stands for the *sh* words. "Watch" was another, standing for the *ch* words, their ease of pronunciation stemming from the occurrence in Yana of the sounds *sh* and *ch.* Yana also had the English *l,* hence he said "last" and "little" and all such words without consonantal change. But Yana has no *r,* "rice" therefore becoming *lice* with him, and "rabbit," *labbit.* The word "dance" presented no difficulty, nor did "Italian," which he said *Itallian;* nor "hot," which he said *haht;* nor "white man," which he called *witeman;* nor was his *wandahlah* far from its original, "one dollar."

Short sentences, many of them, he may have learned as single and whole entities, but without difficulty. "You like him?" he asked plainly. His linguistic mastery of this sentence was no doubt forwarded by his urgent wish to know whether the stranger in question was well or poorly regarded. "Put 'em away!" was another early sentence. He meant, "I have put them away." He was very proud of his first long sentence, "Me bick man, shmoke shigar!" That may well have been a one-time-around sentence, an imitation *in toto* of the words and manner of whatever acquaintance it was who gave him a cigar. *Lashybum* belongs in this category, as do *lassa,* "lots of," and *Skoot!,* "it's good." These sound like Yanaization of slovenly English, learned, it is hoped, not in the museum, but on shopping trips to the "street."

By contrast, most of his English was spoken with separate

syllabic accuracy. It is possible almost to hear one of his friends speaking and Ishi painstakingly imitating, in such words as his *penss,* "pencil"; *bahdaydoes,* "potatoes"; *carrazy,* "crazy"; *wahle Injin,* "valley Indian"; *meanus,* "beans"; *pish,* "fish"; *pike,* "fight"; *knipe,* "knife"; (Yana has no *f*); *milik,* "milk"; *kopee,* "coffee"; *bahnahna;* and *chickana.*

There were phrases and concepts which were mixed English and Yana. His word for fire, *auna,* pronounced "ow-na," occurred in combination with English words, not only in his *crazy-aunatee* trip, but in the phrase, *too much lazy aunatee,* meaning either "a lazy boy" or "a slow fire." Notice that the *z* was mastered, not continuing to appear as *sh.* He also said *him crazy aunatee,* that is, "crazy like fire," or "burning like whisky." *Too much I smoke* meant "fog"; *too much watertee,* "too much rain there is." *Hims good,* or *hims no good,* however the judgment went, speaks for itself. *Die man,* meant "death"; *too much pinna,* "too much pain"; and his inquiry, *Evelybody hoppy?* were among the phrases his friends, far from correcting him, adopted for their own, finding them expressive and endearing as he spoke them, as were his names for them, *Popey, Watamany,* and *Chiep.*

Ishi's *Hullo,* or if the occasion was formal, *Howdado,* were cordially said and accompanied usually with a warm smile. He retained a reluctance to the use of words of farewell. His preferred phrase was a casual, *You go?* or, alternatively, *You stay. I go.* He would add a *Goodboy* when he felt it was expected of him but his heart was not in it. For whatever personal or custom-ingrained reasons, there attached to parting a significance best not accorded recognition in words.

Besides his friends, a Sioux Indian once passed judgment on Ishi. It happened in this way. Pope and Ishi were attending a Buffalo Bill Wild West Show, of which they both were fond. There were a number of Plains Indians in the show. One of them, a tall, dignified man decked out in paint and feather war bonnet, came up to Pope and Ishi. The two Indians looked at each other in silence for several moments. The Sioux then asked in perfect

English "What tribe of Indian is this?" Pope answered, "Yana, from Northern California." The Sioux then gently picked up a bit of Ishi's hair, rolled it between his fingers, looked critically into his face, and said, "He is a very high grade of Indian." When he had gone, Pope asked Ishi what he thought of the Sioux. "Him's big chiep," was Ishi's enthusiastic reply.

Ishi was not given to volunteering criticism of the white man's ways. But he was observant and analytic, and, when pressed, would pass a judgment somewhat as follows. He approved of the "conveniences" and variety of the white man's world—neither Ishi nor any people who have lived a life of hardship and deprivation underrate an amelioration of those severities, or scope for some comforts and even some luxuries. He considered the white man to be fortunate, inventive, and very, very clever; but childlike and lacking in a desirable reserve, and in a true understanding of Nature—her mystic face; her terrible and her benign power.

Asked how he would, today, characterize Ishi, Kroeber says, "He was the most patient man I ever knew. I mean he had mastered the philosophy of patience, without trace either of self-pity, or of bitterness to dull the purity of his cheerful enduringness." His friends all testify to cheerfulness as a trait basic to Ishi's temperament—a cheerfulness which passed, given half a chance, into a gentle hilarity. His way was the way of contentment, the Middle Way, to be pursued quietly, working a little, playing a little, and surrounded by friends.

The figure of Ishi stands, part of it in the sun, varicolored and idiosyncratic and achieved; part in deep shadow, darkened by the extent of our own ignorance and by its own disadvantagements. A biography should include something at least of the nature of these shadows, the unrealized potential, the promise unfulfilled, even in that brightest year of his life, 1914. He had only one name, not the usual two or three. He had only a museum address, although it was in very truth home to him. There was no living person with whom he could, from time to time, revel in a rapid and idiomatic exchange in the childhood tongue. Affectionate and uncorrupt, he was denied the fulfillment of wife and children, or of any sex life whatsoever. Then there was the total lack of immunity to diseases of the modern world, which had been disastrous to thousands of other Indians, and which brought to Ishi illness and untimely death.

Almost a century has passed since Ishi was born, and he has been dead forty-four years, yet he continues to engage the imagination: he was unique, a last man, the last man of his world, and his experience of sudden, lonely, and unmitigated change-over from the Stone Age to the Steel Age was also unique. He was, further, a living affirmation of the credo of the anthropologists that modern man—*homo sapiens*—whether contemporary American Indian or Athenian Greek of Phidias' time, is quite simply and wholly human in his biology, in his capacity to learn new skills and new ways as a changed environment exposes him to them, in his power of abstract thought, and in his moral and ethical discriminations. It it upon this broad base of man's pan-humanity that scientists and humanists alike predicate further progress away from the instinctual and primitive and subhuman strata of our natures.

With little room for choosing, Ishi made choices as courageous and enlightened as the scope of his opportunities permitted. In the Oroville jail he chose life with a strange white man, rejecting the alternative of joining subjugated members of his own race; later he chose the dignity of an earned salary and independence, rejecting government wardship; and when "civilization" bestowed upon him the gift of tuberculosis he chose to fight it according to Popey's instructions and to accept defeat with grace, his concern being to make himself as little a burden as might be to those who cared for him.

Epilogue: DEATH IN A MUSEUM

Ishi developed a hacking cough in December, 1914, and was in hospital for treatment and tests during most of the following January. Retrospectively the doctors knew this illness to have been the probable beginning of an active tuberculosis, but his sputum contained no tubercle bacilli; he was not running a temperature, and appeared to have suffered and recovered from a respiratory infection of a mild and nonrecurring nature. But early spring found him back in hospital once more, and giving a positive reaction to the tuberculin test, although the sputum was still free of bacilli. By late spring he seemed to be recovered and the doctors said the progress of the disease had been arrested. Kroeber left to go to Europe at the end of the semester, not altogether reassured by Ishi's apparent recovery and the favorable medical prognosis—an uneasiness which the event justified. He was not to see Ishi again.

The summer began well for Ishi. He went to live with the Watermans' in Berkeley. They made much of him; he was happy to be part of a household and family, and for several hours most days he worked with Edward Sapir who was spending the summer in Berkeley in order to record linguistic material on the Yahi language from Ishi.

Ishi did not hint that he felt unwell, but in August Waterman noticed that he tired easily and had little appetite. Worriedly, he coaxed him to eat more and to rest, and, when he seemed no better toward the end of the month, took him home to the museum where Dr. Pope could look after him.

To survive our civilization, an early and continuing immunization to it is necessary. There were the six healthy and ebullient

Eskimos whom Admiral Peary brought with him to New York City upon his return in 1897 from one of his early trips which ultimately were to lead to his discovery of the North Pole. All six of them caught colds in Newfoundland and promptly contracted tuberculosis in New York. An employee of the Natural History Museum and his wife, herself half Labrador Eskimo, took care of them in a pleasant home and garden in the Bronx. Their sanguine temper did not desert them, and every care then known was given them, but when Peary returned to the Arctic the next year only one of them, and he a desperately sick Eskimo, went with him. Unless he blessedly died before reaching home, he may possibly have spread the disease abroad amongst his people. Of his companions, four were already dead. One, a child of ten, recovered and grew up to become one of New York City's army of taxi drivers. As for Ishi, he had had the first "common cold" of his life within a few weeks of coming to San Francisco; his first pneumonia the same winter.

Bulletins were sent regularly to Kroeber giving Ishi's afternoon peak temperature, whether he was cheerful or depressed, and any messages that Ishi might have for him. Gifford wrote most of these reports, since he was with Ishi daily; Waterman was teaching in Berkeley and could come to the museum only on weekends. Occasionally it was a doctor, a nurse, or a secretary who wrote. Kroeber must have written in answer two or three times a week. There are repeated references in the correspondence to a two-way exchange: "Ishi is very fond of the purse you sent. He keeps his sacred tobacco in it." "Ishi was very much tickled with your letter and postal, particularly the latter showing a dance figure." From his bed, Ishi could see the steel structure of the new hospital under construction next door. He watched the men at work on the high girders with an amused fascination. *All a same monkey-tee,* he reported. Kroeber was in Germany, in England, and finally back in New York City. The bulletins followed him faithfully: he and Ishi were in touch to the end in a continuing communication of sorts, although Ishi could not read or write, and a continent lay between them.

Ishi had been put in hospital with the return of acute symptoms. He was well taken care of, Popey was at hand, and he knew many people in the hospital, but Gifford and Waterman saw that he was constrained and unhappy, and they recalled the passionate wish of all Indians to be *home* when death comes. They brought Ishi home. In a letter written on September 30, 1915, Gifford tells how they did it:

"Waterman and I have decided to cut out the Pacific Island exhibit for awhile and give the room to Ishi. This is the sunniest room [in the museum]. Here he will be treated as *Ishi*. At the hospital I fear that the nurses were so busy that he was treated simply as a hospital patient, without regard for his personality."

Ethnological and art objects from the Pacific Islands went back into packing boxes in the basement of the museum. Ishi's room was large and sunny, with a wide view overlooking the park, the black mass of eucalyptus trees known as Sutro Forest, and the hospital. Pope visited him several times a day, someone of the museum staff was in and out at all hours, and Warburton nursed him and cooked for him so expertly, and kept his health chart so professionally, that even the exacting Popey could find no fault.

Ishi lived on with good days and bad, stoical, uncomplaining, interested in whatever went on, affectionate and responsive, until the spring. He died on March 25, 1916. Popey, his Kuwi, was with him at the end. Death came at noon, in the time of the year when new clover was painting green his native hills and when Deer Creek and Mill Creek were swollen with the rush of the spring salmon run.

Kroeber and Gifford were agreed that when Ishi died his body should be touched and handled as little as possible. Cremation should follow at once, the crematory furnace being our nearest approach to the out-of-door funeral pyres of ancient Romans and modern Mohaves, of Hindi peoples ancient and modern, and of the Yahi. The ashes should then be buried, the cemetery urn again being our closest equivalent of a basket and a rock cairn—all to accord, as nearly as our ways allow, with Yahi usage. Kroeber wrote to Gifford from New York on March 24, the day before Ishi died:

> Please stand by our contingently made outline of action, and insist on it as my personal wish. There is no objection to a cast (death mask). I do not, however, see that an autopsy would lead to anything of consequence, but would resolve itself into a general dissection. Please shut down on it. As to disposal of the body, I must ask you as my personal representative to yield nothing at all under any circumstances. If there is any talk about the interests of science, say for me that science can go to hell. We propose to stand by our friends. Besides, I cannot believe that any scientific value is materially involved. We have hundreds of Indian skeletons that nobody ever comes near to study. The prime interest in this case would be of a morbid romantic nature. Please acquaint Waterman with my feelings; also Pope. When the time comes, please see that the various people in the hospital are properly thanked. They have been more than good. You can get an individual plot in any of the public cemeteries. Draw upon any money in our keeping for this purpose without question or formality on my responsibility.

Waterman, had he been less upset, would have backed Kroeber and Gifford. But Waterman was taking Ishi's death with so much grief and emotion and sense of guilt that he could be no principle's and no person's ally. He wrote Kroeber: "As you have heard from Gifford, the poor old Indian is dying. The work last summer was too much for him. *He was the best friend I had in the world* and I killed him by letting Sapir ride him too hard, and by letting him sneak out of lunches." It did no good to point out that loss of appetite marked a certain progress of the disease; nor that it was Sapir who, exhausted, brought a day's work to a close before Ishi tired of repeating the beloved words and sounds of Yahi.

Waterman wrote also to Roland Dixon who knew Ishi and had done ethnographic work in country bordering the Yana hills: "He was my best friend." The stark letter leaves no room for the comfortable suspicion of overstatement.

Pope, as will be seen, was as keen as the others that Ishi should reach the Land of the Dead properly prepared and accoutred to take his place amongst the other Yahi Shades. But he was Ishi's Kuwi, and the white man's also. He would have liked to know *everything* about Ishi. As Kuwi, he owed it to the world and to Ishi to know as much as he could by any reasonable means learn. Waveringly, Waterman agreed with him. Alone, and the youngest, Gifford did what he could. His letter to Kroeber on March 30, tells how he succeeded against difficult odds, one serious one being that Kroeber's letter (quoted above) was received too late to help him.

> I took the stand which you asked me to take some time ago: namely, that he [Ishi] have a Christian burial like any other friend. The only departures from your request were that a simple autopsy was performed and that the brain was preserved. The matter was not entirely in my hands—in short what happened amounts to a compromise between science and sentiment with myself on the side of sentiment. Everything else was carried out as you would have done it, I firmly believe. [Ishi] told Pope sometime ago that the way to dispose of the dead was to burn them, so we undoubtedly followed his wishes in that matter. In the coffin were placed one of his bows, five arrows, a basket of acorn meal, ten pieces of dentalium, a boxful of shell bead money which he had saved, a purse full of tobacco, three rings, and some obsidian flakes, all of which we felt sure would be in accord with Ishi's wishes. The remains are to be placed in a niche at Mount Olivet Cemetery. Pope and Waterman decided and I agreed that a small black Pueblo jar would be far more appropriate than one of the bronze or onyx urns. Tomorrow afternoon Pope and I are going down to place the ashes in this jar and put it in its niche. [The inscription on the jar

reads: ISHI, THE LAST YANA INDIAN, 1916.] The funeral was
private and no flowers were brought. Waterman, Pope,
Loomis [of the Academy of Sciences], Loud, Warburton,
Mason [of the Philadelphia Museum], and myself were
official attendants.

Now the law reads that when a person dies intestate and without living blood relatives, such monies and property as may have
been his at the time of death go to the state. The public administrator who is charged with responsibility to see that this transfer
is actually made, has, or had in 1916, certain discretionary powers
also. Ishi's few personal possessions the administrator left with the
museum. There was also Ishi's treasure in the safe in the museum
office, his "counting room"—five hundred and twenty half dollars
in thirteen film cases, each neatly filled to the top. The administrator took half this sum for the state. The other half went where
Waterman knew Ishi wished his treasure to go—to the House of
the Kuwi. So it was that Doctor Moffitt, Dean of the Medical
School, received two hundred and sixty half dollars with a covering note from Waterman: "This [gift from Ishi] is in actual cash,
and I hope you will accept it, though of course it is no return for
the medical and hospital attention that Ishi received. It will serve
perhaps as a recognition of his sense of obligation." Doctor Moffitt
acknowledged the gift, thanking Waterman and explaining that
he was putting Ishi's money in a special fund rather than taking
it as payment of hospital expenses, since there had never been any
idea of charging him. In this way, Ishi's treasure continues to
contribute its bit to the science of healing, a science for which
Ishi himself had so great a curiosity and concern.

Ishi's public missed him. Letters expressing affection for him
and sorrow that he was gone came to Waterman and Gifford. A
few of these blamed the staff for not having taken better care of
him: a museum was not a proper home, they said; there had been
carelessness in allowing Ishi to be exposed to infection; he should
have been taken back to his old home and natural environment.

As far away as Kansas City a group of high school students there, who knew of Ishi from one of their teachers who had spent some time with him at the museum before he was ill, held a memorial meeting for him.

Meanwhile, within the museum walls there lingered a numbing sense of loss, and an unwonted silence no longer interrupted by the soft-voiced inquiry, *Evelybody hoppy?* Eyes were averted from the shut door of the sunny room which had been his. The staff members, even Loudy and Worbinna, were idle, at loose ends.

Gifford ordered the door to the empty room opened, and the Pacific Islands exhibit brought up once more from its basement storage, and reinstalled. At work, the men reminded one another that Ishi himself had warned that it was dangerous to speak of the dead; bad even to think too much about them; that each had his world—the living and the dead—and should be left to it. Grief and mourning there surely must be, but as with all feelings, kept within measure, unindulged. The museum was learning to live without its Wild Man.

As for Ishi's three closest friends, Pope probably missed him, day by day, more than did Waterman and Kroeber, but, almost surely, suffered less than they from a sense of half-realized opportunity in his death. Between Pope's active role as his physician, and his and Ishi's total reciprocal enjoyment of whatever had to do with a bow and arrow—any bow, any arrow—theirs was a rich and fulfilled relation. Pope continued to be beguiled by his Wild Man's aboriginal and romantic differences from himself; and their alikenesses never ceased to thrill him. Of Ishi's death, Pope wrote:

And so, stoic and unafraid, departed the last wild Indian of America. He closes a chapter in history. He looked upon us as sophisticated children—smart, but not wise. We knew many things, and much that is false. He knew nature, which is always true. His were the qualities of character that last forever. He was kind; he had courage and self-restraint, and though all had been taken from him, there was no bitterness in his heart. His soul was that of a child, his mind that of a philosopher.

Waterman and Kroeber, bound to the reticences of Yana etiquette, made no significant public statement upon Ishi's death. He had walked quietly out of the Neolithic world into their world, and once he was settled in the museum, Ishi and the anthropologists took each other pretty much for granted, as one's family is taken for granted, and one's close friend. Four and more moon cycles waxed and waned and returned, while Ishi stayed on, a part of the changing twentieth century—his two friends had ceased to envision a world without him.

Then he was gone, the long journey from the ancient Yana homeland along Mill and Deer creeks to the Land of the Yana Dead completed, his leavetaking from his friends and their world as quiet as his own preferred and understated phrase of farewell:

"YOU STAY, I GO."

John

NOTES

For those who have read closely Waterman's monograph *The Yana Indians*, or who will read it in the future as the principal source for the history of the Yana, it should be said that my account accepts Waterman's dating and time sequence except in two instances, as follows.

The last, or Kingsley Cave massacre, date given, 1871, is construed by me to have preceded the Five Bows incident, date given, 1870. Of the two dates, 1870 will be seen to be the firmer one, but it is the sequence that is of first importance, whether it was 1870, 1871, or 1872. The crucial events may have occurred in any one of these years. The only definite date given for the Kingsley Cave massacre is from a single informant, Norvall, whose oral and unverified recollection in 1915, forty-four years later, was that it had occurred in April, 1871. This would mean, according to Powers' and Segraves' dating, that the last massacre postdated the Five Bows incident and that the concealment was undertaken with a population of more than thirty people, perhaps as many as forty or forty-five; that within a year, thirty or more of this number had perished in the Cave killings; and that perhaps a dozen, conceivably as many as fifteen, survivors were left to enter a second year of concealment. Norvall's date is judged in error vis-à-vis Segraves' and Powers' date.

Waterman undertook to present the oral source material as he got it, warm and alive from the honest memory of living informants, keeping it in their own words, when the account was not too prolix or rambling. No one was more aware than Waterman of the inconsistencies, inaccuracies, and gaping holes in the materials. His task was to record the sources before all the living fragments of recollections were gone. Either he or someone else could, later and at leisure, sift the material for its meanings and non-meanings. Waterman nowhere suggests that he believed that there was any violent convulsion of loss during the period of the concealment such as the Cave massacre would have been. He speaks rather of its course as having been a very gradual reduction of population over the years of the duration of the concealment. It was the understanding also of other people who came to know Ishi well that only a few of his tribesmen were left to go into hiding—not more than the twelve who came to Segraves' cabin, or only two or three or four more possibly, who may have been lurking behind the emissaries, close by but not seen by Segraves.

The second date that I do not use is the one given in the Rafe Johnson story, summarized by Waterman in his monograph (p. 59).

1878—Rafe Johnson, son of old "Peg Leg" Johnson, in company with Jim Melick, lassoes two squaws near Black Oak Mountain. An Indian man is shot through the thigh, and a child is shot through the ankle. One of the women "is taken to Nome Lackee, the other to Redding." [There is an evident mistake here, since the Nome Lackee Reservation was abandoned long before this. Possibly the woman was taken to Round Valley. Information from D. B. Lyon, 1915.]

Lyon was a valuable informant to Waterman on his experiences in the late 'eighties when he was a young boy. He was born too late to know the Rafe Johnson story except through older people from whom he may have heard or overheard some discussion of its several events and aspects.

Shootings and woundings took place in the Yana hills; perhaps also lassoings, but there is no confirming second telling nor has any clue turned up to indicate where this dreamlike episode belongs. If it happened, all or part of it, it must have been before 1878.

Note on the Three Captives, Chapter 5, page 96

The three last Yahi to be taken captive, except of course for Ishi himself, were an older woman, a young woman, and a little girl. Segraves who, with Hiram Good, had made the capture was sure that the young woman and the little girl were Ishi's sisters, and he believed the spokesman for the Yahi to have been Ishi's father. These are not relationships confirmed by Ishi and must be discarded. The spokesman *could* have been Ishi's uncle, and the captives his aunt and cousins. We do not know that they were, nor is it of the first importance to know. The numbers of the band were so reduced that any loss, whether of blood relative or not, was personal and tragic.

Hiram Good "gave" the two women and the little girl to a Mr. Carter who lived, apparently a bachelor, in Acorn Hollow on lower Deer Creek. "About this time," as Segraves told the story, the young woman gave birth to a boy whose father was not Carter, Segraves is careful to say, but an (unknown) "wild" Indian. The baby was named, or nicknamed, Snowdrop. So much for Segraves' account, from which it is to be inferred that the young woman was pregnant when captured.

Stephen Powers published a somewhat variant and a fuller account of Snowdrop's birth. Says Powers:

> Several years ago this tribe [the Yahi] committed a massacre near Chino, and Sandy Young, a renowned hunter of that country, with a companion, captured two squaws, a mother and a daughter, who promised to guide them to the camp of the murderers. They set out at nightfall in the dead of winter. It was sleeting, raining, and blowing that night as if "the de'l had business on his hands." But they passed rapidly on without halt or hesitation, for the squaws led the way boldly. From nightfall until long after midnight they held on their dreary trail, stumbling and floundering occasionally, but speaking scarcely a word; nor was there a moment's cessation in the execrable, bitter sleet and rain. At length they came to a creek which was swollen and booming. In the pitchy darkness it was manifestly impassable. They sounded it in various places, and could find no crossing. While the hunters were groping hither and thither, and shouting to each other above the raging of the torrent, the squaws disappeared. No hallooing could elicit a response from them. The two men considered themselves betrayed, and prepared for treachery. Suddenly there came floating out on the storm and the roaring a thin young squall. The party had been re-enforced by one. The hunters then grasped the situation, and, laughing, set about collecting some dry stuff and making a fire. They were benumbed and half frozen themselves, and supposed of course the women would come in as soon as they observed the fire. But no, they wanted no fire, or, if they did, their aboriginal modesty would not allow them to resort to it under these circumstances. The grandmother took the new-born babe, amid the almost palpable blackness of darkness, the sleeting, and the yelling winds, and dipped it in the ice-cold creek. Again and again she dipped it, while now and then the hunters could hear its stout-lunged protest above the roaring. Not only did the infant survive this unparalleled treatment, but it grew excellently well. In memory of the extraordinary circumstances under which it was ushered into this world, Young named it "Snow-flake" and it is living to this day, a wild-eyed lad in Tehama.

To sum up: the two women and the little girl were taken by Segraves and Good in March, 1870 (date from Segraves). There followed the Five Bows incident two weeks later. Snowdrop (or Snowflake), was born the following winter, and was pointed out to Powers in Tehama in 1872

(Powers). Beyond that, nothing more is known of them. It was presumably Sandy Young who told Powers the story of Snowdrop's birth. At first reading it seems to be an extravagance and a rationalization, but sense lies embedded within its nonsense.

In her own Yahi home, the prospective mother would have been under strict taboo during her pregnancy. For the birth she would have gone to a small separate house with her mother or some other older woman to help her, where the baby would have been delivered, washed in water and ritually cleansed, mother and baby returning to the family house when the navel cord was healed. That a Yahi mother might panic when her time was upon her, choosing the unsheltered and stormy night rather than a cabin shared with the man who was presumably the father of her baby, and with another man, and that she would resort to any stratagem to get away, is not far fetched within the frame of Yana belief in the unwilled power for evil to any man exposed to childbirth.

The simple human truths behind the disguised and lurid story would seem to be that the men were truly concerned for the mother and baby; that the women succeeded in protecting two white men from a contamination they were too ignorant to understand; that in some measure the ritual cleansing of the newborn child was seen to; and that in due course the women with the baby returned to their cabin home with their white keeper.

Note on Other "Wild" Indians, 1911–1927, Chapter 6, page 113

It should be said that the present account has not detailed stories of wild Indians in the Yana hills after Ishi's capture, since, without exception, so far as I know, the stories have been based on meagre, wishful-thinking evidence, such as a fresh barefoot track on a sandbar of Mill Creek, a small fire, still smouldering; a "bed of twigs" within an undisturbed clump of chaparral on Dry Creek; or "signs" of Indian occupation in a cave on Deer or Mill creeks. As late as October, 1927, sixteen years after Ishi's capture, there was a story of evidence of wild Indians published in the *Sacramento Union*. The recent footprints and campfires never turned out to be those of Indians, and the true Indian campsites in and out of caves, which people sometimes came across, were not of recent occupancy. In 1914 Ishi identified *in situ* the caves and villages and camping places that he and his people customarily used, such as the Bay Tree village on Mill Creek, the Three Knolls village, and the last hiding places of the remnant band. None of these hiding places had been disturbed or used since he had last seen them. As for other caves containing bones and artifacts, Ishi said that these were old in his time, that his people never had used them, for they were the ancient homes and burial places of ancestors, taboo to him and his contemporaries. The archaeology which, during the last decade, has been going forward in Yana country under the Archaeological Survey of the University of California, takes its principal orientation from Ishi's, Waterman's, and Kroeber's maps (the last named still in field notebooks), with their identifications of sites, old and modern. What Ishi referred to as ancestral sites have turned out to be archaeologically old, and those where his own generation lived have contained only late-horizon Yahi material.

The virtual certainty that Ishi was correct in believing that no other Yahi was living at least in Yahi country after 1911 rests on the lack of any real evidence to the contrary, and, more importantly, on the smallness of the territory that remained free of white intrusion, every foot of which Ishi knew with exactitude and intimacy. It is inconceivable that another Yahi, unbeknown to him, could have lived there during the years when he never left his homeland, and when its compass became ever more restricted.

BIBLIOGRAPHY

This list of the printed sources that I read and used in the preparation of *Ishi* contains only material of immediate concern to the text of this book. Exhaustiveness of bibliography for the areas of special interest suggested by Ishi's story—toxophily, linguistics, archaeology, and land morphology, are four such—would carry me into fields where I do not have a scholar's or specialist's control either of sources or material. Neither Ishi nor his people would be anywhere within them. So much of the source material for the book comes from the files of the Museum of Anthropology, from unpublished field notes, and from oral report and letters that, as in Waterman's monograph on the Yana Indians, the bibliography is modest and in many ways secondary to the unpublished, handwritten, or face-to-face reporting of event and affect.

The printed sources divide into natural categories of subject matter and interest. One of these, the frontier, has a large literature. My list includes, with one exception, only the intimate accounts of life on the frontier along Old Lassen Trail.

For the sake of brevity, the following abbreviations are used in the bibliography:

UCAS—University of California Archaeological Survey

UC-AR—University of California Publications: Anthropological Records

UC-PAAE—University of California Publications in American Archaeology and Ethnology

FRONTIER

Anderson, R. A. *Fighting the Mill Creeks.* Chico, California, Chico Record Press, 1909.

Bruff, J. Goldsborough. *The Journals, Drawings, and Other Papers of J. Goldsborough Bruff, April 2, 1849–July 20, 1851*. Edited by Georgia Willis Read and Ruth Gaines. New York, Columbia University Press, 1949.

Carson, A. Thankful. *Captured by the Mill Creek Indians*. Chico, California. Privately printed by the author, 1915.

Cook, Sherburne F. *The Conflict between the California Indians and White Civilization, III: The American Invasion, 1848–1870*. University of California Publications in Ibero-Americana, 23. Berkeley, University of California Press, 1943.

Cowan, Robert G. *Ranchos of California*. Fresno, California, Academy Library Guild, 1956.

Curtin, Jeremiah. *Creation Myths of Primitive America*. Boston, Little, Brown & Company, 1898.

Hallowell, A. Irving. "The Backwash of the Frontier: The Impact of the Indian on American Culture," in *The Frontier in Perspective*, edited by Walker D. Wyman and Clifton B. Kroeber. Madison, University of Wisconsin Press, 1957. Pp. 229–257.

Hutchinson, W. H. *One Man's West*. Chico, California, Hurst & Yount, 1948.

Moak, Sim. *The Last of the Mill Creeks and Early Life in Northern California*. Chico, California, 1923.

Powers, Stephen. *Tribes of California*. Smithsonian Institution, Contributions to North American Ethnology, Vol. III. Department of the Interior, U. S. Geographical and Geological Survey of the Rocky Mountain Region. Washington, D.C., 1877.

Robinson, W. W. *Land in California*. Berkeley and Los Angeles, University of California Press, 1948.

U. S. War Department. *The War of the Rebellion . . . Official Records of the Union and Confederate Armies. Published under the Direction of the Secretary of War*. Washington, D.C., 1865–1901. Series I, Vol. XL, part 1, p. 1162; part 2, pp. 28, 637, 874.

Wells, Harry L., and W. L. Chambers. *The History of Butte County*. San Francisco, Chambers, 1882.

Anderson's reporting of fighting the "Mill Creeks" is first hand, uninhibited, and intelligent. It is about Indian fighting as it occurred in Lassen County and thereabouts, told by the sheriff of the time and place. Recommended.

Bruff's *Journals* are not to be missed by anyone with an interest in human behavior. They have been excellently edited and presented.

The Wells and Chambers history of Butte County is early, and rewarding. These early county records, put between covers before details were lost, are the documentarian's delight.

Thankful Carson's story of her capture and escape carries, in its dry literalness, more sense of the terror under which both Indians and whites struggled than do any of the burnished and furbelowed elaborations of the story which the newspapers of the day, and later, printed. Indeed, it was to correct some of their exaggerations that Mrs. Carson was induced, as an old lady, to tell the story herself.

Cowan and Robinson present, very simply, the names and locations and dates of land grants, Spanish and Mexican, in California. More detailed accounts, lists, and documents are available in the Bancroft Library of the University of California; these deal with all aspects of Spanish and Mexican California and the lands beyond.

Powers and Curtin are unique in being gentlemen of parts and of literary competence who traveled in California and wrote about the frontier when, with Powers, it was yet at its rawest, and with Curtin, not long past its first phase. Hutchinson's *One Man's West* contains a vivid chapter on Ishi, among other matters of interest to an understanding of pioneer days and ways. He follows in the tradition of Stephen Powers.

Sim Moak's version of the Mill Creek fighting should not be missed. He is more spontaneous than is Sheriff Anderson, who sees some of the complexities in frontier living. Sim simply lived the life to the full.

Cook's papers in the Ibero-Americana series are dry and statistical, his method factual and scientific. But he treats of material so laden with human struggle and tragedy that one reads on with a fascinated horror.

The War of the Rebellion Records are not recommended reading except to the dedicated student of the period, for whom they are essential source material.

On the other hand, Hallowell's essay "Backwash of the Frontier" contributes a modern, psychologically sophisticated and philosophical scholar's approach. The whole of the book—*The Frontier in Perspective*—of which his is the final essay becomes exciting reading, when, after looking through a microscope darkly at the frontier of Old Lassen Trail, the reader turns to this book's wide-angle, telescopic lens view of the concept *frontier* and its impact on history.

HISTORY

Bancroft, Hubert Howe. *History of California.* San Francisco, The History Company, 1888. Vol. VI, pp. 16–17.

Baumhoff, Martin A. *Excavations of Kingsley Cave.* UCAS, Report No. 30. 1955.

———. *An Introduction to Yana Archaeology.* UCAS, Report No. 40. 1957.

Dixon, Roland B. *The Northern Maidu.* Bulletin, American Museum of Natural History, Vol. 17, part 3, pp. 119–346. 1905.

Garth, Thomas R. *Atsugewi Ethnography.* UC-AR, Vol. 14, No. 2, pp. 129–212. 1953.

Heizer, Robert F. "An Assessment of Certain Nevada, California, and Oregon Radio-carbon Dates," *Memoirs,* Society for American Archaeology, No. 8, pp. 23–25.

———. *Aboriginal California and Great Basin Cartography.* UCAS, Report No. 41. 1958.

———— and A. B. Elsasser. *Some Archaeology Sites and Cultures in the Central Sierra Nevada.* UCAS, Report No. 21. 1953.

Sapir, Edward and Leslie Spier. *Notes on the Culture of the Yana.* UC-AR, Vol. 3, No. 3, pp. 239–298. 1943.

Squier, R. S. *The Manufacture of Flint Implements by the Indians of Northern and Central California.* UCAS, Report No. 2. 1953.

There is not too much to be said to illuminate these references. One turns to the mammoth compilations made under Bancroft to answer a thousand questions of fact. Dixon, Garth, and Sapir-Spier, are historical and enlightening in the particularistic ethnographic detail way of history. Heizer, Elsasser, and Baumhoff are much more interesting, at least to the armchair archaeologist-antiquarian, and to anyone who has found an obsidian arrow point *in situ,* or who has come upon a baffling petroglyphic record carved in the living rock by some unimaginably ancient predecessor who left his mark, whether map, or emblem of worship and divinity, or personal artistic ebullience we cannot now say.

As will be seen also in the next section, the telling of the story of Ishi and his people has had, to date, two florescences, the earlier one ending in the 'twenties. There followed, except for the occasional popular magazine article retelling the familiar tale, a thirty-year silence. A new point of view, new linguistic and archaeological techniques, brought a spurt of further exploration and publication during the 'fifties.

Perhaps it is with Ishi, as with a painter or an author who suffers eclipse, to be rediscovered in a new climate of opinion and values. The first period closes with 1923 and the second opens with publications in 1953, 1955, and 1957 on Yana archaeology; with tape recordings made from the old cylinders, in 1958; the Yana Dictionary in 1960 and this biography in 1961; and the Archaeological Survey has hanging on its office walls maps with many unworked Yana sites, each marked with a small cross—a check mark for work to be done.

MONOGRAPHS, BOOKS, AND ARTICLES CONTAINING
PRIMARY DATA ON ISHI

Kroeber, A. L. "The Elusive Mill Creeks," *Travel Magazine* (August, 1911).

———. "Flint Chipping and Fire Making," *San Francisco Call,* December, 1911.

———. "Ishi, the Last Aborigine," *The World's Work* (July, 1912), pp. 304–308.

———. "The Yana and Yahi," in *Handbook of the Indians of California*. Smithsonian Institution, Bureau of American Ethnology, Bulletin 78 (Washington, D.C., 1925; 2d print., Berkeley, 1953), Chap. 23, pp. 336–346.

———. *Cultural and Natural Areas of Native North America.* UC-PAAE, Vol. XXXVIII. 1939. 3d print., 1953.

Nelson, Nels C. "Flint Working by Ishi," in *William Henry Holmes Anniversary Volume,* edited by Frederic W. Hodge. Washington, D.C., 1916. Pp. 397–402.

Pope, Saxton T. "Making Indian Arrowheads," *Forest and Stream* (December, 1913).

———. *Yahi Archery.* UC-PAAE, Vol. XIII, No. 3, pp. 103–152. 1918.

———. *The Medical History of Ishi. Ibid.,* No. 5, pp. 175–214. 1920.

———. *A Study of Bows and Arrows. Ibid.,* No. 9, pp. 329–414. 1923. 2d ed., rev., 1930.

———. *Hunting with the Bow and Arrow.* San Francisco, James H. Barry Co., 1923.

———. "Archery—Ancient and Modern," *Field and Stream* (February, 1925).

Redding, George H. H. "An Evening with Wintoon Indians," *The Californian,* Vol. II, No. 12 (December, 1880), pp. 563–606.

Waterman, T. T. "The Last Wild Tribe of California," *Popular Science Monthly* (March, 1915), pp. 233–244.

———. "Ishi, the Last Yahi Indian," *The Southern Workman* (Hampton Normal and Agricultural Institute, Virginia), Vol. 46, pp. 528–537. 1917.

———. *The Yana Indians.* UC PAAE, Vol. XIII, No. 2, pp. 35–102. 1918.

The above list constitutes, one might say, Ishi's direct contributions to science and the humanities, and are the fruits of his friends' care that they be recorded and preserved. Alas, the monographs are all long since out of print and to be come by only through the scant chance of the selling and scattering of a private library that happens to contain them. The larger university and public libraries have copies, but not circulating copies.

A first responsibility was to include the material of the monographs in this book, and this has been done. Pope's descriptions, in his *Yahi Archery,* of how Ishi made and shot the bow, and of how he hunted, are in the chapter called "The Craftsman." In this chapter also are Kroeber's accounts of Ishi's arrow making and fire drilling, with additions from Nelson, Pope, and Redding, since no one, apparently, ever achieves an exhaustive description of each step in the preparation and enactment of a craft process—an art as demanding and difficult as that of giving the rules and directions for playing a game of chess. Waterman's *The Yana Indians* is the skeleton and most of the meat of the history of the Yana; its complexity requires that other source material be interpolated to keep at least a calendric order and, when possible, a geographic one.

Pope's book, *Hunting with the Bow and Arrow,* is a somewhat loosened-at-the-seams retelling of the material in his *Yahi Archery.* It, too, is out of print.

The Handbook was reprinted in 1953 after being out of print for many years; it is of use as a dictionary for answers to all manner of questions about the Indians of California.

Pope's *A Study of Bows and Arrows* has to do with Ishi only in small part. It has been reprinted and is more readily available than are the others to toxophilists to whom it is of especial interest. The monograph by Pope on Ishi's medical history has been utilized in this book save for the very technical and harrowing details of Ishi's last illness.

From the several magazine articles have been kept whatever items added to the fundamental corpus of material, which is all in the monographs.

LANGUAGE

Bloomfield, Leonard. *Language.* New York, Henry Holt & Co., 1933.

Jespersen, Otto. *Language.* New York, Henry Holt & Co., 1922.

Kroeber, A. L. "Linguistic Time Depth Results So Far and Their Meaning," *International Journal of American Linguistics,* Vol. 21 (1955), pp. 91–104.

Sapir, Edward. *Yana Texts.* (*Together with Yana Myths Collected by R. B. Dixon.*) UC-PAAE, Vol. IX, No. 1, pp. 2–236. 1910.

———. *The Position of Yana in the Hokan Stock.* UC-PAAE, Vol. XIII, No. 1, pp. 1–34. 1917.

———. *Yana Terms of Relationship.* UC-PAAE, Vol. XIII, No. 4, pp. 153–174. 1918.

———. *Language: An Introduction to the Study of Speech.* New York, Harcourt, Brace & Co., 1921.

———. *The Fundamental Elements of Northern Yana.* UC-PAAE, Vol. XIII, No. 6, pp. 215–234. 1922.

———. *Text Analyses of Three Yana Dialects.* UC-PAAE, Vol. XX, No. 15, pp. 261–294. 1923.

———. "Male and Female Forms of Speech," in St. W. J. Teeuwen, ed., *Donum Natalicium Schrijnen.* Nijmegen-Utrecht, 1929. Pp. 79–85.

—— and Morris Swadesh. *Yana Dictionary,* edited by Mary R. Hass. University of California Publications in Linguistics. Vol. 22. 1960. 267 pp.

Swadesh, M. "Time Depths in American Linguistic Groupings," *American Anthropologist,* Vol. 56, pp. 361–364.

Waterman, T. T. Five Field Notebooks of Texts and Vocabulary Dictated by Ishi. MS 1911.

Linguistics, like mathematics, or like elaborations of kinship analysis, is either your meat and your joy, or it is boring and probably incomprehensible. Bloomfield, Jespersen, Sapir, and Swadesh are all performers par excellence, musicians as it were who through their keen ears and perceptions play a music all their own to the click of cracked consonants, to tone in speech, to changing suffixes, and to the reduction of "impure" or multiple sounds to their phonemic singlenesses.

It was from Waterman's penciled notes of Yahi, done with phonetically simpler tools, that I was able to excavate the one fragment of a longer story that remains to us, indubitably told by Ishi and taken down as told. This is perhaps the place to explain that I have principally used Waterman's spelling of Yāna and Yahi words. Whether Waterman's or Sapir's, I have simplified the technical orthography, to indicate to the non-linguist reader an approximation of how the words actually sounded to the ear.

Swadesh describes glottochronology in his article cited above. Kroeber, literally following in Swadesh's wake, goes on to make some experimentation with the new method, and explains in language accessible to the nonspecialist the usefulness and some of the hazards of this latest linguistic exercise.

NEWSPAPER SOURCES

Files of newspapers are kept in the University of California Library's Newspaper Room and in the Bancroft Library, in the State Library in Sacramento, in county record archives, sometimes in the offices of the newspapers themselves, and in private collections such as the C. Hart Merriam documentary collection which was given by the Merriam family to the Smithsonian Institution, Washington, D.C., which institution deeded the collection, with the heirs' permission, to the University of California. Its materials are chiefly Californian.

Newspapers are likely sources for a first mention of a person or event or for a first picture and hence for confirmation of a date or a circumstance that has otherwise become hazy in memory or lost to it.

It was from the files of the *Oroville Register* that the date of Ishi's appearance at the slaughter house was confirmed. It was in the *Sacramento Daily Transcript,* April 5, 1850, that Indian troubles indubitably Yahi were first mentioned (Merriam Collection). The *San Francisco Call* published the earliest photograph of Ishi to appear in a metropolitan paper: August 29, 1911.

The articles themselves do not for the most part much enlighten a biography such as this one beyond the invaluable dating. One story reads like another—indeed, their source was single: the *Oroville Register,* August 29, 1911. There follows a list of the newspaper articles I read that had to do with the Yahi or with Ishi. The list makes no pretension to completeness of coverage, but the dates and distributions may be of interest.

I remain in comfortable, permanent debt to William Bascom, Director of the Museum of Anthropology, and to the staff of the Museum, for making available to me the old museum files, pictures, and other archival materials. For the rest, I recall with gratitude that James Downs confirmed the all-important date of Ishi's first appearance as it was recorded in the Oroville paper of August 29, 1911; that Mrs. T. T. Waterman supplied pictures not otherwise available; that Samuel Barrett continues the search for the lost motion pictures of Ishi; that Jan Seibert and Evelyn Lilge typed the manuscript, with critical and helpful reactions to it; and that Jessie Rousseau guarded with a benign jealousy the untroubled hours for composition which I craved.

At the University of California Press, there is Glenn Gosling, Senior Editor, whose queries, after reading my manuscript, I found amiable but loaded. They drove me back to wrestle yet another round with the refractory "historical" material. Now, after the fact, I can truly say I am grateful to him; my travail might else have become my readers'. There is also Lucie E. N. Dobbie, Executive Editor, who chaperoned the book through the Press. I soon learned that she cared greatly about Ishi and wished his story well told. This made working with her a most satisfying experience.

As for Ishi's friends, it seems to me supererogatory to mention them here. They *are,* in a sense, the story. It is through them that we know Ishi.

September, 1960

Theodora Kroeber

Theodora Kroeber (1897–1979), wife of Alfred Louis Kroeber, is also the author of *The Inland Whale* (California), and coeditor of *Ishi the Last Yahi: A Documentary History* (California).

Karl Kroeber, son of Theodora Kroeber, is Mellon Professor in the Humanities at Columbia University and coeditor of *Ishi in Three Centuries* (2002).

Lewis Gannett was a critic for the *New York Herald-Tribune*.

Also available from the University of California Press

Ishi the Last Yahi
A Documentary History

Edited by Robert F. Heizer and Theodora Kroeber

"Readers of Theodora Kroeber's *Ishi in Two Worlds* (1961) feel a tie beyond intellectual interest to this last Stone Age California Indian, who in 1911 was found half-starved at Oroville and thereafter lived at the University of California. In her graceful and sensitive study, Mrs. Kroeber gave us an appreciation not only of Ishi's contributions to our knowledge of prehistoric California, but traced his Yahi people's post-gold rush tribulations with advancing white civilization south of Mount Lassen. This newer work is a proper accompaniment to the earlier one. Its documents have immediacy of eyewitness history and show us as much about the backgrounds of white informants as about the Yahi.... The volume's intriguing photographs are themselves effective story-tellers." —*American West*

"His personal story has been told eloquently in Theodora Kroeber's early book. Her present collaboration with the well-known anthropologist Robert F. Heizer has accomplished something different and important. It has brought together not only most of the anthropological articles written by A. L. Kroeber, Waterman, Sapir, Nettl, and others, but also correspondence among Ishi's friends at the time of his death, and any early newspaper articles. The accumulation of accounts written by early California travelers, army officers, and participants in the fierce campaigns against the Mill Creek (Yahi) Indians between 1860 and 1875 documents some of the most tragic and most sickening instances of the hatred many settlers felt toward the Indians and the savagery with which they treated them. The result is a many-faceted volume which supplements the earlier works and provides a solid nugget of original materials about a series of historical events and a fascinating person." —*Choice*

"Brings together the full documentation of Ishi and his Yahi background, providing a vivid portrait of the interaction between indigenous Indian groups and encroaching white settlers. . . . [An] important collection of original source materials." —Library Journal

"These documents record both the chronology of the way anthropologists work and the way Ishi changed in response to Western culture, until his death from tuberculosis in 1916. The book is a penetrating study of the ways that we come to understand what is is to be human—and to be different." —Booklist

In paperback ISBN 0–520–04366–9
At bookstores or order 1–800–822–6657
UNIVERSITY OF CALIFORNIA PRESS
www.ucpress.edu